T0350938

Get the eBooks FREE!

(PDF, ePub, Kindle, and liveBook all included)

We believe that once you buy a book from us, you should be able to read it in any format we have available. To get electronic versions of this book at no additional cost to you, purchase and then register this book at the Manning website.

Go to https://www.manning.com/freebook and follow the instructions to complete your pBook registration.

That's it!
Thanks from Manning!

Reactive Applications with Akka.NET

ANTHONY BROWN

MANNING
SHELTER ISLAND

For online information and ordering of this and other Manning books, please visit
www.manning.com. The publisher offers discounts on this book when ordered in quantity.
For more information, please contact

    Special Sales Department
    Manning Publications Co.
    20 Baldwin Road
    PO Box 761
    Shelter Island, NY 11964
    Email: orders@manning.com

Manning Publications Co.
20 Baldwin Road
PO Box 761
Shelter Island, NY 11964

Development editor:	Christina Taylor
Technical development editor:	Joel Kotarski
Production editor:	Janet Vail
Proofreaders:	Katie Tennant and Toma Mulligan
Technical proofreader:	Karsten Strobaek
Proofreader:	Katie Tennant
Typesetter:	Dottie Marsico
Cover designer:	Marija Tudor

ISBN 9781617292989
Printed in the United States of America
1 2 3 4 5 6 7 8 9 10 – SP – 24 23 22 21 20 19

brief contents

PART 1 THE ROAD TO REACTIVE 1

     1 ▪ Why reactive? 3
     2 ▪ Reactive application design 11

PART 2 DIGGING IN 23

     3 ▪ Your first Akka.NET application 25
     4 ▪ State, behavior, and actors 43
     5 ▪ Configuration, dependency injection, and logging 59
     6 ▪ Failure handling 76
     7 ▪ Scaling in reactive systems 103
     8 ▪ Composing actor systems 127

PART 3 REAL-LIFE USAGE 149

     9 ▪ Testing Akka.NET actors 151
    10 ▪ Integrating Akka.NET 173
    11 ▪ Storing actor state with Akka.Persistence 192
    12 ▪ Building clustered applications with Akka.Cluster 214
    13 ▪ Akka.NET and reactive programming in production 243

contents

preface   xi
acknowledgments   xii
about this book   xiii
about the author   xvi
about the cover illustration   xvii

PART 1   THE ROAD TO REACTIVE 1

1   *Why reactive?   3*

    1.1   The heart of the Reactive Manifesto   4

    1.2   Reactive systems vs. reactive programming   6

    1.3   Applying Akka.NET   7

        Where to use Akka.NET   7 ▪ Where not to use Akka.NET   8

    1.4   How does Akka.NET work?   8

2   *Reactive application design   11*

    2.1   Basic reactive system design   12

    2.2   Reactive e-commerce application with actors   13

        A reactive shopping cart   13 ▪ Changing states of
        actors   15 ▪ Making the purchase   15 ▪ Data transfer
        between services   16 ▪ Scaling work with routers   17
        Wrapping up   18

2.3   Building on reactive foundations   19

*Publishing the e-commerce application to the world   19
Storing state within actors   20 ▪ Scaling out across a cluster
of machines   20 ▪ Continuing to react to environmental
changes   20 ▪ Wrapping up   21*

PART 2   DIGGING IN 23

3 *Your first Akka.NET application   25*

3.1   Setting up an application   26

3.2   Actors   26

*What does an actor embody?   26 ▪ What can an actor do?   28
Defining an actor   29 ▪ Wrapping up   33*

3.3   Deploying an actor   33

*The actor system   33 ▪ Spawning an actor   35
Wrapping up   36*

3.4   Communicating with actors   36

*Actor addresses and references   37 ▪ Sending a message   39
Wrapping up   40*

3.5   Case study: Actors, concurrency, and phone billing   40

4 *State, behavior, and actors   43*

4.1   Preparing for the next message   44

4.2   Setting appropriate runtime behaviors   44

*Switchable behaviors   45 ▪ Become and unbecome   45
Wrapping up   47*

4.3   Finite state machines   47

*Understanding finite state machines   48 ▪ Using finite
state machines in a concurrency model   50 ▪ Converting a
finite state machine into an actor   52 ▪ Using the finite state
machine actor   54 ▪ Wrapping up   57*

4.4   Case study: State machines, states and events, marketing
analytics campaign   57

5 *Configuration, dependency injection, and logging   59*

5.1   Why do you need configuration?   60

5.2   Configuring an actor deployment   60

Understanding Props   61 ▪ Wrapping up   63

5.3   Dependency injection (DI)   64

Introducing dependency injection   64 ▪ *Configuring a
DI container   66* ▪ *Wrapping up   67*

5.4   C8onfiguring with HOCON   67

What is HOCON?   67 ▪ *Loading configuration into
an actor system   69* ▪ *Wrapping up   70*

5.5   Logging   70

Why do you need logging?   70 ▪ *Writing to the log   71*
Customizing a logger deployment   72 ▪ *Wrapping up   73*

5.6   Case study: Configuration and distributed systems   73

6 *Failure handling   76*

6.1   Understanding failures   77

6.2   Handling application-level failures   78

Responding to application errors   79 ▪ *The Akka.NET
supervision tree   81* ▪ *Failing fast   86* ▪ *The actor
lifecycle   88* ▪ *Watching for the deaths of other actors   91*
Interface-level failures   94 ▪ *Wrapping up   95*

6.3   Understanding transport-level failures   96

Writing applications that handle message loss   97
Wrapping up   101

6.4   Case study: Supervision, failure, chat bots   101

7 *Scaling in reactive systems   103*

7.1   Scaling up and scaling out   104

7.2   Distributing work   106

Routers   106 ▪ *Pools and groups   109* ▪ *Wrapping up   111*

7.3   Routing strategies   111

Random routing   112 ▪ *Round-robin routing   113*
Smallest-mailbox router   114 ▪ *Consistent hashing   116*
Scatter-gather first-completed   120 ▪ *Tail-chopping router   122*
Wrapping up   124

7.4   Case 8study: Scaling, throughput, advertising systems   125

8 *Composing actor systems   127*

8.1   Introducing Akka.NET remoting   129

8.2   Preparing to use remoting   130

Installing Akka.Remote   130 ▪ *Configuring remoting for a
project   130*

8.3   Communicating with remote actors   132

Sending messages to remote actors   133 ▪ *Remote deployment
of actors   135* ▪ *Wrapping up   137*

8.4   Elastic scale across machines   137

*Configuring a router to use multiple machines   138
Wrapping up   140*

8.5   Failure handling across machines   140

Supervisor strategies across a network   141 ▪ *Remoting
DeathWatch   142* ▪ *Wrapping up   143*

8.6   Akka.Remote security   143

*Limiting messages that can be sent over the network   144
Restricting available remote actor targets   144* ▪ *Wrapping
up   147*

8.7   Case study: Remoting, network applications, web server,
and backend server   147

PART 3   REAL-LIFE USAGE 149

9   Testing Akka.NET actors   151

9.1   Introducing Akka.TestKit   153

9.2   Unit testing actors   154

Spawning test actors   155 ▪ *Validating internal data   156
Testing FSMs   157* ▪ *Wrapping up   158*

9.3   Integration testing actors   158

Creating test specifications   158 ▪ *Asserting message
responses   159* ▪ *Time-based testing   161* ▪ *Test probes   163
Wrapping up   164*

9.4   Testing distributed applications with MultiNode
TestKit   164

MultiNode specs   165 ▪ *Testing individual actor systems   167
Barriers   168* ▪ *Testing for network failure   169* ▪ *Wrapping
up   171*

9.5   Case study: Testing, test-driven development,
unit testing   171

10   Integrating Akka.NET   173

10.1   Integrating with ASP.NET   175

10.2   Integrating with SignalR   179

*Communicating through an actor   180 ▪ Connecting to
the user's web browser   182 ▪ Wrapping up   184*

10.3   Custom integrations with akka.io   184

*Creating a listening socket   185 ▪ Sending data through
akka.io   188 ▪ Wrapping up   190*

10.4   Case study: IO, integration, IoT applications   190

11 *Storing actor state with Akka.Persistence   192*

11.1   Understanding event sourcing   193

11.2   Using Akka.Persistence   195

*Writing persistent actors   195 ▪ Configuring a journal   199
Wrapping up   201*

11.3   Akka.Persistence performance tuning   201

*Snapshot stores   201 ▪ Async write journals   203
Wrapping up   204*

11.4   Akka.Persistence performance tuning   204

*At-least-once delivery   204 ▪ Upgrade strategies for
applications using event sourcing   208 ▪ Wrapping up   212*

11.5   Case study: Persistence, storage, staged upgrades   212

12 *Building clustered applications with Akka.Cluster   214*

12.1   Introducing Akka.Cluster   215

12.2   Cluster-aware routers   219

*Creating cluster-aware router groups   219 ▪ Creating cluster-
aware router pools   222 ▪ Wrapping up   223*

12.3   Working with cluster gossip   223

*Retrieving cluster state   224 ▪ Handling cluster gossip
messages   224 ▪ Wrapping up   225*

12.4   Cluster singleton   225

Wrapping up   228

12.5   Cluster sharding   228

*Creating a new shard   229 ▪ Communicating with actors
in a shard   232 ▪ Handling passivation in shards   233
Wrapping up   233*

12.6   Distributed publish-subscribe   233

       Topic messaging   234 ▪ *Point-to-point messaging   236*
       Wrapping up   237

12.7   Cluster client   238

12.8   Case study: Clustering, scaling, cluster management   241

13   *Akka.NET and reactive programming in production   243*

13.1   Designing with actors   244

13.2   Handling failure   245

13.3   Designing for scale   246

13.4   Handling configuration   247

13.5   Ingesting data   247

13.6   Testing   248

13.7   Real-time integration   249

13.8   Data persistence   249

13.9   Cluster scale-out   250

13.10   Conclusion   250

       index   251

preface

Welcome, and thank you for purchasing *Reactive Applications with Akka.NET!* I hope that this book lays a solid foundation for you to create applications and services that are truly capable of standing the trials and tribulations of a wide audience, making the most of the Reactive Manifesto along your way.

As software developers, we find ourselves in an interesting time. The significant growth in popularity of computers of all shapes and sizes—whether they're in traditional devices like laptops and desktops, smart entertainment devices such as TVs, or in the booming Internet of Things market—is leading to a wide demand for new and innovative solutions that can handle high rates of data and scalability.

As the demand on internet-capable computers and devices increases, so does the pressure on software developers to create applications that can withstand growth. We need applications that not only stand up to the demands of users, but are also flexible enough to be rapidly adapted and modified in order to change with market trends and needs.

Reactive systems offer applications that can respond to changes in their environment nearly instantly, making you and your applications essential in the software development landscape. I hope this book helps you on your journey to a thorough understanding of reactive applications and how using Akka.NET can alleviate some of the difficulties you've experienced in the past.

acknowledgments

I'd like to thank Manning Publications for giving me the opportunity to write this book. Thanks, too, to Christina Taylor, my development editor, and to Karsten Strøbaek, my technical proofreader. This book would not have been possible without their help.

I am also indebted to the many people who read this book in various stages and provided feedback, including Aaron Watson, Adnan Masood, Adrian Bilauca, Alex Jacinto, Bachir Chihani, Chris Allan, Dror Helper, Jeff Smith, Kevin Partusch, Lucian Enache, Nick McGinness, Ping Xiang, Riccardo Moschetti, and Shobha Iyer.

about this book

As you work through the book, you'll see how the Reactive Manifesto and reactive concepts fit into this new era of software development. In part 1 of the book, you'll see an overview of the reactive approach and why it's needed in the coming years, as well as a more in-depth look at how you can design systems with reactive traits in mind. From there, you'll get acquainted with Akka.NET, an actor model implementation in .NET that allows you to write applications in the reactive style. Following this, you'll build an understanding of the fundamentals of writing applications using Akka.NET before you look at how to apply these principles in the applications you write, thanks to the Akka.NET ecosystem.

Who should read this book?

Reactive Applications with Akka.NET is written for those with little-to-no experience with Akka.NET, the actor model, or reactive systems, who have encountered difficulties in creating applications that are resilient and scalable. Readers should be comfortable with C# or F# and the .NET framework, but no previous reactive experience is needed.

How is this book organized?

This book has three parts spanning 13 chapters. Part 1 sets the stage for moving into a reactive mindset:

- Chapter 1 outlines what it means to be reactive and when you want to apply Akka.NET.
- Chapter 2 focuses on the tenets for designing a reactive e-commerce application, and will teach you how to effectively design such an application with many of the features that Akka.NET makes available.

Part 2 focuses on digging into the details that you need to create fully functional reactive systems in Akka.NET:

- Chapter 3 presents your first Akka.NET application, and will acquaint you with the design patterns typically used when designing reactive systems in Akka.NET.
- Chapter 4 teaches how to selectively receive messages into an actor with switchable behaviors, and will also teach you the basics of finite state machines, including how to model them using Akka.NET.
- Chapter 5 takes a deep look into how you can instrument and operationalize an Akka.NET application through the configuration of individual actors and actor systems as a whole.
- Chapter 6 focuses on how to respond to service failures within an Akka.NET application, delivering an in-depth look from the original source of the failure to typical failure models.
- Chapter 7 looks at the difficulties involved with traditional scaling approaches, and how the Akka.NET approach is different.
- Chapter 8 looks at actor systems and how to link, scale, and create applications that can handle machine-level failure.

Part 3 wraps up the book by offering real-world case studies and implementations:

- Chapter 9 is focused on testing, from designing unit tests for functionality to verifying the functionality of distributed actor systems through multinode tests.
- Chapter 10 helps you integrate Akka.NET with custom protocols, focusing on sending and receiving data, integrating real-time connection mechanisms, and adding web APIs to allow communication with actor systems.
- Chapter 11 teaches how to add a persistent backing data store to an actor to save its state, with a focus on developing evolvable applications using Akka .Persistence and event sourcing.
- Chapter 12 utilizes Akka.Cluster to create elastic and scalable actor systems that span multiple machines.
- Chapter 13 is an end-to-end case study that will allow you to implement everything you've learned while programming one real-world production problem.

About the code

This book contains many examples of source code in a `fixed-width font like this` to separate it from ordinary text.

In many cases, the original source code has been reformatted; we've added line breaks and reworked indentation to accommodate the available page space in the book. Additionally, comments in the source code have often been removed from the listings when the code is described in the text.

Source code for the examples in this book is available for download from the publisher's website at www.manning.com/books/reactive-applications-with-akka-net.

liveBook discussion forum

Purchase of *Reactive Applications with Akka.NET* includes free access to a private web forum run by Manning Publications where you can make comments about the book, ask technical questions, and receive help from the author and from other users. To access the forum, go to https://livebook.manning.com/#!/book/reactive-applications-with-akka-net/discussion. You can also learn more about Manning's forums and the rules of conduct at https://livebook.manning.com/#!/discussion.

Manning's commitment to our readers is to provide a venue where a meaningful dialogue between individual readers and between readers and the author can take place. It is not a commitment to any specific amount of participation on the part of the author, whose contribution to the forum remains voluntary (and unpaid). We suggest you try asking him some challenging questions lest his interest stray! The forum and the archives of previous discussions will be accessible from the publisher's website as long as the book is in print.

about the author

Anthony Brown has been developing software for several years now, predominantly using the .Net framework. Anthony has worked in a number of different industries working as a developer helping to build better telecom systems, mobile apps and games, as well as enterprise systems. He is a regular speaker at user groups and conferences on the latest and greatest tools and techniques to rapidly build systems that work.

Part 1

The road to reactive

This part of the book sets the stage for your journey throughout the book. In chapter 1, you'll learn what it means to be reactive and when you want to apply Akka.NET. Chapter 2 focuses on the tenets for designing a reactive e-commerce application, and teaches how to effectively design such an application with many of the features that Akka.NET makes available.

Why reactive?

This chapter covers

- Understanding the Reactive Manifesto's principles of reactive design
- Using messaging, resilience, elasticity, and responsiveness
- Building reactive systems with Akka.NET

Over the past several decades, computers and the internet have moved from a position of relative obscurity to being central to many aspects of modern life. We now rely on the internet for all manner of day-to-day tasks, including shopping and keeping in contact with friends and family. The proliferation of computers and devices capable of accessing the internet has increased pressure on software developers to create applications that are able to withstand this near-exponential growth: we must develop applications that can meet the demands of a modern populace dependent on technology. Demands range in scope from providing instantly available information to users, to services that are resilient to issues they might encounter from increased usage or an increased likelihood of failure, which may be caused by factors entirely outside of our control. When this is twinned with the demands of a rapidly evolving company trying to beat the competition to find gaps in an ever-changing marketplace, applications must not only satisfy demands imposed by users but also be sufficiently malleable that they can be rapidly adapted and modified to fill those gaps.

In response to this, technology companies working across a broad range of different domains began to notice common design patterns that were able to fulfill these new requirements. Trends began to emerge, which were clearly visible to companies building the next generation of modern applications with a strong focus on huge datasets, up to the petabyte scale in some instances, which needed to be analyzed and understood in record time, with results being delivered to users at near-instantaneous speeds. Systems following these patterns were seen to be robust, resilient, and open to change. These principles were collected together and form the outcomes you can expect when you develop applications by implementing the Reactive Manifesto: a set of shared principles that exemplify a system design capable of standing up to the challenges of today's demands.

1.1   *The heart of the Reactive Manifesto*

At the core of the Reactive Manifesto is an understanding that applications designed to be responsive, resilient, elastic, and message-driven can respond to changes in their environment quickly (see figure 1.1). A change in the environment could include any number of variables, whether it's a change in the data of another component in the system, an increase in the error rate when attempting to process data or communicate with an external system, or an increase in the amount of data flowing through the system across component boundaries.

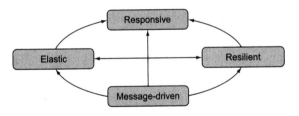

Figure 1.1   Reactive systems: responsive, resilient, elastic, message-driven

The implication is that the most important property of a modern application is its responsiveness: it should quickly respond to requests from users. For example, in the context of a web application, the user should expect to see changes as soon as data is input, whether this is by the application pushing data changes to the user's web browser, or ensuring that such changes can be retrieved quickly when the user next requests the change. The term *responsive* is broad, and its definition in one domain may be vastly different than in another context, so some consideration should be applied to what *responsive* means when applied to your applications. Many of the examples in this book apply to either web applications or real-time data solutions. These two cases themselves include a number of potential interpretations of what *responsive* means. For example, a web application should be responsive by quickly responding to an HTTP request, whereas a data-streaming solution should ensure that data flows at a constant rate in order to prevent a stalled stream, which might have knock-on effects for other components earlier in the stream.

In order to achieve this level of responsiveness, the systems you design must able to handle greater scale. Let's consider the example of a web application again. If it receives more web requests than the server is capable of handling, then it's inevitable that the incoming requests will start to queue up until resources are available to service them. Queuing leads to an increase in response time for users, making the application less responsive. Similarly, in the case of a streaming-data solution, if more events start to flow through the stream, your system must be able to process them within a fixed amount of time; otherwise, subsequent events may be delayed. But it's not enough to constantly provide more computing power; although computing power has dropped in price significantly in recent years, it's still far from cheap. As such, your system should be able to respond to periods of inactivity or reduced throughput by negatively adjusting provisioned compute resources so that you don't have to maintain or pay for unnecessary resources. This scenario relates to designing systems with elasticity: having the ability to expand resources when needed, but otherwise shrinking down to a minimum set of operational resources.

In parallel with elasticity, it's important that systems are equally resilient: they're able to react to a failure, whether it's a failure that originates from within the system, over which you have some degree of control, or from other systems external to yours and over which you have no control. In a streaming-data solution, this might translate into the ability of your stream-processing system to handle receiving bad or invalid data from an incoming data source. For example, with an Internet of Things (IoT) device sending sensor data, your stream-processing solution should be able to handle incoming data that may contain invalid sensor readings caused by a faulty sensor. If your application starts to fail, then this will likely cause knock-on failures in other components within your system. Therefore, a resilient application focuses on the containment of errors in the smallest possible area of the application. Following this containment, it should recover from these failures automatically, without the need for manual intervention. This notion of resilience ensures that the client doesn't end up being burdened with the responsibility for handling failures that may occur in the system.

Finally, driving the concepts you've seen thus far, message-driven systems are the core component that links everything together. By using messaging as the basis of communication between components, the system can perform work asynchronously and in a completely non-blocking manner. It can perform more work in parallel, leading to an increase in overall responsiveness. By using message passing as the basis of communication, you're also able to redirect and divert messages at runtime as appropriate, thus allowing you to reroute a message from a failing component to one that can service the request. For example, if you have two servers, each of which can service a request, then by using message passing, you can change which server receives the request if one server becomes unavailable to service it. Similarly, if you notice one server has become a bottleneck, you can divert a message to another server that's able to service the request. This means that you can dynamically add or remove new instances and automatically redirect messages to the target instance.

You can see how these concepts work together, with messaging being the core building block that powers the resilience, elasticity, and responsiveness of the application. You can also see that elasticity and resilience are shared concerns: when you have the infrastructure in place for resilience, it provides the necessary logic for elasticity. When all of these concepts are linked together, you have applications that are responsive.

1.2   *Reactive systems vs. reactive programming*

The concepts embodied in the Reactive Manifesto are far from new, having evolved over several decades. The Manifesto is itself a formalization of a significant amount of domain knowledge from varying organizations. Due to the relatively broad concepts covered in the Reactive Manifesto, there's some overlap between two related programming concepts: reactive programming and reactive systems.

Reactive programming, like the programming model offered by Reactive Extensions (Rx; a library for developing in .NET), offers a small-scale overview of reactive systems, tailored to how data flows in a single application. Typical applications are driven by a threaded execution model in which operations are performed sequentially in an order that you've defined, leaving you to deal with many of the underlying flow-control primitives needed to synchronize data. In contrast, reactive programming is driven by the execution of code only when new data is available; typically, this is in the form of events arising from a data source. One example is a timer that ticks once every 5 minutes. Using typical programming patterns, you'd have to set up a loop that continuously polls until the minimum time period has elapsed before you progress through your application flow. But with reactive programming, you create handlers that receive an event and are executed whenever a new event is received.

Reactive systems, however, focus on applying the same concepts on a much larger scale involving the integration of multiple distinct components. Many of the applications built today are no longer basic programs, taking in an input and producing an output; instead, they're complex systems made up of arrays of components, where each component could itself be an entire system. This level of interconnectedness brings with it complexities. Systems may not be running on the same physical hardware and may not even be collocated, with one system existing thousands of miles from another. This means you need to consider what happens in the event of failure, or how other system components will respond in the event of a sudden flood of information passing through the system. You saw when we discussed the Reactive Manifesto that these are requirements for a system to remain responsive, and you saw the way to achieve these aims is through the use of a higher-level message-passing-based API.

This is the core difference between reactive programming and a reactive system. Reactive programming involves the notion of events: data that is broadcast to everybody who's listening to that event. Reactive systems are message-driven, with individually addressable components supporting targeted messages. Akka.NET is one example of a tool that simplifies the building of large-scale reactive systems, which you'll see throughout this book, whereas Reactive Extensions is an example of reactive programming, which we won't be considering in this book. The two concepts can be combined, with reactive programming being built on top of a reactive system, or reactive programming existing within a single component of a reactive system. But the combination of these concepts won't be addressed in this book.

1.3 Applying Akka.NET

Akka.NET is a platform on which reactive systems can be built. This opens the door to using it across multiple distinct domains. It has been used in IoT applications, e-commerce, finance, and many other domains. The internal requirements of these applications determine whether Akka.NET is an ideal fit. One concern common to these types of applications is the requirement to update components based on the results of operations of other components. Akka.NET is a powerful tool when you need immediate responses from multiple components all integrated together.

1.3.1 Where to use Akka.NET

One example of where Akka.NET is an ideal fit is in the world of commercial air travel. Here, multiple distinct components produce data at an incredible rate: data that must be processed and delivered to the user as soon as possible. For example, a passenger in the terminal waiting to board a flight needs to know which gate their flight will depart from. Up-to-date information is particularly important in large airports, where it might take 20 or 30 minutes to walk between gates. But a vast number of integrated systems dictate where a flight travels. National air traffic control, which reroutes flights in the event of an emergency and to prevent in-air collisions between planes in a congested airspace, is a factor. The airport's air traffic control, responsible for directing planes to the correct runway, is also a factor; in the case of a large airport, landing on a different runway could direct the plane to a different gate. Other airport operations may divert a flight to a different gate due to a scheduling issue between airlines that prevents a plane from arriving at its planned gate. Similarly, data from the airline's internal systems might force a gate change due to internal scheduling problems. A vast array of data sources publish data that needs to be processed quickly to keep passengers immediately updated regarding any changes that occur as part of the effort to ensure that aircraft are able to turn around and take off again after landing.

Although not all systems are this complex or rely on as many distinct data sources, you can see the pattern of integrating multiple components together into a larger system while accommodating difficulties that might be encountered in the process. An airline, for instance, needs to immediately respond to changes when they're published, to protect the safety and security of passengers and staff.

1.3.2   *Where not to use Akka.NET*

Although Akka.NET makes it easier to build large reactive systems, it brings with it some difficulties. You've seen how complex systems force you to consider their complexities. For example, you must think about partial failures of system components that might impact other components, consider data consistency and how that should be handled in the case of partial failures, and deal with plenty of other issues. Akka.NET brings these difficulties and complexities to the surface as first-class principles, which means that you have to address them. When dealing with them, you'll also unearth a number of other complexities: notably, debugging is more difficult, and you have to think about concurrency. Therefore, for fairly simple web applications that have basic requirements, Akka.NET is unlikely to provide any significant benefits. These include relatively basic CRUD (create, read, update, delete) applications that are backed by a basic database model.

At its core, Akka.NET provides a concurrency model designed to allow multiple components to operate simultaneously. This means that when developing systems with Akka.NET, you need to think carefully about the data in your system. Although Akka.NET removes the possibility of concurrent access to shared data, there's still the opportunity for data races to occur, as well as the potential for deadlocks. For a system that doesn't need to operate concurrently, Akka.NET is likely to complicate matters rather than simplify them.

1.4   *How does Akka.NET work?*

Although Akka.NET itself and how it works might be new to many developers, its underlying principles have been in development for decades, in the form of the *actor model*. As part of the actor model, independent entities, known as *actors*, are responsible for performing work. You can have multiple different types of actors within a system, and each of these types can have multiple instances running in the system. Every actor runs independently of every other actor in the system, meaning that two running actors can't directly interfere or interact with each other. Instead, each actor is supplied with a mailbox, which receives messages, and an address, which can be used to receive messages from other actors in the system. An actor sits idle and doesn't do anything until a new message is received in the actor's mailbox; at this point, the actor can process the message using its internal behavior. Its behavior is the brain of the actor and defines how it should respond to each message it receives. If an actor receives more than one message, the messages are queued up in the order in which they were received, and the actor processes each message sequentially. Each actor will only process a single message at a time, although multiple actors can process their respective messages at the same time. This allows you to create highly concurrent applications without having to concern yourself with the underlying multithreading infrastructure and code that's typically required when developing concurrent applications. It's important to note also that actors are completely isolated, meaning that any internal information or data owned by one actor isn't accessible by anything other than that actor.

You can think of actors as being similar to people with mobile phones (see figure 1.2). Each person has an address through which they can be contacted; in this case, the address is the person's phone number. The person initiating the phone call also has a unique address; again, this is a phone number. By means of those addresses, communication takes place between two people, for example, by sending an SMS with some data in it. The data you might include in an SMS is typically a question, if you want to acquire information, or a statement, if you want to pass information. The SMS you send goes to the other person's mailbox, where they can asynchronously deal with it when they have the resources and bandwidth available. Like actors, every person is an independent, isolated entity with no ability to directly access information belonging to another person. If you want to find out what plans a friend has for the weekend, you don't have direct access to that information; instead, you send them an SMS asking for the information. This is the same pattern you use when sending data between actors: rather than directly accessing an actor's data, you send the actor a message asking for it, and await the response.

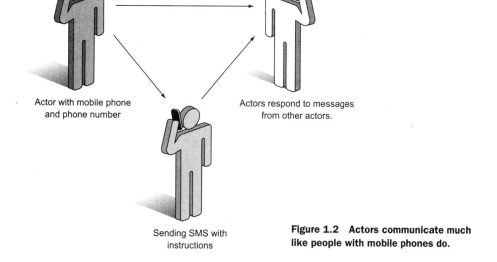

Actor with mobile phone
and phone number

Actors respond to messages
from other actors.

Sending SMS with
instructions

Figure 1.2 Actors communicate much like people with mobile phones do.

Similar to humans, actors can perform a number of operations upon receiving a new message. The simplest operation for a receiving actor is to ignore a message; if it's particularly important, the requesting actor will resend the message and attempt a second time to retrieve a response. Alternatively, upon receiving a message, the receiving actor may choose to send a message elsewhere. This actor might not have all the information available to create a complete response, but it can contact other actors in the system, who might have the information available, after which the receiving actor can act on the message and send a response to the requesting actor. For a particularly intense or long-running task, an actor can spawn another actor that's solely responsible for performing that task. This is similar to how people delegate work to other people if they lack the time needed to perform the task, or if they have other pressing matters to attend to. An actor can also choose how to respond to the next message it receives by modifying its own internal state. This is analogous to hearing new information from a third party that influences your answers to the questions you receive from other people.

The main takeaway when considering the actor model is that its core design principle is to form an abstraction over the top of low-level multithreading concepts to simplify the process of developing concurrent applications. Understanding this, combined with the isolated nature of individual actors, ensures that the systems you build on top of Akka.NET are able to fulfill the criteria in the Reactive Manifesto.

This chapter has shown the core principles that make up the Reactive Manifesto; in later chapters, you'll see how you can apply concepts from Akka.NET to closely align your systems with the aims of the Manifesto.

Summary

In this chapter, you learned

- The driving force behind the move to reactive systems has been the need for systems that are responsive, resilient, elastic, and message-driven, and that can respond to changes in their environment quickly.
- Akka.NET's underlying programming principles are based on the actor model.

Reactive application design

In chapter 1, you saw many reasons why you might want to design an application using the principles laid out in the Reactive Manifesto—reasons primarily driven by the changing face of technology over the past several decades. Whereas computers were once rarities, used primarily by researchers or organizations with sufficient funds, they have since been transformed into the commonplace, with the vast majority of households now having at least one computer, smartphone, or tablet. This number is set to grow with the introduction of the Internet of Things, which is transforming many of the mundane tasks we perform on a daily basis by harnessing the power of an interconnected network of smart devices. This transformation is likely to replicate many of the changes we've already seen in industry over the past few decades, as companies adapt to provide their services in the internet age.

For example, in the world of e-commerce, more and more retailers are providing products and services through online stores. Online shopping has grown, with more consumers opting to use the internet for the majority of their shopping. This has led to a situation in which online retailers are in direct competition with each other. Although this level of competition benefits consumers who can access readily available products with competitive pricing, it puts a huge amount of pressure on retailers to ensure that their online user experience (UX) is near-perfect; otherwise, customers can easily transfer their business to competitors. Research indicates that when consumers encounter errors and excessive page-loading times, they move to competitors with friendlier websites.

2.1 *Basic reactive system design*

Given that the overall aim of the Reactive Manifesto is to provide a responsive experience to the end user, it's apparent that the principles of reactive application design could have significant benefits for the world of e-commerce. You saw the four tenets of a reactive application in chapter 1: it's responsive, fault tolerant, elastically scalable, and message-driven. Of these four, three are directly relevant to an e-commerce website's UX.

If you want to increase the likelihood that customers remain on the website, then you need to ensure that pages load quickly and other actions are performed promptly. If a customer wants to spend money on an e-commerce website, that website should provide a fluid UX; otherwise, the website runs the risk of alienating the user and sending them to a competitor.

An e-commerce website should also be elastically scalable, especially during sharp spikes in numbers of visitors during peak periods of traffic. When you analyze common shopping habits, you see many users accessing websites during a given period, driven by gift-giving holidays such as Christmas, key shopping-discount events such as Black Friday, and so on. In these cases, you want your service to handle the most requests possible. If you have a user spike of an order of magnitude more than normal, you need to accommodate it; otherwise, you run the risk of customers flocking en masse to competing websites.

Similarly, when designing for failure, you want to ensure that even if a non-essential component of an e-commerce website fails, it can still accept the user's payment. For example, if a customer navigates to the checkout page, they shouldn't be faced with errors caused by non-essential features, such as recommendation services or advertising features intended to sell additional products or services. If such components fail, the customer should still be able to complete the purchase.

This combination of requirements suggests that designing an e-commerce application using the principles specified in the Reactive Manifesto may provide substantial benefits. But effectively designing an application using the concepts of the Manifesto can mean significant changes, in terms of both the developer's thought process and the application architecture. In order to better understand reactive application design, in this chapter we'll look at how to design a traditionally CRUD-based application using actors with Akka.NET and the principles from the Manifesto. We'll consider some of the challenges and design decisions you're likely to encounter as you design such applications, as well as how you can effectively design an application using features made available by Akka.NET.

2.2 Reactive e-commerce application with actors

As we've already considered, the way we use computers has rapidly changed over the past several decades, and they're now seen as a commodity that exists in the majority of households, along with internet connection. But users have also become more demanding, requiring more features to enhance their shopping experience. These features include recommendation engines that suggest alternative products, trend calculations to predict which products are due to be the most popular, and integrations with external third-party services that provide additional features and benefits. And e-commerce businesses are interested in gaining insights into how customers are shopping and better positioning themselves to respond to customer demands. This produces high demands on the scalability of both the traffic-handling and application architectures.

Let's consider how you can effectively design a reactive system with an actor-based approach, representing the system entities with actors, in the familiar context of an e-commerce application. If you haven't had the experience of writing e-commerce websites, you've likely used one to make purchases. You saw in the previous section why the world of e-commerce is a strong candidate for reactive application design, where the goal is to create applications that are responsive.

Given that an average e-commerce website is quite large, we won't examine every component within the system; instead, we'll focus on one key aspect of the application: the final purchasing experience. This is the part of the website the user will navigate to once they've finished browsing and are ready to purchase their selected items. This component will have a number of requirements such as providing a shopping cart where users can store items as they browse the site, a checkout where users enter their shipping address, and a payment gateway where users enter payment card details.

Chapter 1 addressed what an actor is and how actors allow you to design applications with concurrency handled transparently for you. It also addressed the requirements of a reactive application and the principles you should adhere to for success. In the rest of this chapter, we'll consider how to incorporate these ways of thinking into a real-life application. We'll also consider how these components would fit into the context of an application designed using Akka.NET, by linking these design ideas to the functionality and features provided as core components of the Akka.NET distribution.

2.2.1 A reactive shopping cart

The first component that a potential customer is likely to encounter is the shopping cart, analogous to the shopping cart in a physical store, which they can use when browsing to collect the items they intend to purchase. Thousands of users may browse the site at once, so your application must support the simultaneous use of thousands of shopping carts. To design this, you'll create a shopping cart, which is nothing more than a list of items and the quantity of items. Each shopping cart is accessed through a unique identifier, which is stored in the user's session. One of the core attributes of actors is the ability to store state, which varies per type of actor. In the case of the shopping cart, you could store a dictionary of the user's session identifier, along with a list of items and quantities. This is how you might model the component if you were to use a database. But actors serialize all incoming messages; only one message is processed at any one time, in order. This means that if lots of users are trying to access their shopping carts at the same time, then they'll have to sit through long queues. This defeats the aim of providing a responsive UX.

But because actors can perform work in parallel and are an incredibly cheap abstraction in terms of memory and computation, you can create many actors to work concurrently. For the shopping cart example, you can create a single actor per shopping cart, responsible for storing a list of items and associated quantities, and the actors are addressed by the shopping cart identifier. You can see an example of this in figure 2.1; each actor is effectively a shopping cart, which is similar to how this might be modeled in the physical world, where you have one physical entity per customer.

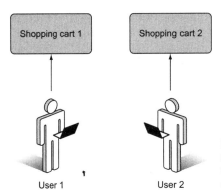

Figure 2.1   Creating one actor per shopping cart allows each shopping cart to be accessed independently of the others. This means there's no contention for resources between User 1 and User 2.

This leads us to the first design pattern you're likely to encounter in an actor-based reactive system. Where possible, you should partition work into actors based on concurrency boundaries; in the case of a shopping cart, a concurrency boundary is an individual shopping cart. Designing systems like this allows for the greatest throughput, ensuring your application remains responsive. It also allows for easier scalability, because you can fine-tune the deployment of the actor to better handle any increased throughput it might experience. The next chapter will look at how to effectively design actors in the context of Akka.NET; you'll also see how to handle an increased throughput by scaling actors out across multiple servers in chapter 12.

2.2.2 Changing states of actors

While a customer is browsing the store, they'll hopefully add items to their cart. There are a number of states a shopping cart can exist in. For example, the two key states are *browsing*, where the customer continues to browse the store, and *purchase-completion*, where the user is completing a purchase. When a user is browsing, they should be able to add more items to their cart; but once they start the process of completing a purchase, you typically don't allow the cart to be modified. This is for a number of reasons, such as the need to reserve items while the purchase is being completed, and computing the cost of the shopping cart contents. You therefore want to prevent new items from being added to the cart while it's in the purchase-completion state.

You saw in the previous section how the shopping cart can be represented as an actor and as part of the actor model. Actors can change their state on demand to respond differently to subsequent messages. Given how this is such a fundamental component of designing actors within actor systems, Akka.NET provides the functionality of switching between states to invoke different behavior and simplify the process of responding to messages. In figure 2.2, you can see how the shopping cart actor can switch between multiple different states.

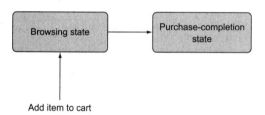

Figure 2.2 The use of state machines with actors in Akka.NET allows you to simplify the process of developing actors with complex internal logic.

This shows another pattern you'll typically encounter with applications written using Akka.NET, whereby you switch between multiple different states as required. Specifying multiple different states allows you to focus on one individual state and the messages it's able to respond to, without needing to consider alternative scenarios simultaneously. This lets you easily understand the logic embedded within actors at a later stage. You'll see how this can be applied to actors in chapter 4, when we consider the importance of state machines in Akka.NET applications and how you can represent them.

2.2.3 Making the purchase

Once a customer has decided on everything they want to purchase, they proceed to the payment stage where you process their choice of payment, typically a credit or debit card. To simplify the development of complex systems involving credit card details, a solution is to integrate with an external payment gateway. You send a request to a third-party service with a token representing the user's credit card details and the total value of the purchase. Given that you're integrating with external services, there's a high probability of failures happening, so you need the system to allow for failure. As you saw in chapter 1, for a system to be truly responsive, it needs to continue to work even in situations where individual components might fail. Due to the high potential for failure when designing complex systems, the Akka.NET mindset is to embrace failure and provide the ability to recover from it quickly.

In Akka.NET, an actor can supervise other actors that are spawned as its children. This design allows for a number of different operations when an actor is discovered to have failed; for example, you may want to restart the actor and attempt to retry whatever work it had been performing, or you might want to stop the actor's operations altogether. By pushing as much work as possible down to child actors, you can isolate failures and allow for a broader approach than retrying the operation, which might be sufficient to resolve the issue. In figure 2.3, an actor has to perform two tasks: upload some data to a web API responsible for processing the payment on a user's credit card, and then send a message to another actor upon completion, informing it that the purchase has been completed. The actor pushes the potentially dangerous work, in this case the web API call, down to a child actor, which is responsible for performing the operation.

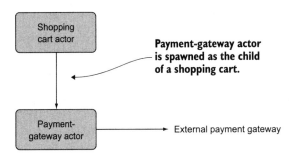

Figure 2.3 Creating child actors allows you to perform dangerous work by isolating it from the rest of the application.

This is another common design pattern in Akka.NET. Because actors are completely isolated from other actors, should one actor encounter difficulties, it won't directly endanger other actors executing as part of an application. You'll see the concept of passing work down to children in chapter 3, when we look at spawning new actors to perform work. You'll then learn how to use actor-based supervision to create fault-tolerant applications in chapter 6.

2.2.4 Data transfer between services

Underpinning the methodology behind designing applications with Akka.NET is the actor model, a concurrency model that solves the problems of coordination and synchronization of operations across multiple threads by preferring isolation. In the actor model, every actor is independent of every other actor, and they communicate by sending messages to each other, in much the same way as humans communicate with each other. This means that when you design applications using Akka.NET, you need to think about how actors talk to each other. Let's consider the example of the payment-gateway actor you saw in the previous section. The payment-gateway actor is solely responsible for interacting with the external payment service, but many components make up the payment flow of an e-commerce website. For example, after a customer has made a purchase, what should the next step be? The logical next step is to fulfill the order speedily. If your e-commerce application is selling digital media, then you may have another actor responsible for assigning privileges to the user's account, which allows them to view the content they've just purchased. Alternatively, if you're selling physical products, then you need to retrieve the products from the warehouse and prepare printed invoices and shipping labels, which will be sent with the purchase.

Because you want to prioritize fine-grained operations within actors, for reasons of scalability and fault tolerance (which I'll address in depth later), you'll have multiple actors responsible for selected operations within the checkout flow. These independent actors need to be able to share results. Each actor has an address associated with it, by means of which other actors can communicate with it; this allows them to pass messages between fixed addresses for actors, rather than having direct references to actors themselves. For example, after the customer has completed their payment and you've verified its authenticity, you pass the message on to the component responsible for fulfilling the order. The payment-gateway actor automatically sends a message to the addresses for multiple other actors in response to payment completion, as illustrated in figure 2.4.

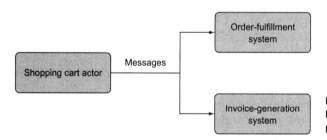

Figure 2.4 Sending messages between actors is a fundamental part of reactive application design.

Messaging between actors is a fundamental aspect of reactive applications designed with Akka.NET; it plays a crucial role in the Reactive Manifesto by providing the foundation on which you create fault tolerance and elastic scalability. As such, you'll see messaging appear in every chapter throughout the rest of the book; but I'll introduce messages in more detail in chapter 3, when you create your first actors.

2.2.5 *Scaling work with routers*

In an e-commerce application, often a single actor is responsible for a certain operation: for example, an actor that performs a search operation for products. But due to the concurrency guarantee offered by Akka.NET, which specifies that only one message should be processed at once, there may be a large queue of messages waiting to be processed by that actor. For the task of product search, you maintain an index of words commonly used so an actor can look up search terms related to certain products. A search actor stores the word index as its internal state and then receives a message to search it for products containing the search term. But if several hundred users are searching for products simultaneously, they may encounter queues as the actor performs each search individually. Although this actor is stateful, in that it stores the product index internally, it is stateless between requests, which ensures that you can easily parallelize the search operation. Figure 2.5 shows that you no longer have a *single actor* processing each message, but instead have multiple independent actors, which are treated as a *single target*.

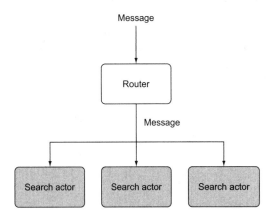

Figure 2.5   **You can parallelize stateless operations by using multiple actors behind a routing proxy.**

The introduction of a *router* allows you to abstract away multiple individual actor instances and treat them all as a single actor, given that you direct messages to the router rather than to each actor sitting behind the router. The use of routers as a means of parallelizing trivial workloads is a common pattern, and you'll see how to use one in chapter 6, when we look at using routers to build scalable applications that respond to an increased number of messages by forwarding messages to other targets.

2.2.6   *Wrapping up*

These are just some of the most basic design patterns you're likely to encounter when designing applications using the fundamentals of the Reactive Manifesto. Figure 2.6 shows a broader picture of the checkout system as a whole, which features the individual components and how they communicate with each other. You can see the customer's shopping cart, where they add items as they browse through the store. After a while, the user is finished shopping and wants to complete their purchase. The shopping cart then transfers into the purchase-completion state, which passes customer payment details to an external payment gateway. When a response comes back from the payment gateway, the application can complete the purchase.

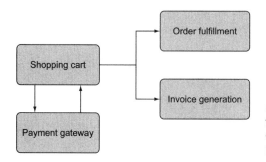

Figure 2.6   A simple e-commerce checkout flow has a number of interconnected components that can be built from the design patterns you've seen so far.

Here, we've considered only some of the basic design patterns; but even simple Akka.NET functionality forces you to consider many of the principles that make up a reactive application. The use of message passing directs you down a systems path that simplifies the process of scalability and fault tolerance; actors force you to think about concurrency boundaries and which tasks can be performed simultaneously; and supervision makes you think about what will happen in the event of the failure of other systems, whether internal or external. Throughout the rest of the book, we'll progressively consider deeper design patterns that help simplify the process of developing larger and more complex systems.

2.3   *Building on reactive foundations*

Although these few components allow you to build an e-commerce system with a wide array of features, many potential enhancements are available for you to take it further. On top of the basic components provided by Akka.NET, there are a number of additional components for building more-advanced functionality. In this section, we'll consider how you can extend your application using these features, and easily build larger and more complex systems that continue to follow the principles of the Manifesto.

2.3.1   *Publishing the e-commerce application to the world*

As it currently stands, the e-commerce application you designed exists solely as an Akka.NET application. A typical system is consumed by a number of different clients including web browsers and mobile apps; this means that you need to add some degree of integration with existing systems. With Akka.NET, you can expose an actor system onto a network using the Akka.Remote functionality, which lets other clients consume your e-commerce application.

Let's consider one of the most typical ways of consuming an e-commerce application: using a website in a web browser. In this case, you need to serve the contents of the application through a secure HTTP interface. Figure 2.7 shows the scenario: a web API that communicates with the Akka.NET application. By using an HTTP-based web API, clients and web browsers can consume your application.

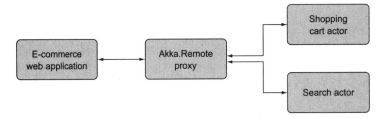

Figure 2.7   Akka.NET applications need to be accessible to a number of clients. This can be achieved through the use of a web proxy in front of the application.

To achieve this level of integration, Akka.NET provides the Akka.Remote functionality, which lets you expose an Akka.NET application over a network connection to other clients. This allows a web proxy to communicate with the actors defined in your web application, such as the shopping cart or payment-gateway actors. You'll see in chapter 8 how to use Akka.Remote to work with existing web API projects.

2.3.2 Storing state within actors

The application you've created has no persistence of state and, instead, stores everything in memory. You'll usually want to persist changing data so that users can modify it. Consider the shopping cart. In an e-commerce store, you want to ensure that there's minimal friction in the buying process. Losing the user's shopping cart is a potential loss of revenue for the business. To avoid data loss, it's important to persist data to a persistent data store such as a database or a filesystem. In chapter 11, you'll see how to use a database to back up the data stored in your actors to create resilient applications with Akka.Persistence.

2.3.3 Scaling out across a cluster of machines

As e-commerce sites continue to grow in popularity, it's likely that your website and e-commerce application will see an increase in traffic volume. This may become too much for a single server to handle, so you'll need to use multiple servers. For this purpose, Akka.NET provides the Akka.Cluster extension, which allows you to treat a number of machines as a cluster. You can run your e-commerce application across all machines in the cluster and scale up the application beyond the limits of a single server. In chapter 12, you'll see how Akka.Cluster lets you build elastically scalable services and systems that scale on demand across multiple machines, as dictated by load.

2.3.4 Continuing to react to environmental changes

The Reactive Manifesto states that an application should react to changes in its environment. In an Akka.NET application, this often means responding to a message from another actor, such as the way multiple actors communicated in the checkout flow. But sometimes changes need to trigger an immediate response; for example, in your e-commerce application, peripheral components may rely on knowing when a customer completes a purchase. Such components might include systems that auto-suggest new products based on historical purchases, or internal systems that adjust pricing automatically based on the number of purchases within a given time period. In these cases, responding to events as soon as they occur lets you build more-reactive applications. Akka.NET provides publish-subscribe functionality, allowing decoupled components to register to receive any messages that are published onto an event bus. In chapter 12, you'll see how the distributed publish/subscribe functionality can respond to changes in the cluster as soon as they happen.

2.3.5 *Wrapping up*

Akka.NET provides a rich ecosystem of additional functionality, much of which is beyond the scope of a simple checkout in an e-commerce application. Given increasingly demanding customers and a more competitive marketplace, it's important to consider how some of this additional functionality can be applied to a simple shopping cart to create a richer experience for users, leading to increased spending on your e-commerce website. These more advanced features will be addressed later in the book, when we look at clustering across machines, persisting actor state to external data stores, and integrating an Akka.NET application with other applications, whether these are new or legacy applications.

Summary

In this chapter, you learned

- Applications that follow the principles of the Reactive Manifesto are responsive, fault tolerant, elastically scalable, and message-driven.
- Several core design patterns can be used to simplify reactive application development: the actor model, using state machines, and using routers.
- When designing a system to benefit from Akka.NET, consider using Akka.Remote to expose your application to other clients, persisting data, scaling services, and incorporating publish/subscribe functionality.

Part 2

Digging in

Part 2 digs down into the details that you need to create fully functional reactive systems in Akka.NET. Chapter 3 presents your first Akka.NET application, taking you through the design patterns typically used when designing reactive systems in Akka.NET. Chapter 4 will teach you how to selectively receive messages into an actor with switchable behaviors, and will also teach you the basics on finite state machines, including how to model them using Akka.NET. Chapter 5 takes a deep look into how you can instrument and operationalize an Akka.NET application through the configuration of individual actors and actor systems as a whole. Chapter 6 focuses on how to respond to service failures within an Akka.NET application, delivering an in-depth look from the original source of the failure to typical failure models. In chapter 7, you'll take a look at the difficulties involved with traditional scaling approaches, and how the Akka.NET approach is different. Chapter 8 looks at actor systems and how to link, scale, and create applications that can handle machine-level failure.

Your first Akka.NET application

3

This chapter covers

- Setting up an actor system
- Defining an actor
- Sending a message to an actor
- Evaluating alternative actor implementations

The first few chapters covered what *reactive architecture* means, as well as the key reasons you'll likely want to use it. You've seen how the aim of a reactive system is to create applications that are responsive to the end user, and how this requires applications to work, even when struggling with the demands of scale or malfunctioning components. We've also covered the key things you need to consider when designing a reactive application.

For the rest of the book, we'll consider how you can write reactive systems that follow the principles laid out in the Reactive Manifesto: guidelines designed to suggest solutions that many organizations have found effective for solving their problems. There are many means of developing reactive systems, but we'll focus on one in particular. You'll use the actor model as the underlying basis for your reactive systems, and the implementation you'll use is Akka.NET, a framework designed for writing concurrent applications using the actor model in .NET.

By the end of this chapter, you'll have a basic actor that can receive messages, and you'll send this actor some messages. You'll then be able to adapt this actor and start to build your own, capable of performing more-complex functions.

3.1   Setting up an application

Akka.NET feels much like a framework, but it markets itself as a toolkit and runtime that form the basis of concurrent applications. Akka.NET requires no special application configuration to run and can be hosted in any of the normal .NET runtime environments, whether console applications, Windows services, IIS, WPF, or Windows Forms applications. Throughout this book, examples are given in the form of console applications unless otherwise specified.

All the components required to run Akka.NET are distributed through the NuGet package management system. Because Akka.NET relies on modern features of the .NET runtime, it requires a minimum of .NET v4.5. Akka.NET also has full Mono support, allowing it to run in Linux and Mac OS X environments.

To install the libraries, a NuGet client is required. Options available for dependency management with a NuGet client include these:

- *Visual Studio package-management GUI*—If you're developing applications using Visual Studio, then dependencies can be managed directly through the references node of a project in the Solution Explorer.
- *Command-line tooling*—In environments where you don't have access to Visual Studio, a number of command-line tooling options are available, including the official NuGet client and third-party alternatives such as Paket.

The only NuGet package required to develop applications in a single-machine scenario is the Akka package. This provides all of the core functionality required to create and host actors, and then send messages to these actors.

3.2   Actors

When considering Akka.NET, it's important to realize that the ideas surrounding the framework are those relating to concurrency. The actor model is designed to allow multiple tasks to operate independently of each other. It abstracts away many of the underlying multithreading constructs that are required to ensure that concurrency is possible. At the heart of this is the concept of an *actor*.

3.2.1   What does an actor embody?

Let's consider what an actor is in the context of Akka.NET. The actor model is a model of computation designed to make concurrency as easy as possible by abstracting away the difficulties associated with threading, including mutexes, semaphores, and other multithreading concepts.

We can think of actors in the same way that we think of people. Every day, we communicate with hundreds or thousands of people using a variety of methods. People send messages to those surrounding them and then react to messages they've received. This communication is all in the form of message passing, where a message can be any of a number of types, such as body language or verbal cues. When a person receives a message, they can process the information and make decisions. The decisions a person makes might include sending a message back to the original sender, such as saying "hello" in response to a greeting, or it may be to interact with other parts of the world, such as tasting or feeling something in order to get more information. Finally, a person can save memories or information in their mind. For example, they're able to recognize faces and names, and store facts for later recollection.

The comparison between human communication and actors can be condensed into three key concepts, which form the basis of the actor model. These three concepts are *communication*—how they send messages between each other; *processing*—how an actor responds whenever it receives a new message; and *state*—the information that an actor is able to store when processing.

COMMUNICATION

When considering the principles of reactive applications, you saw the advantages of using a message-passing architecture to build systems that are scalable and fault tolerant. By default, all actors communicate asynchronously by means of message passing.

Each actor has a unique identifier—an address—through which it can be contacted. You can think of the actor's address in exactly the same way you think of an email address: it provides a known endpoint you can send messages to. The end user can receive their email at any address, and the same is true with an actor's address. You can send a message to an actor's address, and it automatically gets routed to the intended processing for that actor. This address is then connected to a *mailbox*, which is a queue of the messages an actor has received at its address. This mailbox is where every message is added as it's received, until the actor is able to process the messages sequentially.

Email can serve various purposes. It can contain text, media, or even contact information. Akka.NET is similar, but it relies on using data types as the basis of messages. Actors can use any type as the basis of messages, but there's one requirement: messages must be immutable. If a message isn't immutable, then the actor could potentially modify it either while it's in the processing stage or while it's in the queue. In either scenario, this would break the concurrency safety guarantees provided by Akka.NET.

PROCESSING

Once a message has been received, an actor needs to be able to do something with that data. This is the job of the actor's processing component. As a message is received, the processing component is started by the framework, which then invokes the appropriate method on the message object to handle it. Akka.NET provides guarantees that at most one message will be processed at any one time and, due to the queue provided by the framework, that the processing component receives the messages in the exact order they were sent to the actor.

Akka.NET supports different programming methodologies, so there are a number of techniques for using the APIs that best fit different paradigms. For example, the C# APIs revolve around the use of inheritance.

STATE

The analogy of actors as people touched on the notion of memory and information saved in the brain. If you want to access this data, you can't directly query it from somebody else; you need to ask them about data *they* know about. The same concept applies with actors. An actor is free to store whatever state is appropriate, and then forms a sealed boundary around it. The only thing in the application that has access to the data stored in the actor is the processing component associated with that actor.

The primary reason for this is that actors are a construct designed to reduce complexity when writing multithreaded applications. Removing shared access to data reduces vast numbers of potential concurrency bugs, such as deadlocks and race conditions. It also means you can quickly scale up an application built on actors, because you can deploy actors into new locations when required.

COMBINED RESULT

When these three constructs—communication, processing, and state—are combined, you have the concept of an actor: a high-level approach to dealing with concurrency, whether the tasks running concurrently are on separate threads or in separate data-centers. Figure 3.1 shows the interaction between the three key concepts and how they relate to each other. As you can see, the state is entirely enclosed within the bounds of the actor and isn't accessible from outside the actor instance. The only means you have of manipulating or retrieving the data is through the use of behavior, which you define to run within the bounds of the actor. This behavior is then only invoked as required when a new message is received by the actor's inbox.

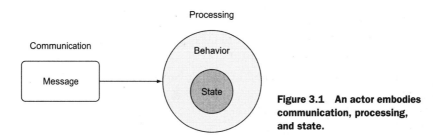

Figure 3.1 An actor embodies communication, processing, and state.

3.2.2   *What can an actor do?*

You've seen that actors are very small isolated entities that share nothing with the outside world, and each of them is scheduled to process the messages in its mailbox. They're like small applications that have built-in communication channels. Because of this, actors are able to perform any operation an application can normally perform. But you can generalize the actions that an actor is likely to perform into three categories:

- *Sending a message*—When you designed a reactive system, you saw that an application is typically built as a data flow, whereby applications propagate events that they've received and responded to. Actors need to be able to send messages to other addresses in the actor system. This task isn't necessarily confined to sending messages to *actors*; it could also include communication through external services with other transport protocols such as HTTP.
- *Spawning other actors*—When an actor is under load with long-running computations and a queue of messages, it can spawn a new actor responsible for handling all of the significant processing. The ability of an actor to spawn new actors also serves other uses, such as having a supervisory actor spawn new children to perform dangerous work that may lead to errors.
- *Setting behavior for the next message*—One key role of an actor is to respond to messages it receives: reactive applications respond to changes in their environment. Changes in an environment are likely to lead to changes in the way messages need to be processed, so actors should be able to set how they process new messages.

These are some of the common tasks that actors perform, but it's likely that your actors will be performing other tasks as well. These might include jobs such as connecting with external web services, interacting with devices such as the graphics on the host machine, and interacting with external input and output on the host machine.

There is, however, a restriction on the kind of work an actor can perform. Actors should avoid performing long-running blocking operations, particularly in cases where a number of actors may all be performing blocking operations. This prevents the Akka.NET scheduler from running any of the processing for other actors. The work that actors do should be asynchronous and operate primarily through message passing. An example of a blocking operation is waiting for a user to enter some text into a console window through the use of `Console.ReadLine`.

3.2.3 *Defining an actor*

Now that you understand actors and how the core components fit together, let's look at how to define an actor. Think again about the similarity between actor communication and how people communicate. Let's build an example with actors to model this interaction. You'll create an actor that represents the sort of actions a person might take after receiving a greeting.

When writing an actor in C#, you rely on the inheritance of certain actor classes and override certain methods that are called whenever a new message arrives. The simplest possible means of implementing an actor is to use the `UntypedActor` class.

Using this approach, you can execute a single method any time a new message arrives, similar to the following:

```
class PersonActor : UntypedActor
{
    protected override void OnReceive(object message)
    {
    Console.WriteLine("Received a message: {0}", message);
    }
}
```

This basic example shows how you create an actor using Akka.NET, but you'll also want to do something with the actor when it receives a message. You can use any type within the Common Language Runtime (CLR) as a message, with the only requirement being that the class must be immutable.

> **NOTE** In the following message classes, I omitted constructor guards, which should be used to verify that you're not, for example, passing a null or empty value where you should be passing an actual value. In a production-quality application, as opposed to demo code, additional checking should be performed to ensure that the application consistently stays in a valid state.

Create two messages that an actor can receive, Wave and VocalGreeting:

```
class Wave {}

class VocalGreeting
{
    private readonly string _greeting;
    public string Greeting { get { return _greeting; }}

    public VocalGreeting(string greeting)
    {
        _greeting = greeting;
    }
}
```

Now the actor can be changed to perform different actions when it receives a message of a given type. For example, when it receives a VocalGreeting message, it can print a message to the console:

```
class PersonActor : UntypedActor
{
    protected override void OnReceive(object message)
    {
    if(message is VocalGreeting)
        {
            very msg = (VocalGreeting)message;
            Console.WriteLine("Hello there!");
        }
    }
}
```

When you create a message for each type, you end up with a lot of duplication in the handling of the message. Here, for example, you've got two types of messages, and in each instance, you need to check whether the message is of a certain type and then cast it to that type. You can also end up with a lot of code duplication when you want to check a condition within the message itself. To prevent this, Akka.NET provides an API that can pattern match on the message type. The following example shows how, using the Akka.NET pattern-matching API, you can invoke a handler, depending on the message received:

```
class PersonActor : UntypedActor
{
    protected override void OnReceive(object message)
    {
      message.Match()
              .With<VocalGreeting>
                    (x => Console.WriteLine("Hello there"));
    }
}
```

Akka.NET also provides a further abstraction on top of the basic actor, which you can use to declaratively handle messages. ReceiveActor combines many aspects of pattern matching while continuing to abstract away much of the logic surrounding message-type handling. Whereas with the simple UntypedActor you had to override a method that would be executed on receipt of a message, ReceiveActor requires you to register a message handler for each of the message types you want to support. The following example shows how the previous example using an UntypedActor can be converted to the ReceiveActor implementation:

```
class PersonActor : ReceiveActor
{
    public PersonActor()
    {
        Receive<VocalGreeting>
            (x => Console.WriteLine("Hello there"));
    }
}
```

Akka.NET is a model for concurrently performing asynchronous operations, and as such is an alternative to the .NET Task Parallel Library (TPL). When dealing with asynchronous operations, you'll typically pipe the results back to the actor's mailbox as a message, but ReceiveActor provides the ability to interoperate with the TPL through asynchronous message handlers. An asynchronous message handler works exactly the same as a regular message handler, except it returns a Task instead of void:

```
class PersonActor : ReceiveActor
{
    public PersonActor()
    {
        Receive<VocalGreeting>(async x =>
```

```
        {
            await Task.Delay(50);
            Console.WriteLine("Hello there");
        });
    }
}
```

The approaches shown so far for creating actors have relied on the use of delegates for handling messages, but Akka.NET provides an additional means of creating actors in the form of `TypedActor`. It allows for stricter contracts for the types of messages actors can receive, by implementing an interface for each of them. When an actor receives a message of a given type, the method implementing the interface for that message type is executed with an instance of the received message:

```
class PersonActor : TypedActor,
                    IHandle<VocalGreeting>
{
    void Handle(VocalGreeting greeting)
    {
        Console.WriteLine("Hello there");
    }
}
```

All of the actor definitions here allow you to build up bigger and more advanced actors, capable of performing more-complex operations. As you've seen, actor definitions are classes in C# that override specific methods. You can store state in an actor using either properties or fields of the class.

When you store state in an actor, it's only accessible from within that actor. It's impossible to access any properties or fields from outside the actor's boundaries. This means that, regardless of where an actor exists, there's no need to worry about synchronizing access to the state, because messages are processed one at a time:

```
class PersonActor : ReceiveActor
{
    private int _peopleMet = 0;

    public PersonActor()
    {
        Receive<VocalGreeting>(x =>
            {
                _peopleMet++;
                Console.WriteLine("I've met {0} people today",
                                  _peopleMet);
            });
    }
}
```

Upon receiving a message, it's common to require some metadata about either the message received, such as the address of the sender, or the actor processing the message, such as the address behavior stored in the actor. In any of the actor types, you can access this metadata through the `Context` property. For example, if you want to identify the sender of a message, you can access it through the Sender property of the context. Given the sender, an actor can send messages in response to a message it received. In human terms, if somebody waves at you, you can say "hello" to that person in response by sending them a VocalGreeting and also waving at them with a WaveGreeting:

```
class PersonActor : ReceiveActor
{
    public PersonActor()
    {
        Receive<Wave>(x =>
            {
                Context.Sender.Tell(
                    new VocalGreeting("Hello!"));
                Context.Sender.Tell(
                    new WaveGreeting ();
            });
    }
}
```

There are many more ways of defining actors that are specific to certain aspects of Akka.NET, but I'll cover those in later chapters.

3.2.4 Wrapping up

In reactive system design, one key consideration is that operations should be done on the level of the smallest unit of work. In the context of Akka.NET, the actor is the encapsulation of that smallest unit of work. Actors are designed in line with the concurrent programming model, so any operations within the confines of an actor are thread safe. Thus, you can scale out your application across as many threads, machines, or data centers as you like, and the framework will be able to handle any and all scaling issues. These are handled by queued messages processed one at a time, ensuring that messages are processed in the same order in which they're received.

3.3 Deploying an actor

Having defined an actor, you need to get it running in your application. Let's dig into the underlying framework and see how you can use Akka.NET to start instances of actors that can react to messages. We'll look at the concept of an *actor system* and how to deploy an actor into one.

3.3.1 The actor system

If actors are people, then actor systems are the countries in which they live. An actor system is essentially the host within which all of your actors are deployed. Once actors are deployed, they can perform any assigned tasks. Like people under governments, actors need some form of management and restrictions in place to ensure that they're good and valuable citizens in society. These tasks fall within the realm of the actor system, which is not only the actor host, but also the scheduler and routing system. You don't need to know about the internals of the actor system to be able to develop applications with Akka.NET, because it abstracts all of that away from the user.

Some of the key roles the actor system is in charge of include these:

- *Scheduling*—Actors, as multithreading constructs, run at a higher level than regular threads, and as such, they need some means of coordination. The actor system ensures that all actors have a fair chance of processing their messages within a reasonable amount of time. It also ensures that heavily used actors can't starve the system of resources, which prevents less frequently used actors from being in a situation where they're not processing data.

- *Message routing*—All messaging through Akka.NET is location transparent, meaning the sender doesn't need to have any knowledge of the location of the recipient. But some part of the system *does* need to know the locations, and this is the actor system. It's capable of routing messages to many different locations, whether they're on a separate thread, running on a remote system, or running on a machine in a cluster.

- *Supervision*—The actor system is also the top-level supervisor of your application, so that, if a component crashes, the actor system can recover it. Chapter 6 looks into this, when you incorporate the notion of fault tolerance into your application.

- *Extensions*—Akka.NET supports a vast range of extensibility points at all stages in the processing pipeline. The actor system is responsible for managing all of these extensibility points and ensuring that any extensions are correctly incorporated into the application.

This is only a small subset of the many tasks the actor system is responsible for. It's common to have only one actor system running per application. On a machine, actor systems are identified using unique names, allowing for the possibility of more than one actor system existing on each machine.

Actors in Akka.NET operate under the concept of a *hierarchy*, whereby each actor is the child of another actor in the hierarchy. This arrangement provides better fault tolerance when you're developing applications; the intricacies of this will be covered in chapter 6. When instantiating an actor system, Akka.NET initially creates a number of actors used by the system. The top-level actors are these:

- `user`—This actor holds all the actors spawned in the actor system. Even if you spawn an actor without a parent, it *does* have a parent in the form of the `user` actor, which supervises all of the top-level actors.

- `system`—This is the top-level actor under which all of the system-level actors are stored—typically actors that are used for tasks such as logging, or those deployed as part of some configuration.

- `deadletters`—As actors are free to send messages to any address at any stage of the application, there's always the possibility that no actor instance is available at the path specified. In this case, the messages are directed to the `deadletters` actor.

- *temp*—At times, Akka.NET spawns short-lived actors. This is typically for scenarios such as retrieving data, which will be covered later in this chapter.
- *remote*—When multiple actor systems are joined using Akka.NET remoting, there are some scenarios in which Akka.NET needs to create actors to perform supervisory tasks when a supervisor exists on a separate machine. In these cases, the `remote` top-level actor is used. This will be covered in chapter 8.

These actors all form part of the actor hierarchy. In figure 3.2, you can see their deployment in the hierarchy of a relatively simple actor system. The actors form a tree structure, similar to a filesystem, with files and folders. The user has deployed three actors into the actor system, `actorA`, `actorB`, and `childA`, which is a child actor spawned beneath `actorA`.

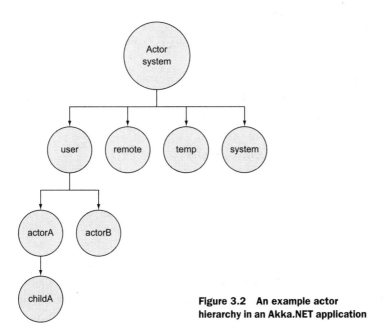

Figure 3.2   An example actor hierarchy in an Akka.NET application

The decision to use actors for all top-level work in Akka.NET ensures that a uniform interface exists throughout the application. `user` actors are free to send a message to any of these system-created actors in the same way that a `user` might expect to send a message to an actor that they have instantiated.

3.3.2   Spawning an actor

In section 3.2.3, you defined a `GreeterActor` that can do some work; now, you need to deploy it into an application so that it can be used. Before you can deploy an actor, you need something capable of hosting it: you need to initialize an actor system. As you've seen, the actor system is the component of Akka.NET responsible for many of the tasks related to how actors are run within the framework.

Instantiating an actor system that hosts actors is a simple task: call the `Create` static method on the actor system. The only requirement when creating an actor system is to name it so that actors can be identified based on which actor system they live in:

```
var actorSystem = ActorSystem.Create("MyActorSystem");
```

An actor system can also be created with a configuration section for customizing parts of the framework (covered in chapter 5). For now, you'll create an actor system without a configuration file in C#, which causes a fallback to the default configuration.

The actor system is responsible for many of the internal tasks and scheduling associated with the Akka.NET framework. As a result, the actor system ends up becoming a heavyweight object, so you typically only spawn one actor system per application. The actor system is also the main means you have of interacting with actors operating within the framework. In the majority of scenarios, it's typical for the actor system to reside either in a static class or in a singleton object, or be injected as a dependency into those methods that require it.

Once an actor system has been created, you're free to deploy new actors into it. For this, you use the `ActorOf` method, which requires the actor type to instantiate as a generic type argument. The following example shows how you can deploy your actor from earlier into the actor system:

```
var actorRef = actorSystem.ActorOf<GreeterActor("actorA");
```

Once the `ActorOf` method has been called, Akka.NET will create and initialize the new actor. You also pass it a string that you can use to uniquely identify a given actor instance within the actor system, `actorA` in this case. With this name, you can retrieve references to the actor instance directly from the actor system.

3.3.3 *Wrapping up*

The actor system forms the basis of the host within which your actors will live. Although you don't need to understand all the intricacies of what happens deep within the framework, it's beneficial to be familiar with some of the features provided by the actor system. The actor system is also the key extensibility point of an Akka.NET application and allows more-advanced features to be implemented, many of which we'll look at in later chapters.

3.4 *Communicating with actors*

Having spawned an actor into your actor system, you'll want to communicate with it. The actor is currently doing no work and just sitting in memory. By communicating with it, the framework will invoke the message-processing on that actor.

As you've seen, the actor model relies on message passing as a means of communication between actors. *Message* is essentially a generic term for a collection of data that's packaged and sent to an actor instance, represented by its address, somewhere in the actor system. You saw in the example earlier that your messages will consist of data types you've created.

3.4.1 Actor addresses and references

Upon spawning an actor, the actor system returns a direct reference to the actor through an IActorRef. This actor reference isn't a direct reference to the actor's location in memory, but rather a reference to the actor as used by Akka.NET. The reference facilitates sending messages to the inbox of the referenced actor. The Akka.NET framework provides a number of built-in means of referencing actors, including actor references for clusters and remote actor systems, but you won't see these until later chapters.

The most commonly used actor reference is LocalActorRef, whose job is to operate on actor systems that function on a single machine. The key component of the actor reference is the storage of the address of the actor itself. Upon deployment, every actor is given a unique address, through which it is reachable. The address is reminiscent of a simple URI that might be used to identify files in a filesystem or web pages on a website. Figure 3.3 shows the four key components of an actor address:

- *Protocol identifier*—This is used to reference how a connection is made to the actor system. It's similar to how *http* and *https* are used in web addresses to identify which system should be used. For a single machine, this is typically through an identifier similar to akka://, but for concepts such as remoting, there are other commonly used identifiers, such as akka.tcp://.
- *Actor system name*—When you create an actor system, you give it a unique name, represented by this part of the address.
- *Address*—This is only used with remoting, but it still forms a key part of the actor path and identifies the machine on which an actor system resides.
- *Path*—The final part of the address is the path, used to identify an actor. All user-defined actors start with /user/ for this part of the path, but other system-defined actors inhabit other root addresses.

All parts form an actor path.

Protocol   ActorSystem   Address   Path

akka.tcp://MySystem@localhost:9001/user/actorName1

Figure 3.3   The four parts of an actor address

Using an actor reference ensures that your application is loosely coupled, but other problems remain. To send a message to a given actor reference, you need to pass the actor reference around the application. Among the benefits of a message-driven architecture is the ability to have loosely coupled systems where actors don't rely on intimate knowledge of other actors. To achieve this with Akka.NET, you send messages to an address rather than to an actor reference directly. Given an address, you're able to send a message to that address. For example, to send a message to `ActorA` in your actor system, you retrieve a reference to its address:

```
var address = system.ActorSelection("/user/ActorA");
```

When you deploy an actor, you see that it's deployed into a hierarchy. If you deploy an actor as the child of another actor, then you can continue to address it, similar to how you find files in a folder in a filesystem. If `ActorA` has a child actor called `Child`, then you can send messages to it as follows:

```
var childAddress = system.ActorSelection("/user/ActorA/Child");
```

The addressing system in Akka.NET also respects the use of path-traversal elements that are typically associated with URIs. For example, a common case is to retrieve the parent of the current actor, so that messages can be sent to a sibling of the current actor. This can be achieved by using the `..` syntax to retrieve an actor's parent:

```
var address = Context.ActorSelection("../ActorB");
```

Actor selection vs. actor references

Although it might seem that the concepts of *actor selection* and *actor reference* are the same, there's a significant difference in that an actor reference points to a specific incarnation of an actor, whereas an actor selection points to an address. This address may be shared with multiple instantiations of an actor. For example, given a *reference* to a specific actor, if that actor is destroyed and re-created, then any messages sent to that actor reference won't be delivered to the target, even if they both share the exact same path across instantiations. But, given an actor *selection*, messages can be sent to it; even if an actor is destroyed and re-created, all messages will be delivered.

This distinction allows for more-complex paths to be used in the context of an actor address. An example of this is the use of wildcards in an actor's path to select a large number of actors at once. When actors have been selected, you can send the same message to all actors encompassed by the wildcard with a single method call. Paths in Akka.NET support two kinds of wildcards in actor addresses, based on a standard wildcard syntax common to other languages and tools:

- `?`—The question mark replaces a single instance of any given character in a path. For example, the path c?t matches paths such as cat, but not coat or cost.
- `*`—The asterisk matches any string of characters usable as a path. For example, the path /parent/*/ sends a message to all children of the actor called parent.

On occasion, it's beneficial to have a *direct reference* to an actor instance rather than a *generic address*. For this, Akka.NET provides a number of means of retrieving a reference from an address:

- *Calling* `ActorOf` *to spawn a new actor*—Upon spawning a new actor, a direct reference to that actor is returned, which represents the incarnation that has been spawned.
- *Sending a message to an actor*—By sending a message to an actor, you can use the `sender` property of a received message to identify which actor replied to the request for information. Akka.NET provides built-in support for this through the `Identify` message, and through an abstraction over the top of this on `ActorSelection`, which can be used to resolve an instance.

Although often it's appropriate to send messages to an address, it can frequently be beneficial to pass around a reference to a specific actor. For example, for a long-running actor that's valid throughout the lifecycle of the application and carries out a specific purpose, it's typical to pass an actor reference in the constructor of those actors that depend on it.

It's important to understand the difference between an actor reference and a simple actor address due in part to the actor lifecycle, covered in chapter 4. But for your purposes, either is an appropriate means of messaging a specific actor.

3.4.2 Sending a message

After spawning an actor into the system, you can communicate with it by sending messages to its mailbox. For this, you need something capable of receiving a message. As you saw in the discussion of the differences between an address and a reference, you can send a message to either. Once an actor is spawned, the actor system returns a reference to that actor instance, to which you can then send a message. The actor reference defines a method called `Tell`, which takes an instance of any type and passes it through the Akka.NET framework. If you're using F#, a custom operator is defined for sending a message. For example, if you want to send a vocal greeting message to the actor you defined earlier, you can do so as follows:

```
actorRef.Tell(new VocalGreeting("Hello"));
```

There may be times when you don't have an actor reference; on those occasions, you'll look up an actor by its address. For this, you need something capable of providing references to other actors. This may be the actor system that's hosting the actor, or it may be the `Context` associated with a specific actor. To select `actorA` that you deployed earlier, you can use the actor system and select the actor by its address:

```
var selection = actorSystem.ActorSelection("actorA");
```

In each of these cases, the actor system provides the root location from which actors will be retrieved, which for the actor system is directly beneath the user actor. But if you had a second actor deployed alongside your first, you could use the first actor reference as an anchor to other actor locations:

```
var selection = actorRef.ActorSelection("../actorB");
```

Once you've got an address, you can then pass messages to it in the exact same way as if it was an actor reference:

```
selection.Tell(new VocalGreeting("Hello"));
```

Actors are designed to completely encapsulate any state, to ensure that nothing outside of the system is capable of mutating it. Akka.NET retains full control over the processing stage, allowing only one message to be processed at a time. This keeps all code thread safe, but it makes it more difficult to access data. To access data from outside the system, you need to send a message specifically requesting that data. Akka.NET provides another method that allows for request-reply scenarios: Ask. This asynchronous method is designed to form a layer of abstraction over the top of the messaging:

```
var response = await selection.Ask(new Wave());
```

Because Ask is an asynchronous construct, you need to factor this into your code so that you await the response to Ask. By default, Ask has a timeout of 10 seconds, within which the actor needs to respond to the initial request message; otherwise, the request will time out with an exception. It's important to realize that the actor receiving the Ask request has no way of knowing that the sender is expecting a reply. It's up to you, the developer, to handle this scenario.

3.4.3 Wrapping up

Messages form an integral part of the design of a system using Akka.NET and are the key to communication between multiple actors, or even other entities outside of the actor system. As such, it's important to model your domain effectively through the commands that actors respond to. In later chapters, we'll look at techniques such as event sourcing and domain-driven design as a means of modeling certain interactions between actors. At this stage, however, it's likely that most actors will be either reacting to events or responding to commands.

Although the term *message* is used, Akka.NET doesn't require anything special with regard to the design of a message; messages can be simple .NET classes or structs. The only requirement when designing messages is that they should be immutable, in order to ensure that the thread-safety guarantees specified by Akka.NET can't be broken anywhere in the application.

3.5   *Case study: Actors, concurrency, and phone billing*

Many modern mobile games operate on a *freemium* model, whereby users play the game for free, but in-game credits are required to perform certain tasks. These in-game credits can be either purchased using real money or earned by performing certain operations in the game, and can then be used to purchase upgrades in the form of visual changes or temporary performance boosts to get through challenging parts of the game. In this case, multiple external sources attempt to credit the user's account; also, the user will try to debit their account. The overall financial success of the company is dependent on selling in-game credits to players, so it's important that users get the credits they're entitled to through performance and by purchase. You also need to ensure that you don't allow users to overspend their credits, and limit their spending potential to the number of credits they have in their account.

You may have to deal with many operations in which you either debit or credit the user's account. It's likely that many of these changes will happen concurrently, with multiple components trying to access the user's credit balance. Because actors help eliminate many of the difficulties you face when developing concurrent, multi-threaded code, you can safely operate on the user's credit balance without worrying about whether other components are also modifying it.

If the billing system is flawed, the business will suffer from lower revenue than expected. Actors operate on a serial stream of messages, and this guarantees that an actor can't modify the same state from two concurrent operations. You can see how to model that in a game backend server in figure 3.4. Here, each actor represents a single user's account in the game. Multiple actors can process work concurrently, ensuring that every user can modify their balance with minimal waiting. Other components in the game can send messages to modify the user's account balance by requesting that the amount be reduced when the user spends their earned credits, or by increasing the balance if the user purchases more credits.

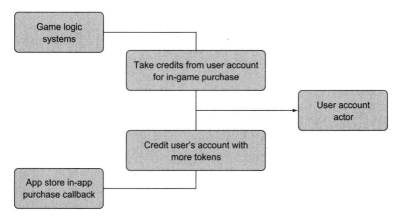

Figure 3.4 The user's in-app purchasing or financial situation can be updated from multiple different sources.

By using actors, you've managed to greatly simplify the complexity surrounding concurrent operations on shared data, all thanks to the principles of the actor model, which sits at the core of Akka.NET applications.

Summary

In this chapter, you learned

- An actor is the smallest unit of work in a reactive system. Operations within the confines of an actor are thread safe.
- You deploy an actor into an actor system, which is the host for all your actors.
- To communicate with actors, you pass messages. Messages are the key to communication between actors and with other entities.

State, behavior, and actors

This chapter covers

- Receiving messages with switchable behaviors
- Understanding finite state machines
- Modeling finite state machines with switchable behaviors
- Building complex finite state machines with `FSMActor`

In chapter 3, we looked at creating actors and sending messages to them. You saw how, using `ReceiveActor`, you can register methods that an actor will execute when it receives a message. In this chapter, you'll learn how to change which methods are executed in response to the messages received at runtime. This will allow you to build complex actors that are responsive and reactive to their environment, in accordance with the Reactive Manifesto.

This chapter also covers how you can generalize actors in various states into a *finite state machine* (FSM). You'll learn how you can create FSMs diagrammatically and how you can convert these diagrams into different actor types, including a new actor type—the `FSMActor`.

By the end of this chapter, you'll have learned how to create actors that fully react to changes in their environment.

4.1   *Preparing for the next message*

You'll remember that the aim of a reactive application is to react quickly to changes in the environment. These changes could require an actor to respond to either expected or unexpected events, with a different behavior executed in response to each type of event.

As an example, consider an actor that represents a water-depth sensor. For homeowners living next to a river, this sensor would be used to measure the current water depth and to warn of heavy rains. On a daily basis, the homeowners would typically log depth values in a database purely for their historical value. But if the sensor receives values that lie outside the expected range—for example, if the river starts to rise due to heavy rains—the sensor needs to alert the homeowners of a potential flood danger.

Here the simplest approach would be for the actor to maintain a set of variables that record both the water's current depth and all the water-depth messages received. To monitor whether the water is at an alert level, you need to store details such as how many messages the actor has received that contain readings over a specified level. Although this is a potentially workable option, it causes problems related to the maintenance of the codebase. As a developer, your aim should be to reduce the complexity of potential solutions, not increase it. When you have to analyze all the variables stored in your actor to determine its current state, the simplest parts of the application become harder to monitor.

In chapter 2, you learned about the pipeline of steps carried out by an actor. When the framework receives a message, the actor associated with that message stores it and invokes a handler, a specific behavior, as its response.

In our homeowner example, you could create multiple handlers for the water-depth sensor, one for each of the possible states being monitored. For instance, homeowners might monitor two states, a normal state and an alert state. When the actor executes normal-state behavior, it processes messages by appending the result to a database table. But if the actor receives a value higher than a specified water level, it will switch into an alert state. When it's in an alert state, the actor will send an urgent notification to the user warning of possible flooding, which will then require extra actions in response.

4.2   *Setting appropriate runtime behaviors*

The concept of behavioral changes forms a key part of building easy-to-maintain applications with Akka.NET. As you've learned, an actor's lifecycle consists of four stages: define, deploy, message, and become. In chapter 3, you learned how to define, deploy, and message actors, but you haven't yet examined how to perform the become operation. So in this section, you'll focus on how actors dynamically change their behavior at runtime.

4.2.1 Switchable behaviors

In the previous chapter, we considered how actors communicate in a manner similar to how people do; both actors and people communicate asynchronously through message passing. We looked at how people respond when they receive a message. Sometimes, because of the state they're in, they aren't able to respond to a message in the same way that they would normally. For example, if somebody waves at you while you're asleep, you're not aware of the behavior, so you inadvertently ignore the message.

The same is true of actors in Akka.NET. Sometimes an actor isn't in a situation where it makes sense to process a message. For those situations, Akka.NET offers *switchable behaviors*, which allow an actor to process messages only when it's in the appropriate state. So when an actor switches into a new state, it can continue processing the messages received in the previous state, or it can receive an entirely different set of messages.

4.2.2 Become and unbecome

When you defined an actor in chapter 3, you used the UntypedActor, which invokes a method upon receipt of a message. With Akka.NET, you can choose to change a message handler dynamically at runtime through the use of switchable behaviors. The only requirement for a message handler to switch behaviors is that it must retain its method signature. Therefore, a new message handler must take an Object as a parameter and return void. In order to switch to a new message handler, you set it using Become.

Let's consider an example. You can use an actor to provide access to a database, although in certain circumstances the database might not be reachable by the application. In cases where you can't reach the database, any connections will time out, so the application needs to wait several seconds every time it tries to access data. This wait time breaks one of the aims of the Reactive Manifesto: to ensure that applications remain responsive even in the face of failure. Thus, you can create an actor that has two possible states: operating normally, or failing. If the database is unreachable, you can return either cached data or a message informing the requesting actor that the database is unreachable.

Let's create an application that responds to a GetData message. If the database is unreachable, the application returns a DatabaseNotAvailableMessage; otherwise, it returns a GetDataSuccess message:

```
class DatabaseActor : UntypedActor
{
    protected override void OnReceive(object message)
    {

    }

    public void Reachable(object message)
    {
        message.Match()
            .With<GetData>(x =>
```

```
                           {
                                var data = Database.Get(x.Key);
                                Sender.Tell(new GetDataSuccess
                                    {Key = x.Key, Data = data});
                           })
                        .With<DatabaseUnavailable>(x => Become(Unreachable));
    }

    public void Unreachable(object message)
    {
        message.Match()
                .With<GetData>(x => Sender.Tell(
                                        new DatabaseUnreachable()))
                .With<DatabaseAvailable>(x => Become(Reachable));

    }
}
```

You can also use Become and Unbecome within the ReceiveActor. You saw in the previous chapter how the ReceiveActor registers message handlers that operate whenever it receives a message of any type. You can, however, choose to add each of the handlers within a method. As long as you call this method from the constructor, it will work as expected. Moving the handlers into a new method allows you to change the currently applied message handlers at runtime. When you call Become within a ReceiveActor, you need to supply a method that takes no parameters and returns nothing. When you call Become with a new method, it calls that method to register all the message handlers. You can use the same techniques as in UntypedActor to add the message handler to a stack:

```
class DatabaseActor : ReceiveActor
{
    public void Reachable()
    {
        this.Receive<GetData>(x =>
            {
                var data = Database.Get(x.Key);
                Sender.Tell(new GetDataSuccess
                        { Key = x.Key, Data = data});
            });
        this.Receive<DatabaseUnavailable>(x => Become(Unreachable));
    }

    public void Unreachable()
    {
        this.Receive<GetData>(x => Sender.Tell(
                    new DatabaseUnreachable()));
        this.Receive<DatabaseAvailable>(x => Become(Reachable));
    }
}
```

The circuit breaker pattern

Although this example of switchable behaviors might seem simple, it forms the basis for a frequently used pattern in Akka.NET. The goal of the Reactive Manifesto is to create applications that are responsive regardless of circumstances, such as a failing state. In the case of a database, you only know it's unreachable by trying to access it. If it fails to respond within a given time limit, then you know that the connection has failed, and you can then avoid retrying every request.

The *circuit breaker pattern* is inspired by the principles of the circuit breaker found in electrical wiring installations. In these systems, at the first sign of a fault, a circuit breaker automatically cuts off the power supply, acting as a failsafe that could potentially save lives. The circuit breaker pattern follows the same principle. In the event of a failure, the circuit breaker automatically forces the application to "switch off." This ensures that timeouts don't affect other actors that are requesting data from, for example, a database.

Although we won't cover the circuit breaker pattern in depth here,[a] it's important to note that even more-complex constructs can be built quickly and easily using some of the most basic elements of the Akka.NET framework.

---

[a] A thorough guide to the circuit breaker pattern can be found on the Microsoft Azure website, at https://docs.microsoft.com/en-us/azure/architecture/patterns/circuit-breaker.

The concept of switchable behaviors in Akka.NET forms an important part of building systems that follow the principles of the Reactive Manifesto. Switchable behaviors allow you to specify the messages an actor can receive, without undue complications regarding the internal state.

4.2.3 Wrapping up

Switchable behaviors are a great feature. They enable you to write actors that react to their environment—and they let you write cleaner code. You've learned how to write actors that can switch their message-receiving behavior at runtime, thereby allowing a different set of message types to be received. In the next section, you'll look at a broader range of switchable behaviors, namely, FSMs, which you'll find extremely useful in a concurrency model like Akka.NET.

4.3 Finite state machines

When you develop an application, you often need to identify a behavior as being in one of several key states. For example, if you're designing an application that directs calls to call-center workers, you need to identify which state an agent is currently in. They might be on a call, on hold, finishing a call, on a break, offline completely, or in some other scenario. But there are only a finite number of states that an agent can be in, so it's possible to model those states, as well as the events that cause transitions between states. For example, if you have a call-center agent who's currently on a call, then they won't be able to answer an incoming call. *Finite state machines* allow you to model this behavior effectively using a common diagrammatic format that makes it easy to view the events that cause transitions within a system.

4.3.1   *Understanding finite state machines*

The example involving a call-center agent compares well with an FSM, but it's a relatively complex example to start with. Instead, we'll start with something simpler.

An FSM is composed of events and states. An *event* can be thought of as a signal used by the current state to transition to a new state. A *state* is a group of actions that are executed, depending on the event received. Once a state receives an event, it can perform one of three options: it can ignore the event, remain in the same state, or move to a new state.

Let's consider the example of a turnstile gate at an entrance to a theme park or sports stadium. The aim of a turnstile is to keep people out until they've provided a ticket, required to unlock the barrier. When a ticket is scanned at the turnstile, assuming it's valid, the barrier transitions into the unlocked state. When it's in the unlocked state, the individual is free to enter the stadium. As soon as one person has passed through the turnstile, it automatically locks to prevent the next person from entering. Sometimes, when someone walks up to the turnstile, they might not have a valid ticket. In that situation, you want to prevent the barrier from unlocking, ensuring it remains in the locked state. Of course, you might accidently scan a ticket more than once; in that case, you don't want to lock the turnstile before the guest has entered.

We can represent these states in a *state transition diagram.* A state transition diagram shows all the states in which your system can exist, as well as the events that cause the changes between states. In the turnstile example, your system can only be in two possible states: locked or unlocked. In the transition between those two states, there are only two events: either the user rotates the turnstile, or the user scans their ticket. When the user scans a valid ticket, the turnstile transfers into the unlocked state. When the user then pushes the turnstile to rotate it, it should let them pass, as well as transition back to the locked state. If the user pushes on the gate when it's in the locked state, it should stay in the locked state. Similarly, if the user scans their ticket multiple times, it should remain in the unlocked state as it waits for the user to pass through the gate (see figure 4.1).

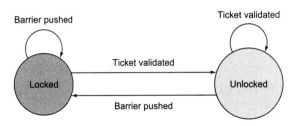

Figure 4.1   A simple FSM for a ticket turnstile, showing the two possible states and the transitions between them

A text-based description of an FSM can be difficult to understand, but it's possible to represent the state machine diagrammatically with a state transition diagram. In a state transition diagram, you draw the state machine as a directed graph, where each vertex is a state, and each edge is an event. This provides a visualization of how each event causes transitions between states. Each edge is marked with a label that signifies the type of event received. You can see the transition by finding the current state vertex and then tracing the edge that has a label matching the event name. An event edge can transform the state machine into either a different state or the same state.

Typically, when you build an FSM, your system will automatically need to enter a certain state as soon as it starts up. We refer to this as the *default state*, and it can be represented on the state transition diagram as a small black spot with an arrow pointing to a state. This small spot symbolizes the initial entry location for the state machine and signifies that it should automatically move into the new space. Figure 4.2 shows the turnstile state machine with a default state marker, which indicates that the locked state is automatically entered when the FSM is started.

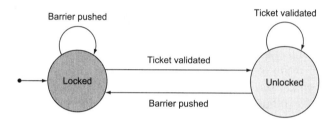

Figure 4.2 An enhancement of the turnstile FSM showing the initial state of the system

Although state transition diagrams are a valid means of representing FSMs, there are many other ways of representing them, such as the commonly used *state transition table*. This is a textual representation of the behavior changes encompassed within a state machine. A state transition table also makes it easier to include details of the effects that could occur between transitions. This might include, for example, some communication with an external information source, or in the case of the turnstile, telling a locking mechanism to unlock when the unlocked state is entered. You can represent the turnstile state machine as a state transition table, as shown in table 4.1. The information represented in both the diagram and the table is identical; they simply provide two different views of the available information.

Table 4.1 State transition table for a turnstile showing the current state and the next state it transitions to upon receiving a message

Current state	Input	Next state	Output
Locked	Ticket	Unlocked	Unlock lock
	Turnstile pushed	Locked	Nothing

Table 4.1 State transition table for a turnstile showing the current state and the next state it transitions to upon receiving a message *(continued)*

Current state	Input	Next state	Output
Unlocked	Ticket	Unlocked	Nothing
	Turnstile pushed	Locked	Lock turnstile

4.3.2 *Using finite state machines in a concurrency model*

Finite state machines are important building blocks upon which you can build complex asynchronous systems. Let's take, for example, an actor that's responsible for loading some state from a database. You've seen how important it is to ensure that the behavior of actors is asynchronous, so all actors can make progress. Given this requirement for asynchronous behavior, you need to consider how best to handle the messages an actor receives.

As soon as your actor is initialized, it will immediately retrieve its internal state from a database. This asynchronous operation completes when the database passes the state back to the actor as a message. Unfortunately, this leads to a potential problem. What happens if another actor sends your actor a message before your actor has received a reply from the database? In this scenario, your actor receives a message that it's unable to process, because it's currently in the middle of performing its initialization.

You give your actor two key states: initializing and initialized. Figure 4.3 shows this situation in a state transition diagram. The actor is first set to the initializing state. When it's in this state, the only message that you care about is a response from the database containing its initial state. In this example, the input that causes a transition is a message containing a response from the database.

Once your actor has received the response from the database, it can parse the data and set its initial state. The actor is then in its initialized state, which ensures that it's able to respond to messages that it would normally experience during its lifecycle.

Although this demonstrates how to design an actor that can switch between states even while it's performing an asynchronous operation, there's still a problem. The actor currently ignores any messages that were received while the actor was in the initializing state. Figure 4.3 shows a timeline of messages received during the actor's different states. Currently, its initialization state will simply dismiss any other message

Figure 4.3 An FSM for an actor loading data into memory

that isn't a response from the database. Usually, you don't want to ignore messages, because your application assumes that the actor is able to process any new messages once it's created and initialized.

STASHING

To remedy this problem, you need to store any messages the actor has received but can't yet process. You could store these in a queue on the actor, as state internal to the actor. But then you have to manually process these messages when you receive a response message. Akka.NET provides a solution in the form of a *message stash*. Think of a stash as a temporary message store, where messages can be stored while maintaining the order in which they were delivered. A stash works with the mailbox of the actor to ensure that you're able to temporarily stash away messages until a more appropriate time.

In order to create a stash on an actor, you need to ensure that your actor implements an interface. Currently, Akka.NET provides an unbounded stash, which doesn't set any limits on the maximum number of messages that can be stashed. In order to implement the interface, the only requirement is to add a single property to the actor. The simplest actor definition that also has a stash attached to it is shown in the following example. In this scenario, you create an actor in exactly the same way as in chapter 3, but it has one minor modification in the form of the addition of an interface implementation:

```
public class StashingActor : UntypedActor,
                                IWithUnboundedStash
{
    public IStash Stash { get; set; }
}
```

Now that you've got an actor with a stash attached to it, you can delay the processing of messages. Expanding on your simple actor definition, you can add two message handlers. Then, whenever the actor receives a message that isn't a database payload, it'll stash it for later. When it does receive the payload, it will perform two operations. It will change its behavior into a different message handler, in this case the Initialized message handler. It'll also unstash all its stashed messages. When these messages are unstashed, they're prepended to the mailbox associated with that actor. Prepending these messages ensures that they'll be processed in the same order in which they were delivered:

```
    private void Initializing(object message)
    {
        if (message is ReadComplete)
        Become(Initialized);
            Stash.UnstashAll();
        else
            Stash.Stash();
    }
    private void Initialized(object message)
    {
```

```
        //Process messages normally here
    }
```

When you want to retrieve messages from the stash, you do so in one of three ways:

- `Unstash`—Prepends only the oldest message from the stash
- `UnstashAll`—Prepends all the messages from the stash while also retaining their order
- `UnstashAll` *with predicate*—Prepends all messages from the stash for which the predicate returns `true`, while also retaining their order

The use of stashing is not something that's limited to changing state. The stash is accessible within the actor at any time, allowing it to retrieve messages from the stash whenever it wants to add stashed messages back to the queue.

Stashing forms one of the key parts of actor implementation when you're working with FSMs, as it allows you to delay the processing of some messages until the actor is in the correct state to do so. This lets you build a more complex state machine, one capable of dealing with significant amounts of asynchronous code, while also ensuring that the code stays manageable and easy to understand.

4.3.3 *Converting a finite state machine into an actor*

As you've seen, FSMs are an essential component for developing concurrent applications with Akka.NET. Although you could develop an FSM in the actor using state stored within it, you can also use an actor's behavior-switching capabilities. Given either a state transition diagram or a state transition table, you can port the FSM to an actor.

Let's work with the turnstile example once again, in which you have two states: locked and unlocked. You also have two events: rotate the turnstile and scan the ticket. You can represent each state as your message-received behavior when using Akka.NET. This means that if you use a `ReceiveActor`, for example, you can create two methods in your actor definition that represent actor states. In this case, they'll be called `Locked` and `Unlocked`, according to the states in your state transition diagram. This leads to an implementation similar to the following code example, which shows the two states of your actor:

```
class TurnstileActor : ReceiveActor
{
    void Locked()
    {
    }

    void Unlocked()
    {
    }
}
```

Given your actor with its possible states, you need to look at the events the actor receives and how they should affect the current state. An event in an FSM can be thought of as an external influence, designed to show a change in the world in which your system is running. This definition of an event in an FSM matches the definition of an actor when used in the context of the Reactive Manifesto. As such, you can model your events through the use of messages.

Examining the state transition diagram, you only have two events that cause transitions in your system: a guest pushing against the turnstile or a guest scanning a valid entry ticket. You'll create classes to represent the possible events; in both cases, they'll be class definitions with no data associated with them. You can call them `Ticket-Validated` and `BarrierPushed`. The following code example shows the events and how simple their definitions are. When naming events, you may have noticed a common trait. Events are always historical facts that have taken place within your system and, thus, are named accordingly:

```
class TicketValidated { }
class BarrierPushed { }
```

Now that you've got the states and events defined, you can look at the state transition diagram to see how your actor should react to the messages received. As you saw in figure 4.3, an arrow represents a state transition. An arrow from a vertex to itself (labeled "Other" in the figure) can be thought of as a null operation; it won't have any effect on the current state, so, typically, you can ignore it. You can see that the `Ticket-Validated` event in the `Locked` state will cause a transition to `Unlocked`, and the `BarrierPushed` message will lead to the `Locked` state. In each of these states, you only have one message that you need to react to, so you can create them as a single message handler delegate. The following code example shows you how to set up handler delegates to ensure that they only react to their own specific message:

```
void Locked()
{
    Receive<TicketValidated>(msg => Become(Unlocked));
    Receive<BarrierPushed>(msg => { });
}

void Unlocked()
{
    Receive<TicketValidated>(msg => { });
    Receive<BarrierPushed>(msg => Become(Locked));
}
```

Continuing through the state transition diagram, you see the entry state, represented by a black dot pointing to a given state. In this case, it's the `Locked` state. So your actor should immediately be placed in the `Locked` state to ensure nobody is allowed in without a valid ticket. You do this by directly placing a call to `Become` in the constructor of the actor. This specifies that an actor should use this specific behavior for the very first message it receives:

```
public TurnstileActor()
{
    Become(Locked);
}
```

Although that's all the information you can glean from your state transition diagram, there's still one other feature that needs implementing. Remember that the state transition table can contain more data than the diagram. In this case, it's an external change that needs to occur when the actor enters the Unlocked state: it needs to communicate with the turnstile locking mechanism to unlock it for one turn to allow the user to enter. You can do that by adding information to the body of the Unlocked state method. In this case, you'll call a method on an object, which will inform it of the unlocking action:

```
void Unlocked()
{
    Barrier.Unlock();
    Receive<BarrierPushed>(msg => Become(Locked));
    Receive<TicketValidated>(msg => { });
}
```

4.3.4 *Using the finite state machine actor*

FSMs are incredibly useful components when you're writing asynchronous applications, and although you can replicate simple state machines using switchable behaviors, there are limitations involved with them. For example, an actor can't perform operations as it transitions out of a given state. You also have one other problem with your current implementation. In Akka.NET, you have the concept of *supervision*, which you'll learn about in chapter 6. For now, you only need to know that when an actor throws an error, it restarts in a new state. This means that it loses all its data and associated state when it restarts.

To address these issues, Akka.NET provides an actor specifically for the purpose of creating an FSM: FSMActor, a generic class requiring two type arguments. You need to supply the type of the actor state as well as the type of data the actor stores. The following example shows how you can begin converting your turnstile actor to use FSMActor. This code snippet simply defines your actor as an FSM that has all states deriving from ITurnstileState, with the actor storing data of type ITurnstileData:

```
class TurnstileStateMachine : FSM<ITurnstileState, ITurnstileData>
{
}
```

You can now define data structures that are used to represent the states and data stored in the actor. You'll start by defining a base interface that all of its possible states can inherit from. Following that, you'll create two classes that implement the interface and represent the states, namely, Locked and Unlocked. You'll also create a class within which you'll store state. Although you don't need to store any data in your FSM, you'll create a class that it could use as a data storage location:

```
interface ITurnstileState { }
class Locked : ITurnstileState
{
    public static readonly Locked Instance = new Locked();
}
```

```
class Unlocked : ITurnstileState
{
    public static readonly Unlocked Instance = new Unlocked();
}

interface ITurnstileData { }
class TurnstileData : ITurnstileData { }
```

When you create states, an important consideration is how Akka.NET compares the states in the application. By default, C# uses reference equality to compare the two states. To ensure the states are compared correctly, you should implement `Equals` on each state to ensure you choose the correct state.

Once you've implemented equality, you can register each of the states and a handler in the constructor of the actor. Use the `When` method on `FSMActor` to register a handler that executes when a message is received and the actor is in that state. The handler is invoked with two pieces of information: the current actor state and the received message. Once it receives a message, it can then pattern match on the possible messages received and handle them appropriately. Every message handler has to return the action that should be undertaken as a result of the message. This is usually one of two methods: either `GoTo`, which transitions the actor into a new state, or `Stay`, which keeps the actor in its current state. You can build your state machine further by using these features to register the two handlers you'll need for the `Locked` and `Unlocked` states:

```
public TurnstileStateMachine()
{
    When(Locked.Instance, @event =>
    {
        if(@event.FsmEvent is TicketValidated)
        {
            Console.WriteLine("Ticket was validated");
            return GoTo(Unlocked.Instance);
        }
        return Stay();
    });

    When(Unlocked.Instance, @event =>
    {
        if(@event.FsmEvent is BarrierPushed)
        {
            Console.WriteLine("User pushed barrier");
            return GoTo(Locked.Instance);
        }
        return Stay();
    });
```

After registering the handlers, you need to perform a number of other operations before the actor is usable. You first need to tell the actor what the initial state and internal data should be, which you manage with the `StartsWith` method. Once you've performed all of your configurations, you need to initialize the actor and ensure it's ready to receive any messages sent to it. This is managed with the `Initialize` method:

```
StartWith(Locked.Instance, new TurnstileData());
Initialize();
```

When developing applications using FSMs, you can also set a timeout on an individual state. If a message hasn't been received within a fixed timespan, then the actor will send itself a StateTimeout message. This message can be handled like any other and can be used in pattern matching. To use the StateTimeout functionality, you pass a TimeSpan to the When method, which specifies how long the actor should wait before sending a timeout message. For example, when you may want the turnstile to stay unlocked for only a limited period of time. To accomplish this, you can create a timeout on the Unlocked state and handle the message in the state message handler:

```
When(Unlocked.Instance, @event =>
{
    if(@event.FsmEvent is BarrierPushed ||
       @event.FsmEvent is StateTimeout)
    {
        Console.WriteLine("Barrier will now lock");
        return GoTo(Locked.Instance);
    }
    return Stay();
}, TimeSpan.FromSeconds(10.0));
```

You saw that one of the problems when using switchable behaviors is the limited potential for performing operations on a state change in an actor. FSMActor helps solve this problem by registering a function that executes every time a transition occurs. When this function is called, it receives the previous state as well as the next state. This allows operations to happen between state transitions. For example, in the turnstile actor, you want to tell the locking mechanism to unlock upon transition from Locked to Unlocked, and to lock on the transition between Unlocked and Locked:

```
OnTransition(OnTransition);

private void OnTransition(ITurnstileState prevState,
        ITurnstileState newState)
        {
            if (prevState is Locked && newState is Unlocked)
            {
                BarrierLock.Unlock();
            }
            else if (prevState is Unlocked && newState is Locked)
            {
                BarrierLock.Lock();
            }
            else if (prevState is Locked && newState is Locked)
            {
                Console.WriteLine("The barrier gate is still locked");
            }
            else if (prevState is Unlocked && newState is Unlocked)
            {
                Console.WriteLine("The barrier gate is still unlocked");
            }
        }
```

`FSMActor` allows you to develop more-complex FSMs that are easier to scale when using more states with more-complex transitions. `FSMActor` is less frequently used than `ReceiveActor`, but it can form a solid foundation upon which you can build complex state-based asynchronous systems.

4.3.5 *Wrapping up*

This section covered a lot of content. You've looked at how, using FSMs, you can generalize the ideas surrounding the states and behaviors that an actor can exist in at any given time. You've seen how you can represent these states and transitions, both textually and diagrammatically, through the use of state transition tables and state transition diagrams. Finally, you've examined how these representations can be converted to Akka.NET using actors' built-in features that help manage complexity.

4.4 *Case study: State machines, states and events, marketing analytics campaign*

In this chapter, we've considered how you can model some common objects using state machines. You've seen how to represent a turnstile as a set of finite states, as well as the events that cause transitions between states. These principles can be extended to larger and more-complex applications that have a limited number of states. One practical example is the management of complex marketing campaigns.

For businesses to thrive, they need to retain customers and potentially convert them from occasional users to recurring users who pay monthly for a service. One way to achieve this is to incentivize the user by offering promotions, based on their previous usage of the application or service. For example, if a user signs up for a service but doesn't use it, then the business might want to provide them with a user guide to help them make the most of the service. Similarly, if the user signs up as a free user but doesn't convert to a paying user, then the user could be targeted with a promotional campaign offering them a discount code. Marketing campaigns that start small can quickly grow into complex systems that depend on a number of different variables, such as the date or how long it's been since the user last used the service.

As these campaigns are typically made up of a number of states, along with events that cause transitions between these states, you can think of a marketing campaign as a state machine, which means you can encode the logic in an actor. In figure 4.4, you can see how push events flow within the actor. These events include information relating to how the user uses the application, such as how long it's been since they last used it, and whether they pay for the service. The actor can use its current state to work out how to process incoming events, and whether the user should be notified of a discount available to them or be sent more information on the service.

In this example, the overall state of the marketing campaign would be difficult to represent in a database table, but using an actor that allows for on-the-fly configuration of its behavior vastly simplifies processing incoming messages.

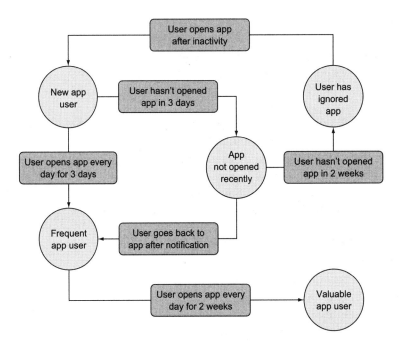

Figure 4.4   A marketing campaign application can quickly become complex. Marketing departments will want to provide targeted information to individual users based on how they've been using the app.

Summary

In this chapter, you learned

- How to model real-world situations using state machines
- How to diagrammatically explain a state machine using state transition tables and state transition diagrams
- How to create a simple state machine using the behavior-switching functionality of Akka.NET
- How to create more-complex state machines using the finite state machine actor type

Configuration, dependency injection, and logging

> ## This chapter covers
> - Configuring actor deployments
> - Using dependency injection
> - Using Akka.NET's logging system

You've learned how to deploy simple actors in Akka.NET, and in the remainder of the book, we'll look at how you can create actors that solve more-complex problems. First, you need to understand how to inject configuration into Akka.NET, as a way of controlling how scenarios are handled in the framework.

In this chapter, we'll look at how to instrument and operationalize an Akka.NET application. It's important to have thorough instrumentation and logging in place, even when developing simple actor applications. Akka.NET provides abstractions to develop distributed applications, but this comes with inherent downsides. You saw in chapter 1 that one of the principles of the Reactive Manifesto is the use of asynchronous message passing for communication between components in a reactive system. Because messages are passed asynchronously, there's no notion of the typical flow control that you get with applications that rely on synchronous method calls. Although asynchronous message passing provides a foundation for reliable and scalable systems, it also prevents you from effectively debugging applications using a debugger. Instead, it's important to have thorough logging and instrumentation in place, which allows you to understand the system as a whole, rather than as isolated components. This chapter focuses on how to use Akka.NET to monitor and instrument an application with centralized logging. We'll also look at how to effectively tailor an application to different environments by configuring the actor system, as well as the context in which the system operates. This chapter isn't a comprehensive guide to all means of configuration in Akka.NET, but rather is a baseline on which later chapters will build when introducing additional configuration options.

5.1   Why do you need configuration?

The actor systems you've used so far have been relatively simple, with only a few actors communicating and with few messages being passed between them. In later chapters, the number of features in the systems we look at will increase, which means an increase in system complexity. This chapter provides a firm basis for handling that increased complexity.

Let's consider for a moment the actors you deployed into your system. They required no customization. But the simplest actor configuration will fail when you deploy more-complex actors. For example, how do you handle a case in which you want an actor to distribute its messages to other actors, thereby increasing the amount of work that can be done in parallel? And how does an actor handle a failure? These are just two of the scenarios you'll configure in your actors. In later chapters, you'll see more uses for actor configuration when we look at remote actors and failure handling. In this chapter, we'll look at creating more-complex actors, such as those with many dependencies.

Not only can you configure actor deployment, you can also modify the way the actor system itself runs, without the need to recompile the application. As you'll learn, you can change how Akka.NET deploys an actor into the actor system; for example, you can create a cluster of actor systems, or change where actors are deployed within the cluster. For now, we'll look at one of the most essential parts of an Akka.NET project: logging. You'll learn how to use Akka.NET configuration to customize loggers and how loggers can be used in an application.

5.2   Configuring an actor deployment

In each of the actor examples you've seen so far, all deployments into the actor system have been through the generic method `ActorOf<T>`. In these cases, `T` is the type of the actor being instantiated. But sometimes you'll want to change how the actor is deployed by Akka.NET, for example:

- *Custom constructor*—When Akka.NET deploys an actor using `ActorOf`, it uses the default constructor of the actor. For more-complex actors, you may need to pass some dependencies into the constructor, so you'll need to tell Akka.NET how to instantiate the actor.

- *Custom mailbox*—The mailbox is the internal component responsible for receiving messages for an actor. Although the mailbox isn't directly used by the developer, it forms a key component of the actor itself. Often, an actor will need to use a mailbox other than the default one, as when some messages have a higher priority than others and need to be processed first.

- *Deployment location*—An actor is typically deployed into the local actor system. But as you'll see later, an actor can be deployed into several other locations, including a remote system or even a cluster of actor systems.

- *Custom dispatcher*—The dispatcher is responsible for the thread on which an actor processes its messages. For example, if you're defining an actor that processes many messages, it may need more resources than other actors. The dispatcher for that actor can be set to use a dedicated thread to process messages.

These are some of the more common requirements you'll need when configuring an actor. Whereas the custom mailbox, deployment location, and custom dispatcher are only used in advanced actors, the custom constructor is frequently used, as it allows you to directly inject dependencies into the deployment itself. Throughout the rest of this section, we'll look at configuring the Akka.NET framework to create and deploy an actor into an actor system.

5.2.1 Understanding Props

In previous chapters, you saw that after defining an actor, you need to effectively deploy it into an actor system. Deploying an actor means that it's given an address and a mailbox that can receive messages from other actors in the system. In order to deploy an actor and instantiate it, you used the `ActorOf<T>` method on the actor system instance. For all the examples so far, `ActorOf` has been sufficient, as it simply takes an actor type as a generic parameter and uses the default constructor.

But this generic method doesn't automatically spawn the actor into the system. Instead, it creates a template for how the actor should be deployed. The template provides a reproducible way of creating an instance of the actor. The template, then, is similar to a recipe. A recipe isn't a meal in itself, but simply a series of reproducible steps one follows to create a meal. By providing food and something capable of "defining" the food, such as a chef, you can create the same meal repeatedly. Now consider what happens when something goes wrong in a restaurant, as when a waiter drops a meal. The restaurant can create a new meal, because it has the recipe.

The same principle applies to actors; for example, consider the scenario in which an actor unexpectedly stops because it encounters an error. We'll look at how Akka.NET responds to failures more in a later chapter, but for now, we'll consider the easiest and most common approach to handling failures. The Reactive Manifesto encourages building applications that respond to failures in the system. One way of responding to a failure is to simply restart the actor, in the hope of regaining a known working state. But for this you need a template to provide a reproducible deployment. The term *reproducible* in this setting means that the actor must end up in the same state as when it was first deployed.

The "recipe" that can produce an actor in Akka.NET is known as `Props`. `Props` is used heavily in Akka.NET and is a requirement for complex actors. For now, we'll focus on the simpler aspects of using `Props`, such as creating actors with complex constructors.

CREATING PROPS

Due to the multithreaded nature of the code in which `Props` is used, every `Props` instance is immutable and requires factory functions to create an instance. Let's take another look at the `PersonActor` example from chapter 3, where the actor defines a behavior for what happens when it receives one of two messages. If it receives a wave message, it sends a vocal greeting back to the original sender; if it receives a vocal-greeting message, it writes the content of the message to the console.

Normally, when spawning an actor, you'd use `ActorOf` with the actor type as the generic parameter. But you can create the `Props` object for this actor in a similar way by using the generic factory method for this actor type, assuming you have a default constructor on the actor that takes no parameters. Then you receive the `Props` object, which you can use to spawn an actor internally:

```
var personProps = Props.Create<PersonActor>();
var personActor = system.ActorOf(personProps);
```

But this doesn't change anything for when you want to deploy `PersonActor`, and you had to write more code to do the same job. Custom `Props` become useful when you want to do something complicated that's outside the scope of what Akka.NET can manage by default. For example, let's modify the `PersonActor` definition to take a dependency on a string that the actor will use to communicate with another actor. Akka.NET needs some way of knowing what string it should pass into the constructor. You can manage this in one of two ways: by providing an expression that's used when an actor instance needs to be created, or by specifying the type name along with an array of parameters.

The simplest way of providing this string is by creating `Props` with the type of the actor and an array of parameters. For example, if you want to use the string "Hello from Props!", you can create `Props` as shown in the following code. In this case, you provide the type of the actor to `Props` using the `typeof` keyword. You also create an array of parameters, which in this case is the string constant "Hello from Props!":

```
var personProps = Props.Create(typeof(PersonActor),
    "Hello from Props!");
```

This approach is by far the simplest, but you give up the ability at compile time to check that you're either providing all of the required parameters or that all parameters are of the correct type for the actor definition. To alleviate this difficulty, Akka.NET allows you to specify an expression for creating an instance of the actor.

When you want to deploy or redeploy that actor definition, Akka.NET will evaluate that expression and use the returned instance in the actor system:

```
var personProps = Props.Create<PersonActor>(
    () => new PersonActor("Hello from Props!"));
```

SPAWNING AN ACTOR WITH PROPS

Having created a `Props` object, you can spawn it in a way similar to how you spawned actors using the actor type. In this case, rather than using a generic method, you can use the `ActorOf` method and pass in the `Props` object. You can also create it with a name, exactly as when you deployed actors. The following example deploys your more-complex actor using the `Props` object you built earlier. As you can see, there's very little difference in the process when creating actors using `Props` versus directly deploying actors:

```
var personActor = system.ActorOf(personProps);
```

A WARNING ABOUT PROPS

As you've seen, when you use `Props`, you can use an expression to create an actor instance. You can then create a `Props` object with this expression and use that to spawn an actor. But there's no guarantee that you'll spawn the actor as soon as you create the `Props` object. In order to remain performant, many operations in Akka.NET are evaluated lazily. One example of this is when you want to retrieve the original sender of the current message using the `Sender` property. This is only evaluated when it's needed, which means that if you pass the `Props` object, you create a different actor to spawn it, and then the `Sender` will be different than what the receiving actor expects. You can solve this problem by retrieving a reference to the current value first, as shown in the following code:

```
var sender = Sender;
var props =
    Props.Create(() => new LoadTestingActor(sender));
```

There are other scenarios in C# where you might encounter this problem, most notably when using an `index` variable in a loop. In such situations, it's important to realize that the `Props` are not evaluated immediately, which might lead to unexpected values.

5.2.2 Wrapping up

In this section, you've seen how Akka.NET can spawn an actor by using a template known as `Props`. You've seen how to create `Props` for a given class with a complex example. In the next section, we'll look at how to spawn complex classes using a dependency injection (DI) framework.[1] Although `Props` might seem difficult or even dense at the moment, you'll explore in later chapters just how important `Props` is when Akka.NET scales up actors or handles failures. At this stage, however, the main

---

[1] This book isn't doesn't provide a thorough introduction to dependency injection, but only provides the basics needed to begin using it. If you're interested in learning more about DI, see Dhanji R. Prasanna, *Dependency Injection: Design patterns using Spring and Guice* (Manning, 2009), or Mark Seemann and Steven van Deursen, *Dependency Injection in .NET* (Manning, 2018).

use of `Props` is as a means of deploying actors with more dependencies, as provided through the constructor. You'll see in the next chapter how to use dependency injection to automatically inject dependencies into `Props`.

5.3 Dependency injection (DI)

In previous chapters, you saw actors that had no external dependencies and that were simple to deploy into an actor system. Then you saw how Akka.NET creates a template for actor deployment, and how you can interact with templates to provide additional dependencies into an actor's instantiation. Sometimes, actors grow and require more and more dependencies on external services. As dependencies increase, you start to generate more-complex chains of dependencies, so that one dependency requires others. Typically, you'd approach this problem by using a dependency injection framework, which can automatically create any dependencies you require.

The same principles apply to Akka.NET, and you can use dependency injection to create the `Props` object that you used as a template. In this section, you'll see how to create an actor using the principles of dependency injection, thereby providing a number of external dependencies that are consumed by the actor instance.

5.3.1 Introducing dependency injection

Among the tasks an actor can perform is to work with external dependencies. For example, you may have a database actor that forms the basis from which other actors in the system communicate with the database. Or, you may have an actor that's in charge of performing interactions with a web service. In these cases, you deal with dependencies that you may want to quickly and easily configure, so that later you can replace them with something else.

Let's consider your database actor again. When it communicates with the database, it probably performs the operation with a well-known abstraction over the top of it. For example, you may already be using Microsoft's Entity Framework or even a custom-written API using raw SQL queries. Regardless of the technology, you probably tend to use a built-up abstraction because of its simplicity. But there may be times when you no longer want to use that abstraction to retrieve data from the database, such as during testing. When you write tests, you don't want to interact with external services, for a number of reasons:

- *Time to execute*—External dependencies are typically served over high-latency connections, such as a network or internet connection. If every test needs to use these connections, it can lead to a significant increase in the amount of time a test suite takes to execute. This is something you don't want, as you seek quick feedback from tests.
- *Difficulty in setting up data for tests*—Once you've got a test with a dependency on an external service, in order to achieve predictability, you need to have an understanding of the data in the source. This means you need to configure the

data source to add new test data or retrieve stale data before you're able to run a test.

In testing, when you have a dependency on an external service, you should replace it with something that optimizes system efficiency and throughput. Although this can be configured manually, a DI framework allows for the easier resolution of complex dependency graphs. A *dependency graph* is the chain of dependencies that builds up as dependencies depend on other services. For example, you may have a dependency on Gmail within your application, but Gmail itself might require an abstraction over the top of an email client.

Possible uses of dependency injection go far beyond just testing; for example, if you have an application that can run in different environments, you could switch dependencies on a per-environment basis. If an application can run in a number of different cloud hosts, such as Amazon Web Services or Microsoft Azure, you might use different logic for performing certain operations, such as retrieval of the current machine's IP address.

Scenarios such as these are where dependency injection can be useful. By registering a concrete instantiation of a dependency, such as a class, against a template of the dependency, such as an interface, you can separate the implementation of the dependency from how you use it.

You'll see throughout this section how you can manage complex dependency graphs in Akka.NET by using a DI framework. In particular, we'll look at containers and how they can be used to provide dependencies to an actor when it's spawned.

DO YOU NEED DEPENDENCY INJECTION?

Many developers swear by dependency injection as a means of creating testable code; but before deciding to use it, you should consider whether it's truly necessary. Akka.NET presents a different approach to concurrency by using actors, which were typically not considered when dependency injection became popular.

With actors, you have to be cautious of anything that can be a potential source of state sharing. You saw in chapters 2 and 3 how you should design actors so that they don't share any state between them, which promotes better scalability and fault tolerance. This goes against the structure of DI frameworks: they use a dependency, which is shared across many instances, for as long as possible. Also, you don't know how long an actor might be in use. Some actors may reply to a single message and have a lifetime of less than a second, while other actors may stay active for long periods of time with potentially no downtime. This poses a different set of challenges that some DI frameworks may not be tailored for.

Before using dependency injection in Akka.NET, you should consider whether it brings significant advantages to your codebase, especially when being careful about dependencies is a major consideration.

5.3.2   *Configuring a DI container*

In Akka.NET, you can use several DI libraries, with the option of including adapters for others, if they're not already provided. All the adapters are available through NuGet, along with a number of community-contributed alternatives. Some available adapters include Ninject, Castle Windsor, and Autofac; in this section, we'll use Autofac. The only key difference in the API is how you register dependencies in your framework.

Your first step is to install the Autofac library from NuGet, along with the adapter for Akka.NET. In the same way that you installed the Akka.NET project in chapter 3, you need to install the Akka.DI.AutoFac NuGet project. This will add the DI library to your project, if it's not already included. Before you can create actors with automatically resolved dependencies, you need to configure the container. The container is the component responsible for mapping a required type onto a type instance.

We'll continue with how you can insert extra dependencies into your actor system. In this case, you'll register every request for a string to provide a simple instance of a string. This is something you wouldn't typically do with a DI container; instead, you'd provide more-complex type definitions. In Autofac, you can quickly create a container and supply an instance to use for a given type:[2]

```
var containerBuilder = new Autofac.ContainerBuilder();
    containerBuilder.RegisterInstance<string>(
  "Hello from a DI container");
  var container = containerBuilder.Build();
```

Now that you've got a container, you can create type instances with it. The Akka.NET framework will also use the container to create instances of actors. In addition, you need to register the container with the framework. To do this, create a dependency resolver specific to your chosen DI framework; in this case, an `AutoFacDependencyResolver`, when created, will be automatically registered to the actor system, enabling it to create actors:

```
var propsResolver = new AutoFacDependencyResolver(container, system);
```

As you saw earlier, you need a `Props` object in order to spawn an actor. When you want to create an actor using the DI framework, you use an extension method provided on the `ActorSystem`. Once you've retrieved a reference to the DI extension, you simply call the `Props` method with the type you want to create as a generic type argument. The following example creates the `Props` for `PersonActor` by retrieving all the dependencies from the provided container. To create the `Props` object, you retrieve the `Props` from the context using the Akka.NET DI features:

```
var props = system.DI().Props<PersonActor>();
```

---

[2]   For a more in-depth guide on how to use Autofac as a DI framework, see the official documentation available at http://www.autofac.org.

Once you've retrieved the `Props`, you can use it the same way as previously. Also, you can use `Props` to deploy the actor in the same way as you did when manually generating actors.

5.3.3 Wrapping up

This section focused on how to configure and manage complex dependency graphs for actors in Akka.NET by using a DI framework. NuGet supplies a number of DI frameworks for which bindings and thorough documentation are available for Akka.NET. The same principles apply regardless of which framework is used, allowing for your choice.

This section also marks the end of your introduction to configuring independent actor deployments using `Props`. Throughout the rest of the book, you'll see more examples of how `Props` is used to provide additional functionality to an actor's deployment, such as with remote actors or clustered actors. In the rest of this chapter, we'll look at further configuration in Akka.NET using HOCON, which you'll use to configure system-wide settings for actors.

5.4 Configuring with HOCON

Many libraries and frameworks today use something like XML or JSON for storing and providing configuration data. Typically, the data includes configuration variables that might need to be changed, depending on the environment at runtime, or that need to be frequently changed without requiring recompilation. However, XML and JSON are far from ideal for storing configuration data.

Both XML and JSON were designed as data interchange formats for sending data between multiple applications. These formats are intended for high-speed serialization and deserialization, but they're difficult for humans to read and write. For example, XML is a verbose format with significant amounts of repetition that the user is required to write. Also, it's far from intuitive for the user to compose, due to the potential confusion of when to use attributes on data or when to use nested elements. JSON removes much of the verbosity associated with XML, but it still suffers from problems. The lack of comments can cause issues, particularly when you're documenting complex configurations. Furthermore, the format can be difficult to understand when you're dealing with data that doesn't naturally map onto the types provided by JavaScript.

To address many of these issues, Akka.NET uses a configuration file format known as *HOCON*, which stands for *Human Optimized Configuration Object Notation*. The key point is that it's human readable and was designed from the ground up to be easier to read and write than many other formats.

5.4.1 What is HOCON?

HOCON is a configuration file format that was designed as a superset of JSON. As such, you may notice some similarities between a HOCON file and a JSON file. But

HOCON improves upon JSON by removing a lot of the noise that doesn't add value for a human reading it. It removes the leading and trailing braces and adds other features, such as comments, which ensure that developers can explain certain program decisions in their configuration files.

Let's take a look at a simple HOCON file to see how certain constructs can be expressed in it. The following example shows a file that's been tailored to demonstrate many of HOCON's features. The first point to notice is that HOCON resembles a JSON file. In fact, since HOCON is a superset of JSON, valid JSON can also be used to configure Akka.NET.

```
akka {
    # Project details
    project {
        name = "Cooking"
        description = ${my.organization.project.name} "is a tool to ensure
     the correct preparation of bearnaise source ;)"
    }
    # Team members
    team {
        members = [
            "Bob"
            "Fred"
            "Alice"
        ]
    }
}
akka.team.avgAge = 26
```

You can see a lot of similarities between JSON and HOCON, but some key changes ensure that HOCON is human readable. For example, there's no need to supply opening and closing braces. The separator between keys and values has also changed from a colon to an equals sign. These are the two most noticeable changes, but many other features also assist readability. In the preceding example, you'll notice a number of nested sections, each of which has only one key in it. To simplify cases such as this, HOCON allows you to specify paths where each path segment is separated by a full stop. The two following examples both resolve to the same configuration object:

```
akka {
 cluster {
  roles = []
 }
}

  akka.cluster.roles = []
```

Sometimes, you may need to convey additional information about decisions within the configuration; for example, you might need to specify a detail about the structure of a configuration string for later users. In such situations, you can use a comment to express your intent. It's no different in Akka.NET, and you're free to use one of two commenting styles. Comments may start either with a double forward slash (//), similar to C-style languages, or with a hash character (#), similar to languages such as Python and Bash. In the following example, you add a comment above a key value, which is used to describe the intent of the definition. Comments extend through the length of a line, and a comment ends when it reaches a line separator.

```
#Specifies the roles which this node belongs to
    akka.cluster.roles = []
```

In Akka.NET, you'll also want to configure timeouts and the intervals between certain operations. The other common configuration formats approach this problem of measurement units by using milliseconds or seconds as their values, leaving you to work out which is required from the documentation. HOCON, though, supports the use of certain measurement units in program values. For example, the following time values lead to the same value being made available in the configuration:

```
akka.cluster.seed-node-timeout = 120 s

    akka.cluster.seed-node-timeout = 2 m
```

These are some of the features of HOCON that we'll use throughout the rest of the book, but there's plenty more to discover and use.

5.4.2 *Loading configuration into an actor system*

Now that you've seen what the HOCON format looks like, you can use it in an actor system. You can retrieve the configuration from a couple of different places in an application. At the simplest level is the ConfigurationFactory.Parse method, which takes in a string containing the HOCON definition. As a layer of abstraction on top of this, you can also retrieve the configuration from a resource file embedded in the application. The final option is to retrieve the configuration from an Akka element stored in the application's App.config file as CDATA. For now, we'll use the .NET file APIs and ParseString to retrieve the configuration from a file stored in the current directory. Assuming that the configuration file is in the same directory as the executable, you can load it in as follows:

```
var configString = File.ReadAllText("actorsystem.conf");
var config = ConfigurationFactory.ParseString(configString);
ActorSystem actorSystem =
    ActorSystem.Create("configuredActorSystem", config);
```

Because Akka.NET starts the components (such as logging and other components) in the actor system, the components will overwrite their default values with the values provided in the configuration file. Because all components in Akka.NET use default values, this means you don't need to create a configuration file with every value for every component; instead, you'll fill the configuration with values that you need to change.

5.4.3   *Wrapping up*

You've seen some of HOCON's features and how HOCON differs from other file formats typically used by applications for configuration. You examined how the features provided by Akka.NET and HOCON allow you to write an application configuration that's tailored to the environment in which it's running. Finally, you looked at the Akka.NET API, which allows you to load a configuration into an actor system when it's created. HOCON is a feature-rich configuration format that provides many more features outside the scope of this section, including merging keys and more-advanced key replacements. Up until this point, you haven't needed to configure some of the internals of the actor system, because Akka.NET has provided a configuration file with reasonable defaults, which is used as a backup if you don't provide your own settings. As you use more-advanced features of Akka.NET, you'll modify these settings, such as how actors get created if they're in a cluster or a remote actor system. The next section describes a simple, real-life example of using HOCON to modify a basic section of the framework, the logger.

5.5   Logging

You've seen how to configure the actor system in which your actors are running, thanks to the HOCON configuration available in Akka.NET. Next, you'll see how to create a configuration file and alter how key parts of the system operate. In this section, we'll focus on the logging capabilities of Akka.NET and how to use logging to view the state of the actor system. You'll see how to access Akka.NET's logging utilities, as well as how to configure the log sink to use a different logging system.

Logging is one of the most important operations you'll use in any Akka.NET application to handle some of the problems that arise with asynchronous and distributed systems. In this section, we'll look at how to configure logging in Akka.NET and how to use logging functionality from within an actor to send messages to your configured log sink.

5.5.1   *Why do you need logging?*

Logging plays a valuable part in any application, providing insights into how your system is running at any point in time. But it's especially important in the case of actor systems or, more generally, asynchronous systems, because of factors peculiar to asynchronous systems. A synchronous system provides a linear flow through the system at the cost of a reduction in scalability and fault tolerance, as you saw in chapter 1. But as asynchronous systems allay this determinism, they make it difficult to get a thorough, deep understanding of your system.

For example, consider the flow of a message as it proceeds through a number of stages in a processing pipeline. In the message flow shown in figure 5.1, messages are processed or modified in one actor before being passed to the next. In a synchronous system, you can iteratively step through each of the processing stages before arriving at the final result. At each stage, the workload is visible, and you can see the results at

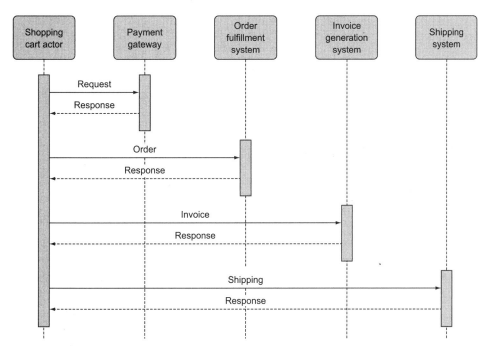

Figure 5.1 Messages flowing through a processing pipeline

that stage. Asynchronicity forfeits this and gives you benefits related to scalability and fault tolerance in its place. Using logging, you can see the flow of messages through the chain of actors, revealing potential sources of failure when the system's running. By using logging in messages, you can see where messages might be directed to targets other than their intended destination, or even where messages aren't reaching any target.

This is just one example of when logging can be used. The vast number of other uses relate to this same concept, which is that logging provides better visibility if/when something goes wrong in an environment where you can't use a debugger. In the event of a failure in the system, you can consult the history stored in the logs and step through the circumstances that led to the system failure.

5.5.2 Writing to the log

Before an actor can write to the Akka.NET log, it needs to retrieve access to the system logger. The logger is retrieved through the static `GetLogger` method on the `Logging` class. From there, the actor passes in a logging target. In this case, it uses its context. Internally, the factory method will retrieve the logger:

```
private readonly ILoggingAdapter _log = Logging.GetLogger(Context);
```

Having retrieved the logger, an actor can write to the log by using any of the methods provided. For example, to write a message at the Debug log level, it calls the Debug method with a string to print. Akka.NET formats the string to provide additional information, such as the thread on which the actor was running, as well as the address of the actor that logged the message, before it's written to the log.

> **LOGGING IS ASYNCHRONOUS** Like many other components in Akka.NET, logging is completely asynchronous. Within the logging system, an actor is responsible for receiving log messages that it then writes to the log output. This means that sometimes, as your system is being shut down, messages going into the log may not reach their final destination, leading to the apparent loss of messages.

5.5.3 *Customizing a logger deployment*

As mentioned in section 5.4.3, Akka.NET uses reasonable default values in situations where no other values are provided. This is no different for cases when a logger isn't provided. By default, Akka.NET creates a logger that prints all received messages to the console. So, if you want to direct all logged messages to the console, you can leave the configuration as is. But in a production deployment, you'll want to log messages to a centralized server, where they can be more easily processed and read. Although Akka.NET doesn't provide the infrastructure to directly log messages to a centralized system, it provides adapters that can perform the task. In this example, you'll use the NLog logging library, which appends log messages to various sources, including files on the filesystem, databases, and even emails. For now, we'll use a simple logger that directs the output to an output file.[3]

The first step is to add the logging library to the project. You can do this from NuGet by adding Akka.Logger.NLog. To customize some of the core components, create a file called NLog.config and add it to the project. The NLog.config file provides details of how to handle certain log messages. For example, it can specify that debug messages go to one location, such as a database, and error messages go to another, such as a text file. For now, you'll use a simple config file that sends all log messages to a text file:

```
<?xml version="1.0" encoding="utf-8" ?>
<nlog xmlns="http://www.nlog-project.org/schemas/NLog.xsd"
      xmlns:xsi="http://www.w3.org/2001/XMLSchema-instance">
   <targets>
   <target name="logfile" xsi:type="File" fileName="file.txt" />
   </targets>
   <rules>
   <logger name="*" minlevel="Info" writeTo="logfile" />
   </rules>
</nlog>
```

---

[3] This is a relatively simple example of a logging output. More-complex outputs are available, but they won't be covered here. For more information on configuring and using NLog, see the NLog project site (http://nlog-project.org/).

Now that NLog is configured in your application, you can configure Akka.NET to use it as the sink to which all logs are sent. This is done by modifying the configuration object that you pass into the actor system when you create it. To change your log providers, you can add an array of possible Akka.NET loggers:

```
akka {
    loggers = ["Akka.Logger.NLog.NLogLogger, Akka.Logger.NLog"]
}
```

There are further settings that you can modify that also affect the logging behavior of the application. For example, sometimes you may not have an actor instantiated at the address to which you sent a message. In this case, the message would get diverted to a special actor known as `deadLetters`. You can configure the logging functionality of Akka.NET so that it outputs a message to the log whenever messages are undelivered:

```
akka {
    actor.debug.unhandled = on
}
```

> **CREATING CUSTOM LOGGERS** Although Akka.NET provides a wide variety of adapters for commonly used logging libraries, there may be a situation in which it doesn't support your choice of logging library. For example, you may be using a custom-developed solution for your business, or an infrequently used library. Akka.NET provides an extensibility point for creating a custom logging adapter that receives messages from your Akka.NET application and outputs them to your logging library. This is out of the scope of this chapter, but we'll come back to it later in the book, when we talk about how to extend the Akka.NET library and its components.

5.5.4 Wrapping up

In this section, you've seen the benefits of using logging when you're dealing with an asynchronous system, and how it allows you to gain better insight into how an application is working and whether it's operating correctly at runtime. You saw how logging works in Akka.NET through the actor system and how an actor sends messages to logging. Finally, you saw how to change the output destination for any log messages you write in the actor system.

5.6 Case study: Configuration and distributed systems

In any modern application development workflow, it's common to have a variety of environments that are used at different stages of the development pipeline, for example, development, test, and production environments. But it's unlikely that configuration is common across all environments. When logging in a development environment, you can log to the local development machine; but in a production environment, you'll probably be aggregating all of your logs into one centralized log-management service, allowing for simplified problem tracking in the event of production issues. Similarly, if you're persisting data into a database or alternative data storage location, you'll want to ensure that production data and test data are stored in separate data stores, and for testing purposes, you may not want to persist data at all.

In this chapter, you saw how configuration components work in Akka.NET; the configuration tooling allows you to change application parameters without having to recompile the application. This allows you to change the configuration file for different environments, and the changes will be reflected in the application.

As part of application configuration, there are typically two categories of configuration parameters: application settings and environment settings. *Application settings* are the parameters responsible for driving business logic. For example, in a machine-learning component, this includes the configuration of machine-learning models. These are parameters that might change frequently as the application is used, but will remain stable across environments. *Environment settings* describe how the application interacts with other systems in the environment, including connection strings to databases and the keys needed to consume external APIs. These are configuration parameters that should change between environments.

Akka.NET HOCON configuration simplifies this usage by allowing you to overwrite configuration parameters, depending on the environment. In figure 5.2, you can see a configuration file shared across all the environments. This includes the common configuration elements, notably, the application settings. You can also see that there's an additional configuration file that's different for each environment and that contains the settings for each independent environment. Internally, HOCON configuration merges the two files—the shared configuration and environment-specific configuration—into a single configuration file.

This ensures consistency across environments for configuration parameters in applications that still need some simplified runtime modification. You can also easily modify the environment-specific settings and ensure that there's no possibility of settings from one environment making their way into another environment.

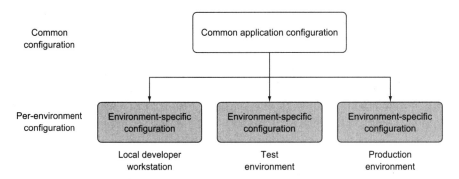

Figure 5.2   A modern application needs to run in multiple contexts, either local, test, or production. It's important to be able to configure the application for each environment without needing to recompile.

Summary

In this chapter, you learned

- The importance of monitoring and logging in asynchronous systems
- How Akka.NET provides a centralized logging point for collecting both system and application logs
- How to configure an Akka.NET application to suit the environment

Failure handling 6

This chapter covers

- Discovering where failures happen in asynchronous systems
- Understanding how actors in Akka.NET handle failure
- Dealing with failures in Akka.NET

First, you learned how to create simple actors in Akka.NET; then, you learned how to create more-complex actors that can react to changes in their environment by using state machines. Next, you learned how actors are configured in Akka.NET by using `Props` for individual actor deployments and HOCON for configuring the internals of the actor system. You know how to implement the principles of reactive systems. In chapter 3, you saw how to build actors that communicate asynchronously through message passing, which forms the building blocks of reactive applications.

In this chapter, we'll look at how you can implement one of the building blocks that sits on top of the message-passing layer, and how an Akka.NET application can respond to service failures. Throughout this chapter, we'll look at what a failure typically involves, especially in the context of distributed environments running

Akka.NET. Then, you'll see how an actor system reacts to failures to ensure operations without requiring frequent human intervention.

6.1 Understanding failures

As the applications you write become increasingly complex, with more moving parts, there's more potential for errors to occur at many different points in the stack. If you want to write applications that can operate for extended periods of time with minimal downtime, then it's important that they deal successfully with failures.

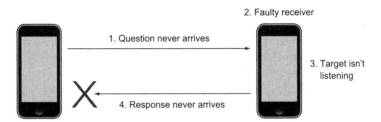

Figure 6.1 During a typical phone call, there are numerous reasons why you might fail to receive a response to a question.

When you make applications asynchronous, you increase the failure potential in the system, at the same time making it harder to find the root cause of the issues. Consider the scenario where you make a phone call to someone not visible to you. During the phone call, you might ask the other person a question. In an ideal situation, the person will hear the question and respond directly, but if you don't receive a response, you're presented with a range of possible circumstances that may have lead to this scenario (see figure 6.1):

- *The other person didn't receive the question.* Although you asked the other person a question, there's no way of knowing that the other person did in fact receive the question.
- *The other person didn't understand the question.* You asked the other person something that they didn't understand, either at all or in the given context. In this scenario, the other party might not know how to respond to the question, so they choose not to respond.
- *The other person is preoccupied with something else.* When you're talking to someone on the phone, you can't see that person, and so you don't know what they're doing at the moment. They may have had to temporarily put down the phone to respond to a more urgent matter.
- *Something serious might have happened to the person.* Once again, you can't see what the other person is doing at the time you ask them a question. If you ask them to do something, but something unrelated has just caused them harm, then

they won't be able to respond to you and will need attention from somebody nearby before they can respond to your question.

- *You never received their reply.* The other person received the question, formulated the response, and then replied, but the response was lost because the phone signal was too weak to transmit it.

All of these failures directly translate to failures that you may see in the world of asynchronous systems development. These are scenarios that you should plan for and attempt to mitigate throughout the design process of your applications. The Akka.NET framework provides features to help developers create applications that stay responsive, even in the face of failure. Throughout the rest of this chapter, we'll look at three key elements of writing failure-resistant applications: supervision trees, failure recovery, and message delivery. These issues are faced on a regular basis by all asynchronous applications and not just those written with Akka.NET.

6.2 *Handling application-level failures*

First, we'll look at failures that your application itself can cause. These are failures of application logic caused by attempting to perform an operation when the system isn't in a valid state. Common examples include trying to access data stored on objects that are currently null references, and invoking a method at the wrong stage in the application's lifecycle. The lifecycle of an application can be thought of as an original starting state with a number of transitions leading to a finished state. Figure 6.2 shows how you modify a state by performing operations on the data.

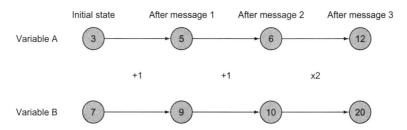

Figure 6.2   variable's state can be considered as a series of events applied to an initial state.

Sometimes you'll encounter problems with transitioning into a new state. If you're performing a number of potentially dangerous operations, you don't want to leave the system with only half of them completed; you could quickly find the system in an indeterminate state. Figure 6.3 shows a number of operations that are applied to an object until it encounters an error. The object is set to a local state before encountering the error, which it tries to recover from. After this, there's no guarantee that any operation it executes can be deemed valid, because the object existed in an indeterminate state.

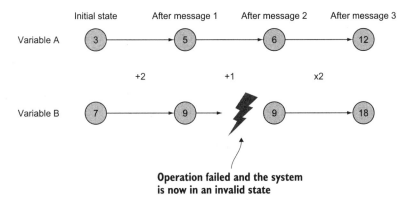

Figure 6.3   An event that fails to apply a change to a variable's state leaves the system in an invalid state.

In this section, we'll look at how severe these kinds of issues are, as well as how you can recover from them normally. You'll see the Akka.NET approach to dealing with errors and the shift in mindset necessary when you're designing applications capable of recovering from errors on their own, without human interaction.

6.2.1   *Responding to application errors*

Programming languages have always provided options for dealing with errors. Relatively simple languages, such as C, rely on the use of an integer to represent an error status returned from a function. Later programming languages provide more-advanced means of handling scenarios where the application is in an invalid state. One example is using *exceptions* to convey in-depth information relating to an error. For example, a common exception in C# is the `NullReferenceException`. The issue that causes this exception is trying to use an object that hasn't been initialized and is still null. When the application runs, it tries to retrieve data stored at that address and is unable to, because nothing exists at that memory location. This exception is probably encountered because the application is in an invalid state. This is a classic example of an application error. There are many possible causes of such an error, but the root cause is that the application performs an operation that forces the system into an invalid state at some stage in its lifetime.

This is a scenario that you'll probably encounter frequently in the world of technology. Let's consider for a moment the sheer complexity of a modern-day application in relation to the universe in which we live. For an application that has six 32-bit integers, there are more than 6×10^{57} possible states in which those six integers can exist (2^{32}-bit arrangements per number with six possible arrangements, giving $2^{32 \times 6}$), but the earth on which we live has only 1.33×10^{50} atoms. Given how many potential states six integers can end up in, it's not unreasonable to think that a more complex application could end up in a broken state, especially because you have neither the computational resources to check every state, nor an understanding of what should happen in each state.

But there *is* one state in which we know an object is almost guaranteed to work, which is the very first state that it exists in once the object has been created. This is an approach to solving technological problems that is used fairly frequently. For example, if your computer starts behaving erratically or slowing down, the first thing you do to eradicate the problem is to restart the machine in the hope that it will return to a known good state, typically the state in which the system was started. Despite a number of tries, this might not work, and the problem might not be solved; you can then try to freshly install the operating system (OS) in an effort to return the whole machine to a known state.

Due to the isolated nature of components in Akka.NET, this is an approach to maintaining fault tolerance that proves to be viable. With tightly coupled applications, it's unlikely to be possible to re-create selected components. But the loosely coupled message passing architecture of Akka.NET ensures that you can remove components temporarily in an effort to fix them. You need a way to signal to the system in charge of monitoring for failure that the component has failed. Fortunately, such a system is provided by the .NET framework, as we discussed earlier, in the form of exceptions. Exceptions are considered to be fatal errors and lead to the whole application crashing if they're not handled. But in Akka.NET, unhandled exceptions are considered to be a crash of the internal logic of the application.

A number of other problems can also result in errors; for example, a logic error when an actor receives and processes a message. In this case, there's little you can do to manage the situation at runtime, other than failing the entire application. An example of such a failure might be that you used some hardcoded logic that divides a number in the message by a constant number in the actor. If this constant number has been initialized to 0, then it will always lead to problems when that type of message is received by the actor. There's no operation you can perform that can alleviate this situation. Instead, you need to redeploy the application with the required fixes in place.

Another potential failure scenario is transient system failures. A *transient failure* is one that may only last for a certain period before being fixed, without the need for any external interaction. An example of this is if your system communicates with an external service, such as a web API or a database. These services may be afflicted by errors that then propagate throughout your system. You saw in chapter 4 how you can address issues relating to transience by using finite state machines to create objects resembling circuit breakers.

From a black-box perspective, there's no single means of determining the source of the application error; instead, you take the same approach across all three scenarios in the hope that the issue isn't threatening the integrity of the application. You can restart the failing actor to refresh it into its original state. This is not to say that continuous restarting of the actor is the solution to the problem. If it's a continuous logic problem, you need to address the logic bugs. This requires the thorough instrumentation of your codebase, through the logging functionality you saw in chapter 5, so you can understand why actors are restarting and how to fix the application.

6.2.2 *The Akka.NET supervision tree*

You saw in chapter 3 what happens when you deploy an actor into an actor system, and the hierarchy of actors that forms when you deploy each new actor as a child of another. The benefits involve scoping actors into related groups so you can build up an effective hierarchy (see figure 6.4). But this is only one advantage of designing systems in such a manner.

Upon spawning an actor into a given context, whether that's into the actor system's root level or as the child of another actor, that actor is configured to have a parent responsible for monitoring its status. Let's take an example from the world of business. If you're looking for employment, you have one of two options: you can either create your own company, or you can join an existing company. Regardless of which option you choose, some-

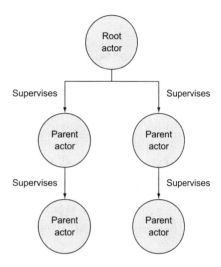

Figure 6.4   The Akka.NET deployment tree lends itself to a natural hierarchy of supervision in the event of errors.

body sits in a position above you in the hierarchy, some person whom you directly report to. If you've joined a company, then you probably have a manager who has control over one area of the company. If something that you're working on goes seriously wrong, then you tell your manager what happened and look at what steps can be taken to get the work back on track. This might involve several options, including firing you or the whole team, or your boss reporting the issue to his boss. You may be at the top of the tree, either by starting your own company or by being promoted up the hierarchy so that you don't *appear* to report to anybody, but you still have to report to the government and its offices about your activities as a company, which is in charge of sorting out any serious problems that may arise.

The same idea is used in Akka.NET. When an actor encounters a serious error, it tells its parent that something has gone wrong, and the parent decides on the best choice of action. By default, Akka.NET will restart the child in the hope that this will fix the issue; but if the error continues to be received, it will escalate the issue to the next parent in the hierarchy. This escalation will be continuously executed until the problem is solved—a technique that's also used in many OSs to ensure that a single application failure doesn't cause the entire OS to crash. The most notable OS kernel that uses this method is the Linux kernel.

Internally, Akka.NET handles this behavior through *supervision strategies*, which tell the framework how it should respond when it detects the failure of an actor's processing stage. A supervision strategy consists of four key components, which are used to make decisions as to what should happen following an error: the actors on which to perform the action, the action to take depending on the failure, the maximum allowable number of the same type of error, and the timespan in which those errors occur.

SPECIFYING THE ACTORS TO RESTART

The first component of the supervision strategy is the actors on which actions are performed in the event of failure. Akka.NET provides two key options in the framework: the one-for-one strategy and the all-for-one strategy. You can add more, but the two provided cover almost all the common actions that are frequently required. In the one-for-one strategy, only the failing actor and actors deployed under it are restarted. Figure 6.5 shows which actor is restarted in the case of a failure. As you can see, once Child A is deemed to have failed, the action is performed on it.

The all-for-one strategy, however, performs the action on the failing actor as well as all of its siblings. Figure 6.6 shows the case where Child A fails. Once Child A is considered to have failed, the resulting action is performed on it, but it is also applied to Child B and Child C.

Typically, the only supervision strategy you'll need to use is the one-for-one strategy. The all-for-one strategy is used by actors that have a tight coupling on key components with their siblings. This might, for example, include the need to recompute a shared resource that all actors need in order to process messages. You saw in chapter 3 how Akka.NET provides sane defaults for configuration settings, and it's no different in the case of supervision. By default, Akka.NET uses the one-for-one strategy for any freshly deployed actor.

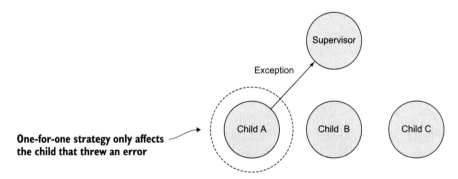

Figure 6.5   The one-for-one strategy will apply the given action only to the child that encountered a problem.

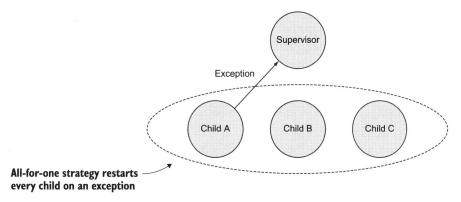

All-for-one strategy restarts
every child on an exception

Figure 6.6 The all-for-one strategy will also apply the given action to all the siblings of the actor that encountered an error.

CHOOSING WHICH ACTION TO TAKE

Upon detecting a failure, Akka.NET needs to know what to do next, as determined by the `Decider` component of the supervisor strategy. The `Decider` is a simple component that supplies a directive to Akka.NET by means of a `Directive`. Akka.NET provides four directives to indicate to the framework how it should respond to a failure:

- *Resume*—The actor will ignore the error and continue on to the next message in its mailbox without performing any special operations relating to the error.
- *Restart*—The actor will restart in an attempt to resolve the error, but the actor won't attempt to reprocess the same message and will instead restart with the next message in the mailbox as the first one it will process.
- *Stop*—The actor will shut down safely and won't receive any more messages. Any messages in its queue will be considered undelivered, and the undelivered-message error will be written to the log.
- *Escalate*—Sometimes, an error might be so serious that the supervisor has only one possible action: tell its supervisor that something has gone wrong. The parent will decide on the best course of action for the error. Then, the supervision strategy of the parent will be used, depending on the error.

In Akka.NET, `Decider` is a simple function you can pass into your supervision strategy that returns a `Directive` when presented with an exception. The `Decider` checks what exception has been invoked in the actor and returns the appropriate `Directive`. You can create a `Decider` that responds to some of the typical failures your system might experience.

Let's consider the example of the shopping cart from chapter 2. Each shopping cart has an associated actor responsible for communicating with the external payment service to settle the final bill for the contents of the shopping cart. There might also be other actors deployed as children of that shopping cart. For example, you might have an actor responsible for applying discounts to the cart contents. Because the payment service is typically provided by an external entity, the data that comes back might not always be in the expected form. In that case, it will probably cause an issue in the actor, leading to an exception. As you've seen in this chapter, an exception will cause the actor to crash and a message to be sent to the parent asking how it should respond. You have a choice of supervision strategies: either restart the faulty actor or restart all child actors. This scenario is an ideal case for using the one-for-one restart strategy, because the other child actors won't be restarted as a result of the payment-service actor failing. But if the child actors communicated with each other and shared state among themselves, then you'd want to restart all of them, as they could have an invalid shared state.

Sometimes errors don't affect the overall operation of your actor. For example, when using a payment service through the network, your system might encounter a response timeout. Although you could restart the actor, it's likely that any other services will simply resend their request if they don't get a response in a predefined time period, ensuring that you don't need to restart the actor. You can build this logic into a `Decider`. If you get a `TimeoutException`, then you simply resume processing messages through the actor, but if you get an `ArithmeticException`, then you restart the actor:

```
Decider.From(exception =.
    {
        if (exception is ArithmeticException) return Directive.Restart;
        else if (exception is NullReferenceException) return
    Directive.Resume;
        else return Directive.Resume;
    });
```

The `Decider` is the core of the supervision strategy and allows you to specify issues and remedy them in the most appropriate way. This, along with the supervision strategy, is all that's required to effectively handle errors in your actors, providing an easy way of managing issues that arise. Although you can create your own custom `Decider`, if you use the default supervision strategy in Akka.NET, then it uses a `Decider` that restarts every actor, regardless of which exception is raised.

CUMULATIVE ERRORS

So far, we've considered what happens with errors caused by an actor's state becoming corrupt; but there are other categories of errors, as you saw earlier. What happens if the state of the failing actor is corrupted because of a corrupted state in its parent? In this case, there's no possibility of the actor recovering from the failure, because it's been incorrectly configured by its parent. You need to restart the parent as well and escalate the issue. You can specify that if the actor must restart a given number of times within a given time period, then it will escalate the error to its parent. By default, Akka.NET uses 10 restarts in a one-minute period to determine whether the next exception should be propagated up the hierarchy.

PIECING IT TOGETHER

You've seen the components that make up the supervision strategy of an actor. You can now piece these together and see how to use them in an actor. We'll continue to use the example for which you've already designed `Directives`. First, create a `Supervisor-Strategy` based on all the parts you've seen so far. In this example, you tell the supervisor that it should restart only the failing child and leave the siblings alone. You also say that, in the event that it restarts more than 10 times, the issue should be escalated to the supervisor's parent. Finally, you only want to restart in the event that the child actor throws an `ArithmeticException`; if the actor throws an `ArgumentException`, then the supervisor should simply ignore the message and continue as though it never received the message. The following code shows how to define this `SupervisorStrategy`. You can see the use of the `OneForOneStrategy` as the basis from which you build the rest of the components. The `Decider` is created from a function passed into `Decider.From`. This function requires you to return a `Directive` based on an `Exception` that's passed to the function:

```
new OneForOneStrategy(10,
                    TimeSpan.FromMinutes(1.0),
                    Decider.From(exception =>
    {
        if (exception is ArithmeticException)
            return Directive.Restart;
        else if (exception is NullReferenceException)
            return Directive.Resume;
        else return Directive.Resume;
    }));
```

Now that you've created a supervisor strategy, you need to associate it with an actor. There are two approaches you can use: you can associate the strategy with the actor itself, ensuring that it's responsible for its own supervision settings; or the supervisor strategy can be configured at the point when the actor is deployed, leaving the deployer responsible for configuring how its child should act in the face of a failure.

The first course is by far the simplest, requiring you to override the `Supervisor-Strategy` method on an actor. This method is then called in the event that an exception is thrown during the processing of a message. In the following code, you make the actor responsible for the `SupervisorStrategy` in the event of a failure:

```
protected override SupervisorStrategy SupervisorStrategy()
{
    return new
        OneForOneStrategy(10,
                    TimeSpan.FromMinutes(1.0),
                    Decider.From(exception =>
        {
            if (exception is ArithmeticException)
                return Directive.Restart;
            else if (exception is NullReferenceException)
                return Directive.Resume;
            else return Directive.Resume;
        }));
}
```

You saw in chapter 5 how to change details of an actor's deployment with `Props`, which you pass into the actor system when you want to spawn an actor. You can specify the supervisor strategy on the `Props` so that it's decided by the actor responsible for deploying it. In the following code, you specify the supervisor strategy as part of the `Props`. If you've got a `DatabaseCommunicationActor` responsible for communicating with a database, you can create the `Props` for it by using the `Create` factory method. Once you've got the `Props` responsible for creating the actor, you use the fluent API to create a new `Props` object with the supervisor strategy on it. The supervisor strategy is declared in the same way as in the previous example:

```
Props.Create<AnomalyDetector>()
    .WithSupervisorStrategy
    (new OneForOneStrategy(
      10,
      TimeSpan.FromMinutes(1.0),
      Decider.From(exception =>
      {
          if (exception is ArithmeticException)
              return Directive.Restart;
          else if (exception is NullReferenceException)
              return Directive.Resume;
          else return Directive.Resume;
      }))); 
```

Both of these approaches have advantages, and the decision of when to use which is influenced by the usage of the actor. Some actors are designed for general use in multiple different components in the same system. That would impose differing constraints on how the actor should react in the event of a failure, depending on its role in the system. In that case, an actor shouldn't be responsible for specifying how it reacts to a failure; instead, that responsibility should go to the component that wants to spawn the actor into its context. But if you've written an actor for a specific purpose, which relies on restarting in a specific way, then you're likely to associate the supervisor strategy with the actor itself. This ensures that all the spawned actors of that type will be spawned with that same supervisor strategy, leaving it suited to homogeneous collections of actors.

6.2.3 *Failing fast*

Programmers often interact with a number of APIs on a daily basis, many of which perform some potentially unsafe operations in the course of their lifecycle. You'll see some of the many possible errors throughout this chapter. In every case where these errors result in an unrecoverable or unexpected error, APIs in high-level languages such as C# typically throw an exception.

This use of exceptions is designed so that the caller of the API has its control flow diverted and is prevented from the intended order of execution. To regain control of the situation, the approach taken is to wrap the calls to the API in a try-catch block. Following this, exceptions are handled by an exception handler specific to the type of exception thrown. The exception handler performs operations to recover from the exception by either retrying the operation again or logging some details of the exception. Then, the exception is wrapped in an enclosing type to provide meaningful information to the user. Finally, either this new exception is thrown or the original exception is rethrown.

This approach has a number of disadvantages, the first of which is the obfuscation of the intent of the business logic expressed in the code. With error-handling code, you surround your cleanly factored code with code that provides functions that will only be executed in exceptional circumstances, rather than allowing developers to focus on the core intent of the code. If you add error-handling code, you may create a codebase that's more confusing for developers, because it imposes an understanding of the implicit details of API methods and where they can fail. This is information that's typically not made immediately obvious in documentation.

Another source of pain when using this approach is the potential for logs to quickly become polluted with multiple messages reporting the same source of errors but at different points in the error-handling hierarchy. For example, a log message may be generated at the most deeply nested point where the error is generated, as well as the place where this rethrown exception is then caught. The log will then contain two messages with different information relating to the same error.

Also, in the event that an exception is logged only at the top of the error-handling chain, there's potential for lost context. If the original exception is generated but not included in any more-generalized API exceptions, it becomes significantly more difficult to drill down to the original source of the error; you only know which API method led to the failure.

The final issue is potentially the most significant. If you perform a number of method calls, one following the other, and following each method call you modify state, in the event that the final method call throws an exception, this will prevent it from setting its final state. This leaves the system in an indeterminate state, where the application has left one state but hasn't entered a new state, creating difficulties further down the line. If you now call that API again, there's no guarantee that it won't provide invalid results every time it's called.

You've seen how Akka.NET provides supervisors that prevent the whole application from being brought down when an exception isn't caught by an exception handler. Relying on this feature, Akka.NET advises that you not use any behavior blocks at all, instead allowing supervisors to deal with errors. This approach is known as *fail-fast programming*, because after an error occurs, the system is immediately informed of the failure. Then, you let the supervisor deal with the specifics of what to do to recover. This ensures that when the supervisor receives an error, it's the only thing that logs the error and the reason for it, right where it occurs, whether it was an inability to connect to an external database or an attempt to divide by zero. Then, assuming the error can lead to an invalid state, the actor can be restarted to a known good state to prevent knock-on effects.

This approach to programming has shown significant benefits historically when developers design applications built on actor systems, but it does involve a significant change in the fundamental concepts of writing code.

THE ERROR KERNEL PATTERN

The approach of restarting actors as soon as an error is encountered can lead to issues, in particular relating to actors that are required to store lots of state. Because Akka.NET actors exist wholly in memory, if an actor is restarted, then it loses all of its associated state. This causes problems, because you rely on restarting actors so frequently in Akka.NET. The common approach to dealing with this problem is to use the *error kernel pattern*, which forces dangerous work down the actor hierarchy to child actors. Then, in the event that the child fails, the error is isolated, ensuring that the parent doesn't end up losing its long-term state.

6.2.4 *The actor lifecycle*

In chapter 3, you saw how to spawn a new actor into the actor system, which internally creates an actor instance. In this chapter, you also saw how actors can be shut down and restarted when a failure is detected. There are two different ways of shutting down an actor, depending on the severity of the situation:

- *Passing a poison pill message*—Akka.NET provides a number of messages that can be sent to actors and processed before reaching the internals of your actor. One example of this is the poison pill message that's identified by the `PoisonPill` class. The actor processes any messages in its mailbox until it reaches the poison pill message, which shuts down the actor before it processes any messages that arrived in the queue after the poison pill. With the `PoisonPill`, you can send messages to a single actor or a group of actors as you would send any other messages.
- *Using* `Context.Stop`—If an actor needs to stop immediately after processing the current message, it can use the `Stop` method on its internal actor context. Here, it passes in the `ActorRef` relating to what it wants to shut down, and then the framework handles the shutdown of the actor.

THE LIFECYCLE

You've seen how an actor can be created by calling `ActorOf` in the framework, which will cause an actor to be instantiated. You've also seen how an actor can be killed either programmatically by itself or by other actors, or by the framework when it detects a failure. Actors in Akka.NET operate and transition through a number of states during their lifecycle. Figure 6.7 shows the states an actor can exist in, as well as how to move between those states.

The core state is the actor's regular operating state, but it must take a number of steps to get into such a state. When an actor is spawned into the actor system, it has a *starting state*. At this point, any configuration the actor needs during its lifecycle is prepared, after which it's ready to start receiving messages. From here, it moves into the

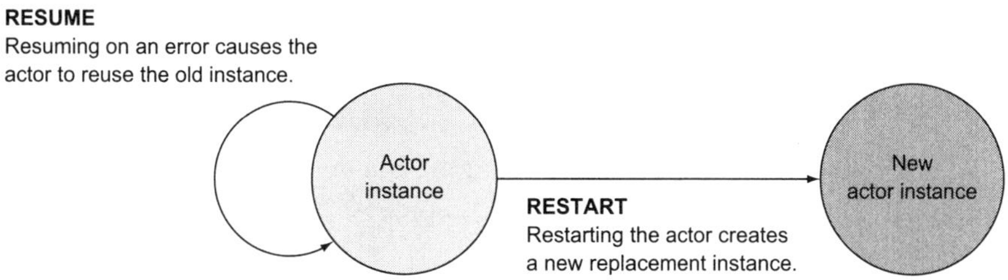

RESUME
Resuming on an error causes the
actor to reuse the old instance.

Actor
instance

RESTART
Restarting the actor creates
a new replacement instance.

New
actor instance

**Figure 6.7   The two most common options in the event of an error cause the actor system
to reuse the old actor instance or create a new one as a replacement.**

running state, where the processing loop is invoked any time a message is received in
its mailbox. Eventually, the actor is likely to be terminated, either gracefully by its own
choice, or forcefully by a supervisor. Following either of these cases, the actor then
transitions into the *terminating state* before ending up in the *terminated state*. When the
actor is in the terminated state, messages addressed to it won't be delivered and
instead are passed on to the deadLetters actor that logs these events.

SPECIFYING THE TRANSITIONS AN ACTOR TAKES

When you create a class for an actor, you can specify operations that should be undertaken at points during the actor's lifecycle. For example, it can be useful to perform
actions before an actor starts up, such as sending a message to other actors in the system. This can be achieved by overriding certain methods on the base actor class,
which are invoked by the framework at stages in the actor's lifecycle. Figure 6.8 shows
the state transitions throughout an actor's lifecycle from the starting phase, through
the receiving stage, and on.

In this chapter, you've seen how the framework can restart an actor once the
framework decides that it has failed. It can be beneficial to know whether an actor has
been restarted, as well as the reason for doing so. This can be achieved by overriding
the PreRestart method on the actor. The PreRestart method then provides the

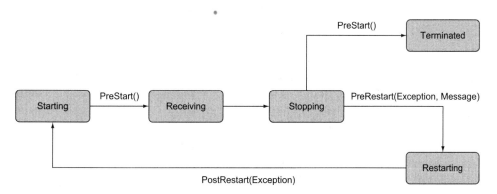

Figure 6.8   Actor lifecycle stages

Exception that caused the actor to restart, as well as the message that led up to the exception. This allows for rescheduling the failing message so that the actor can make another attempt at processing it. You've seen that the common approach to dealing with failure is to restart the failing actor, because a known good state could allow it to process the message successfully. By obtaining the message that led to failure, you can send the message to yourself and attempt to process it in its new state. This is what you do in the following example, in which you receive the message that caused the crash and schedule it to be added to the mailbox, ready to be processed again:

```
protected override void PreRestart(Exception reason, object message)
{
    Self.Tell(message);
}
```

When an actor is assigned to a periodic task, you can use Akka.NET's scheduling capabilities to deliver a message to that actor at periodic intervals, thereby invoking a regularly scheduled behavior. For example, you may want to synchronize the actor's internal state with an external service once every second. To achieve this, the actor sends itself a message once every second, to which is added logic so that the actor's state is accessed safely and with the same concurrency guarantees as other messages. To ensure that this message gets scheduled when the actor starts up, you can use its PreStart method. This method is called following the actor's creation and before it starts receiving messages. It's called every time the actor starts, whether that's a restart or a fresh start. In PreStart, you can initialize any resources that are likely to last the lifetime of the actor. One example of this is a timer, which is required for synchronization. The following example shows an actor that's responsible for performing an operation on a recurring schedule. You create a scheduled message in the PreStart method and, following this, the actor will receive that message on a regular schedule:

```
ICancelable _synchronisationTick;

protected override void PreStart()
{
    var scheduler = Context.System.Scheduler;
    scheduler.ScheduleTellRepeatedlyCancelable(
        0, 500, Self, SynchronisationTick.Instance, Self);
}
```

After the continuously scheduled message is registered, the message should stop when the actor stops, so the scheduler doesn't keep sending the message to it. The Post-Stop override is available to dispose of resources that are no longer needed. The last example showed the actor creating a recurring task and storing a handle to it in the actor's state. Now that the actor has finished its work, it can dispose of the scheduler that's sending it a message. The following example shows how, by using the PostStop method, you can safely access the state of the actor and modify it, in this case by disposing of the scheduler. You can use the PostStop method for other purposes also; for example, you can send a message to other actors to notify them that this actor is terminating.

```
protected override void PostStop()
{
    _synchronisationTick.Cancel();
}
```

These are the core functionalities of the actor lifecycle in Akka.NET. You've seen how, by overriding the methods in the actor definition, you can gain insight into the operation of the actor. You've also seen how to safely access the internal state of the actor to ensure it can initialize and dispose of resources used throughout its lifecycle.

6.2.5 *Watching for the deaths of other actors*

In Akka.NET, it's not just the parent of an actor that can watch for its failure; through a concept known as DeathWatch, other actors can monitor an actor and be notified if it fails. Using DeathWatch, when the framework discovers that an actor has failed, it sends a message to all actors who have subscribed to that notification.

Actors can sign up for DeathWatch notifications through their own context in the actor instance. You saw in chapters 3 and 4 how to use the Context in the actor to perform certain core operations; DeathWatch is no different. With the Watch method, you can supply an ActorRef, which will be monitored, as will the ActorRef of the subscriber. Then, if the watched actor fails, the subscriber will receive a Terminated message in its mailbox, containing the address of the actor that was terminated.

DEATHWATCH AND THE REAPER PATTERN

In Akka.NET, sometimes you have to wait until a number of core actors in the actor system have shut down before you can shut down the entire actor system. It's important to understand what it means for an actor to be *finished*. The simplest clue is that its mailbox is empty, but this doesn't cover all possibilities. You might *think* an actor is finished because its mailbox is empty, but it might be in either of two other situations:

- *It's still processing the last message.* The actor might have emptied its mailbox, but if it's doing some intensive computation as a result of a final message, it may not be safe to shut down the actor system just because its message queue is empty.
- *It hasn't received all of its messages yet.* In a similar vein, if an actor depends on receiving a message from another actor earlier in the chain, then it may not be safe to shut down the actor just because its message queue is empty; it may not have processed even one message yet.

Earlier in the chapter, you saw the various ways you can shut down an actor, one of which is with the PoisonPill message. You can send an actor a number of messages it should process, followed by a PoisonPill message. You can then say with a degree of certainty that when an actor has died, it has managed to complete all the work sent to it; it's *finished*. Figure 6.9 shows a message queue of work an actor must do before you shut it down.

But you likely have more than one actor sitting at the core of the actor system, and you can only safely exit after *all* of these actors are done. You need to form a barrier that you can only pass after all core actors have finished their work. You can extend

Figure 6.9 The `PoisonPill` ensures that all messages in the queue are processed before an actor is shut down.

the approach you've used so far, where an actor does some assigned work and is shut down once that work is complete.

The DeathWatch concept outlined earlier can be used here. You can create an actor whose job it is to DeathWatch each of the core actors you're interested in (the *reaper pattern*). Once the reaper actor gets a message informing it of the death of all the core actors, then it's safe to pass the barrier. You can see the reaper pattern illustrated in figure 6.10. The regular hierarchy of actors is positioned below the parent actor, but you also see the reaper actor, waiting for the deaths of the other actors.

You can create a reaper actor that watches other actors and then safely executes operations once all their work is complete. The reaper actor takes a collection of actor paths that it watches for deaths. It then subscribes to DeathWatch notifications for all of these actors, before listening for the terminated events. When it receives a `Terminated` message, it removes that actor from the collection of watched actors and checks to see whether it needs to wait for any other actors. If it doesn't, then it exits the barrier.

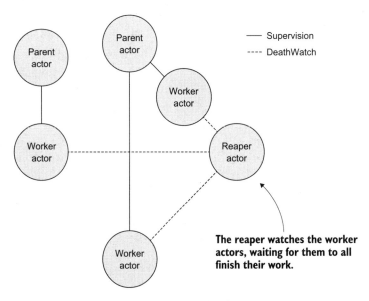

Figure 6.10 The reaper pattern is an application of DeathWatch that allows you to know when all actors have finished working.

First, create a reaper actor responsible for watching all the core actors. The following code snippet shows the initial actor definition with the constructor. The only data you need for this actor is the list of actors it'll be watching, which you supply as a set. Then, in the constructor, you subscribe to DeathWatch notifications for each of the actors you're interested in. This is done by calling `Context`. Use the `IActorRef` to watch for the actors you're interested in:

```
public class ReaperActor : ReceiveActor
{
    readonly HashSet<IActorRef> _watchedActors;

    public ReaperActor(HashSet<IActorRef> watchedActors)
    {
        _watchedActors = watchedActors;
    }

    protected override void PreStart()
    {
        foreach(var actor in _watchedActors)
        {
            Context.Watch(actor);
        }
    }
}
```

Next, add the correct handler for the `Terminated` message. Upon receiving a `Terminated` message, you need to remove the associated actor references from the set of references the `ReaperActor` is watching. If that set is now empty, then you can safely say that all the work has been successfully completed; now, you can safely stop the whole actor system without worrying about whether there's any work still going on:

```
Receive<Terminated>(terminated =>
{
    _watchedActors.Remove(terminated.ActorRef);
    if (_watchedActors.Count == 0)
    {
        Context.System.Terminate();
    }
});
```

This pattern shows how you can use the built-in lifecycle monitoring tools as a means of watching for the work completion of actors. The reaper pattern allows you to safely perform actions once all work has been completed. The key benefit of using Death-Watch, as opposed to other techniques, is the built-in consideration for failure. If you were to design such a pattern using message passing, you'd have to factor in the potential for the actor to fail before ever sending a completed message, meaning you'd need to add timeouts to ensure your actor didn't get stuck in a state where it was waiting for a message it would never receive.

6.2.6 *Interface-level failures*

So far, you've seen what happens if an actor encounters an error because it's in a faulted state; but there's another error state you need to consider, one caused by a user providing invalid input to your actor.

A common pattern seen when developing APIs is something like the following. A method or function takes a number of arguments; the API then progressively checks each parameter to the method to ensure it's deemed valid. This might include checking to see whether a parameter is null or matches a validation scheme. In the event that a parameter isn't valid, then an exception is thrown, such as an `ArgumentNullException` or just an `ArgumentException`:

```
public void RegisterUser(string email, string password)
{
    if (email == null)
        throw new ArgumentNullException("email");
    if (password.Length < 8)
        throw new ArgumentException(
            "Provided password is too short", "password");
}
```

But this approach falls apart when you consider the message-passing approach of Akka.NET. The interface is called by simply passing a message rather than directly invoking it. If you then request data from the actor, you could still be passing invalid data. As such, you need to change the way you consider these errors.

Earlier in this chapter, you saw what happens when an application error occurs: the supervisor is contacted with a notification of the failure and is then responsible for deciding on the appropriate course of action. The sender of the message doesn't know whether or not an exception was thrown, leaving you unsure of whether a receiving actor succeeded in processing the message.

This presents problems with knowing whether the information sent to the target actor was valid for the API. You saw in chapter 3 that when you send a message to an actor, you can send it in the form of a fire-and-forget manner through the use of `Tell`; but it's also possible to use `Ask`. Ask allows your system to asynchronously send a message to an actor and await a response. You can use this communication channel to surface any validation errors to the party that can deal with them in the most appropriate way.

Akka.NET provides the `Success` and `Failure` classes for this purpose. These two classes are used to encompass all the possible outcomes of calling an API through a message-based protocol. A target actor can either return a `Success` message with a result that indicates that the sent data is valid and everything has executed successfully, or the actor can return a `Failure` message that can contain exceptions, providing more details of the validation failure.

Let's revisit the API for registering a user with an email address and a password for an example of how to design actors that respond with the details of user-induced errors. The actor first validates that the information provided by the user passes all the required checks. In this case, it'll ensure that both the email address and password provided by the user are valid.

The actor receives a `UserRegistration` message containing the desired username and password. When it receives this message, the actor performs some simple validation, and in the event that the email isn't in the correct format or the password isn't valid, it replies with a failure message. Otherwise, it continues with the execution and processes the request by storing the message in a database of users. Upon completion, it returns a `Success` message informing the caller that their response was successful:

```
Receive<UserRegistrationInformation>(registration =>
{
    if (ValidInput(registration))
    {
        var accountInfo = RegisterAccount(registration);
        Sender.Tell(new Status.Success(accountInfo));
    }
});
```

A client can use this actor to understand whether information passed to it was correct and in the expected format by asking the actor for a response. Upon receiving the response, you can see whether it was successful, or examine the cause of an error the actor saw:

```
var response =
    await userRegistration.Ask(
        new UserRegistrationInformation(
            "newuser@google.com",
            "P4ssw@rd"));

if(response is Status.Success)
{
    //Handle successful account creation
}
else if(response is Status.Failure)
{
    //Handle invalid input case
}
```

Using this approach to error handling combined with that of the previous section implicitly creates two error channels, which presents you with further benefits. Errors encountered due to an invalid state in the actor or due to a failure to communicate with other services are errors that the user will be unable to deal with and that will degrade the UX for your service or application. But if the user provides an invalid email address, this is a situation that can be remedied.

6.2.7 *Wrapping up*

In this section, you've seen how Akka.NET can help reduce the impact of application-level failures by isolating errors and encapsulating them in the smallest unit of work. Having all potentially error-causing logic hidden deep in one actor means you can let it fail if something goes wrong, because another actor is responsible for watching that actor and restarting it to a known working state. You've also seen how to deal with API-user errors such as when a user supplies an address in an invalid format.

6.3   *Understanding transport-level failures*

So far in this chapter, we've focused on code-based failures, but there's more to actor systems than just the code. You also need to consider how your systems handle failures induced by the distributed environments in which they're running. The most critical failure you need to consider is message-delivery failure, because you want to guarantee that two actors are able to communicate with each other.

Let's consider what happens when you send a letter through the postal system. You wrap your message in an envelope that informs the delivery mechanism of the target, and you leave it in a known location for the delivery system to pick it up. From there, you have no knowledge of whether or not the target received what you sent. This is one of the key disadvantages of asynchronous systems such as Akka.NET. Due to the large infrastructure between the point from which a message is sent and the point at which it should be received, it's possible that the message might not reach its intended destination safely. These sorts of issues are as common in software development as in the physical message-delivery world, so it's important that you write systems that can cope with such failures in the most appropriate ways.

In the vast majority of cases, you're unlikely to lose a message, especially in the scenarios you've seen so far, which have featured actors running across multiple threads on a single machine. Thinking back to the water-depth-sensor example of chapter 4, consider that there might be a message sent between a sensor and the system that fails to be delivered. In this case, you end up having to use a potentially low-quality network connection through which you send messages. This vastly increases the probability of message loss due to the additional levels of complexity through all stages of the pipeline.

For most sensor data, such as for capturing light or humidity readings, it's unlikely to matter if a message is lost, especially if the volume of data is sufficiently high that you can afford to lose 1 out of every 100 data points. But some sensors are much more important. For example, if a motion detector picks up movement suggestive of an intruder in a house, an immediate reaction is necessary. In this case, you want to ensure that a message is delivered to an actor capable of dealing with the event.

In the systems you've built so far, you've relied on Akka.NET to guarantee that a message is delivered; but such guarantees are nonexistent in Akka.NET as it simply follows the at-most-once delivery guarantee. This guarantee says that a message will be sent and passed through the system. But if the message gets lost at any stage in the pipeline, then the sender won't receive any feedback about the failure. You hope that each message is only processed once, but this uncertainty can be a source of difficulties.

Throughout this chapter, you've seen a variety of failures that an actor can face during its lifecycle. You've also seen some of the potential failures in a generalized asynchronous system, such as a phone call. In all these cases, the key problem is that you don't know what state the remote actor is in. It could be in a faulted state, meaning that it's incapable of processing messages; or the communication link between the two actors might have failed; or communication might have failed in only one direction. You're simply unable to determine the state of remote actors, so you can never know whether an actor has received a message, whether it successfully processed a message, or whether it failed to send a successful acknowledgement in response.

To work around this lack of acknowledgment, instead of using the at-most-once delivery strategy, you can switch to the at-least-once delivery strategy. This technique involves sending the same message to a receiving actor multiple times until the sending actor receives confirmation that the message has been successfully processed, at which point any further message-sending will cease. This delivery strategy ensures that the target actor will eventually receive the message, although the target actor might end up receiving several copies of the same message. By sending the message a number of times, you counteract any problems with transient errors across the communication link, thereby allowing at least one of the messages to reach its intended destination.

6.3.1 Writing applications that handle message loss

The actor systems you've written so far have dealt with failures that could be caused by your code, but a modern application always sits on top of several layers of infrastructure, including the CPU internals and the OS, and is dependent on a network connecting multiple machines. You've seen the problems that can arise from this supporting infrastructure, which is capable of inducing failures. You've also seen how Akka.NET handles sending messages, as well as how you can send a message without knowing whether its delivery was a success or a failure.

Although the delivery guarantees of Akka.NET can't be changed, you can turn an at-most-once delivery guarantee into an at-least-once delivery guarantee. In this section, we'll look at how you can build a tool that will let you communicate without worrying about the communication layer.

You'll need an API capable of repeatedly sending a message until it receives a completion acknowledgement. To that end, you'll create an actor that will repeatedly send a message, and then attempt to receive an acknowledgement message in return. In the event that your actor doesn't receive a response within a set time period, it will automatically resend the message, repeating the process until it eventually receives an acknowledgement, or until it sends the maximum allowed number of messages without acknowledgement.

As you've done before, you'll first consider the states that your message-delivery actor can exist in. Typically, its main state will be the one in which it sends a message and awaits a response. In this state, it's capable of accepting one of two messages: either one from the intended recipient notifying it of a successful message receipt, or a timeout message informing the actor that it should send another message. If the actor does receive an acknowledgement message, then it should shut down, because it

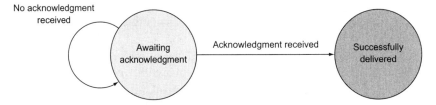

Figure 6.11   The state machine for an actor providing at-least-once delivery is simple, requiring only two states with two possible events.

has nothing else to do. If, however, it fails to receive an acknowledgement across several timeouts, then it will respond to the original sender with a delivery-failure message. You can view these states and their associated transitions in figure 6.11.

The first thing to consider is the messages you'll send between the actors. As shown in figure 6.11, a number of events cause state transitions, notably the Acknowledgement and ReceiveTimeout events. These two messages make clear the various state transitions, as you saw in the discussion of interface-level failures. Also, Success and Failure messages are provided by the framework, enabling your message-delivery actor to inform the sending actor of a successful message delivery.

Because of the potential for failures in asynchronous systems, Akka.NET provides an API that allows you to specify, after a certain period of inactivity, that a Receive-Timeout message must be sent to an actor. This provides a means of developing actors that can respond to situations where the length of time required to send and deliver a message is important.

You need a message that tells the resending actor that the target has successfully received the message, and that it can stop sending messages. You'll now define a simple class that informs the target that it has successfully received a message. In the following code snippet, you'll define just such a class, called Ack, which doesn't need to hold any additional data associated with the received message:

```
public class Ack
{
    private static readonly Ack _instance = new Ack();

    public static Ack Instance { get { return _instance; } }
}
```

Now that you have all the messages used as state transitions in your state machine, you'll need to implement each of these states. As is the case with the actor model, you'll define an actor capable of doing this resending work, which then leaves the original sending actor free to process other work while the resend actor attempts to communicate with a target. The resend actor needs the destination of the message, the message itself, the maximum number of retries it should attempt, and the timeout between retries. Because the actor will be designed with a single purpose, that is, to handle one message and then stop, you'll rely on the constructor to pass in these required arguments.

The following code example contains the initial actor definition as set forth in the constructor. You'll notice that a ReceiveActor has been selected for the target you'll be sending the message to, rather than a reference to an actor in the form of an IActorRef. In chapter 3, you learned about the difference between an IActorRef and an ActorSelection. An IActorRef contains information about the creation of an actor, so if it restarts, then this reference will change. In this scenario, you want to guarantee that you can send the message to the target regardless of failures, such as network failures. But if you used an IActorRef, you wouldn't be accounting for the possibility that the actor fails and is restarted. In the constructor, you'll also notice the use of the SetReceiveTimeout method, which tells the framework that the actor should receive a ReceiveTimeout message after the period specified in the timeout:

```
public class GuaranteedDeliveryActor : ReceiveActor
{
    readonly ActorSelection _target;
    readonly object _message;
    readonly int _maxRetries;
    int _retryCount;
    readonly TimeSpan _messageTimeout;

    public GuaranteedDeliveryActor(ActorSelection target,
                                   object message,
                                   int maxRetries,
                                   TimeSpan messageTimeout)
    {
        _target = target;
        _message = message;
        _maxRetries = maxRetries;
        _messageTimeout = messageTimeout;
    }

    protected override void PreStart()
    {
        SetReceiveTimeout(_messageTimeout);
        _target.Tell(_message);
    }
}
```

Because this state machine has only one core state, you don't need to use any of the finite state machine features; instead, you can use a basic actor. You've seen figure 6.11 that there are two core events that the message-delivery actor needs to handle: a ReceiveTimeout message and an Ack message. If it receives a ReceiveTimeout message, then first it checks whether it's reached the maximum number of retries. If it has, then it follows these steps: it notifies the original sending actor that the message delivery failed; it cancels the message; it receives ReceiveTimeout messages; and it shuts the actor down. If, however, it has retries remaining, it again attempts to send the message to the target and increments the retries counter. This means you have a receive handler for the timeout messages:

```
Receive<ReceiveTimeout>(_ =>
{
    if (_retryCount >= _maxRetries)
        throw new TimeoutException(
            "Unable to deliver the message to the target in the specified
     number of retries");
    else
    {
        _target.Tell(_message);
        _retryCount++;
    }
});
```

You also need to handle where the message-delivery actor receives an Ack message in response from the target. In this case, as shown in the next code snippet, it informs the sending actor that it has successfully sent the message, and then it cancels the ReceiveTimeout messages, before finally shutting down. Once again, this leads to a fairly simple receive handler:

```
Receive<Ack>(_ =>
{
    SetReceiveTimeout(null);
    Context.Stop(Self);
});
```

Finally, having completed such a system, the message-delivery actor needs to confirm delivery. It needs to tell the sending actor that it has contacted the required target, which it does by sending the Ack message to the Sender (sending actor):

```
public class BillingActor : ReceiveActor
{
    public BillingActor()
    {
        Receive<RequestNewPayment>(payment =>
        {
            Sender.Tell(Ack.Instance);
        });
    }
}
```

It's important to consider the operations that the target actor undertakes upon receiving a message from the message-delivery actor. The target actor could process the same message many times over multiple timeouts if it doesn't send its acknowledgment back within the timeout period. To get around this problem, you can filter out messages that the target has already processed, possibly by passing an identifier to uniquely identify a message, and then storing a set of processed messages in the target actor. Alternatively, you could design your target actor so that receiving the same message twice will lead to the same outcome. This property is known as *idempotence*.

You've now seen how to define an actor that provides a best-effort at-least-once delivery guarantee and that will repeatedly attempt to send a message to a given target.

6.3.2 *Wrapping up*

This section focused on how to build applications that stay resilient and reliable even in the event of failures outside of your control, as in the underlying infrastructure that connects actors together. You've seen how Akka.NET deals with sending messages; you've also seen the limitations of this method and how you can address these limitations to ensure successful message transmission. This is a topic we'll come back to in later chapters, where you'll discover an implementation that's available in Akka.Persistence, one of the many Akka.NET plugins.

6.4 *Case study: Supervision, failure, chat bots*

Modern applications have become increasingly complex and dependent on a variety of other systems for their successful operation. Even a relatively simple application needs to interoperate with a database and, potentially, external APIs. However, APIs are now being developed that will open up more-complex domains and techniques to a broader audience, thus simplifying the development of enhanced projects.

One example of these new developments is the proliferation of conversational user interfaces in the form of chat bots. These interfaces require an understanding of the way natural human language works. Natural language processing (NLP) is a fundamentally difficult problem to solve due to the complexities of human language. On top of the difficulties of processing the text itself, your system need to understand the intent of the text and what the user wants the system to do.

A number of companies have started providing APIs capable of figuring out the intent of text so that the user's original text can be compressed into a more manageable dataset. But it's also possible that these external services could fail at any stage. If they do fail, you need to continue to process the user's request. If you don't handle the failure correctly, the user could be presented with internal error messages or, even worse, the user could end up without a response and the application could hang.

Using the supervision components of Akka.NET, you can let it handle the exceptions you don't expect. The common means of communicating with natural-language-intent APIs is by using an HTTP API. An HTTP API could present a variety of issues: there may be network issues that cause timeouts or no responses; there may be authentication issues if you fail to supply passwords when they're required; or there may be errors generated by the remote system if the text you supply is invalid. In all of these situations, you still want to tell the user something meaningful in response to their questions, rather than simply leaving them without any further information.

Figure 6.12 shows how you can assign tasks to a dedicated actor that's responsible for performing the required work and communicating with an external service. In the event that an unexpected error is encountered, Akka.NET will process the failed actor. In a typical situation, this involves restarting the actor and hoping that the issue was transient. But, given that APIs are commonly billed based on the number of operations performed against them, you would shut down the actor calling the API if it

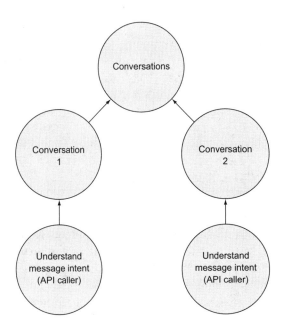

Figure 6.12 **Designing a strong actor hierarchy simplifies the process of reacting to failure in such a way that it doesn't affect other parts of the running application.**

encounters an exception caused by invalid text, because you know that this is an unrecoverable error.

Supervision ensures that you can write systems that aren't overly dependent on external services, as failure handling is a component that lies at the core of the Akka.NET API.

Summary

In this chapter, you learned

- How the complexity of modern systems leads to an increased likelihood of failures
- How Akka.NET helps to reduce the likelihood of system failure by isolating component failures
- How Akka.NET enables you to intelligently recover from errors
- How to handle failures not only in your own systems, but also in the systems with which yours interact

Scaling in reactive systems

This chapter covers

- Evaluating the difficulties of traditional scaling approaches
- Comparing the Akka.NET scaling approach to traditional methods
- Using routers in Akka.NET
- Dynamically scaling actors to react to load changes

In chapter 1, you embraced the goal of building responsive systems to ensure the best possible UX. In chapter 3, you saw how a message-passing architecture lets you break free of systems that rely heavily on blocking API calls. You also saw, in chapter 6, how you can ensure that your applications continue to work in gray-sky as well as blue-sky conditions. By considering where failures are likely to occur and using the failure detection and recovery tooling in Akka.NET, you can respond to errors in your application before they significantly impact your application's performance and negatively affect the end user's experience. Now, we'll look at how you can handle increased traffic and prevent the extra pressure from affecting the performance of your application.

In recent years, with increased computer and internet use in the home, many traditional retailers have started offering their products for sale on the internet, and many retailers such as Amazon operate exclusively on the internet. Some find that the number of customers attempting to access their site isn't linear over the course of the year, with significant spikes around holidays or during sales: for example, Black Friday and post-Christmas sales. Retailers offer discounts on products to draw in new customers and encourage them to spend money. When these sales offer significant discounts, there's a corresponding increase in the number of users trying to access the online store. Most of these visitors likely want to make a purchase, but if the website struggles under the increased load, then it's likely that many visitors will simply stop trying to access it and instead buy the product from a competitor. A consequence of a degraded UX is that many users could be driven away, leading to a loss of revenue for the retailer.

Providing users with a solid experience even when the system's under an intense load is just one of the plusses of a scalable system. There are benefits to be found on the micro as well as the macro levels. Many applications have a relatively fixed number of users at any point in the day. For example, an application designed for employees in the UK is likely to see its full usage during the normal working hours of 9 a.m. to 5 p.m. GMT; but outside of these hours, there might be only a handful of users online. With a scalable solution, you can scale the application down when you see periods of extended quiet and, as a result, save both money and resources.

7.1   Scaling up and scaling out

E-commerce markets are likely to experience large spikes in their number of users. For example, an online retailer may be about to reveal a new product, begin a sale with significant discounts, or enter a gift-giving period such as Christmas. Online marketers need to provision the resources capable of serving an increased number of requests to their websites. The simplest and most frequently used approach is to purchase a faster server for their website to run on, called *scaling up*, where you improve the resources that are currently available (see figure 7.1). If the number of requests is limited by the number of CPU cycles it takes to generate a response, then by using a CPU that can go through more cycles every second, you're able to reduce the time it takes for a response to be generated.

Although this approach might be the simplest for existing legacy codebases, there are many disadvantages to it: even scaled-up resources still have a limit, as you saw in chapter 1. Throughout the history of the semiconductor, and the CPU in particular, the number of transistors has increased every year in line with Moore's law. But, in recent years, the increase in transistor count hasn't led to an increase in speed; we're no longer making CPUs faster. If you rely on buying faster CPUs to scale up your applications, you're going to reach the point where you have the fastest processor available, with no room for growth and scaling beyond that.

You also need to consider how to move your application over to a faster machine in such a way that it doesn't negatively impact your application's availability. If you only have one instance of the application and rely on moving to a faster processor every

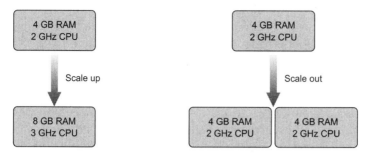

Figure 7.1 Scaling up means you use bigger machines, while scaling out means you use greater numbers of smaller machines.

time it needs to be scaled, then you'll incur an amount of downtime when the application is shut down, as either its host machine is upgraded or a virtual machine is shut down and restarted. This presents an even more frustrating experience to the user: rather than accessing a slow but usable system, they're instead unable to access the system at all.

Scaling up is also very difficult or even impossible to do in an automated manner, depending on the underlying changes that have to be made to the hardware on which the application is running. You saw in chapter 1 that the defining characteristic of reactive applications is that they're able to react to the changing environment in which they're running. In this case, the environmental change is the sheer pressure of increased load. A truly reactive application is nearly autonomous and can handle this increased load dynamically. The scaling-up approach makes this incredibly difficult and requires system administrators to monitor the system and make preemptive changes based on guesswork or assumptions.

Rather than simply trying to work faster to free up resources for the next batch of work when it arrives, an alternative approach is to provide more resources and process work concurrently. This approach means you scale out resources rather than modify already provisioned resources. For example, if an online retailer sees an increased load, they make a second server available to serve a request, with clients being directed to whichever server is least busy. Although this won't result in requests being processed any faster than they were previously, twice the amount of load will be handled. This approach, *scaling out* (refer back to figure 7.1), provides an easier means of scaling resources, and a greater ability to handle an increased load.

You saw that the scaling-up approach could lead to downtime due to transferring the application over to a new machine. This is a problem that you won't encounter when scaling out, because you add more resources to a pool of worker actors, so you still have a worker available to service requests while new resources are allocated. Although the service may experience delays as the scaled-down service copes with the increased load, once the new workers are available, the load is balanced and the response times drop down to the values expected prior to the spike.

You also saw that, when scaling up, it's incredibly difficult to dynamically allocate fresh resources when they're required. But when you simply increase the number of services running, scaling out is easier to automate and more manageable.

Although scaling out presents many benefits, it also poses a number of challenges from a programming perspective in handling increased concurrent workflow. For example, when scaling up, you don't need to worry about two operations modifying a piece of data simultaneously, because you're not running two operations at the same time. Fortunately, Akka.NET's actor model helps resolve this difficulty. By isolating a state to a single actor, you can ensure that there's no contention between multiple instances for a shared resource, which could lead to a bottleneck.

This chapter focuses on how, using Akka.NET, you can scale out actor instances effectively, in harmony with the Reactive Manifesto's aim of being responsive even when you encounter significantly higher amounts of traffic than you designed for. The key component that will help you in this regard is *routers*, used to distribute the work across multiple actors.

7.2 Distributing work

While scaling up the machines on which you run Akka.NET is a perfectly viable option, it isn't the preferred option for the reasons just stated. You want to build systems that can cope under any conditions they're presented with, and if the environment changes, then they should react in a way that provides a good UX. As you've seen, the scale-out option allows you to provide that. This is especially true in Akka.NET, where you have an isolated state that's inaccessible by other actors. This means that you can safely scale out your actors without worrying about concurrency bugs. Figure 7.2 illustrates scaling up versus scaling out.

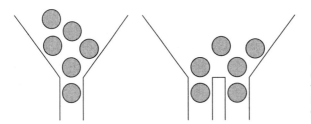

Figure 7.2   Actors can be thought of as funnels: scaling up creates a faster flow rate, whereas scaling out is similar to adding multiple channels to a funnel.

7.2.1 Routers

If the goal is to perform work in parallel, the easiest way to achieve it is by having multiple instances of an actor able to process messages directed to the same target. Remember that, when choosing where to send messages, you can use wildcard paths, which will send a message to all actors whose paths match the wildcard address. But you may want more control over how you process parallel workloads. Consider a further example: a tool designed to stress test how a website handles increased load, by

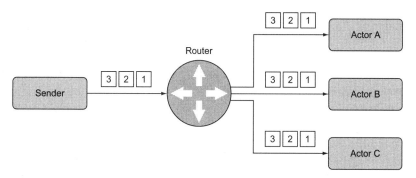

Figure 7.3 The broadcast router sends the received message to every routee actor.

sending many requests simultaneously. Although you could use the wildcard-address approach, it can be slow when there are complex paths to match; it only provides basic message-delivery techniques; and it's tightly coupled with the actor hierarchy architecture.

You need a way to distribute work evenly across a number of worker actors. Akka.NET takes care of this with routers. The concept of a router is quite simple: it wraps a number of actors to use as a single target to which messages can be sent. Messages can then be distributed to all workers, as specified in the routing strategy. Routers can be configured either mostly through configuration or entirely in code. Distributing work to all actors referenced by the router is referred to as *broadcast* in Akka.NET, and the *broadcast pool* provides the infrastructure to distribute work in this way (see figure 7.3).

You can use HOCON configuration to configure the router. In chapter 5, you saw the HOCON format and how it's used in Akka.NET to allow for the configuration of core Akka.NET features. To define a router in HOCON, you create a HOCON element, with the element key being the path to the router. This path has the same syntax as actor addresses shown in figure 3.3, so you can use wildcards in the address if the router is nested under multiple other actors. Every router configuration needs at least the type of router; but routers may also need additional configuration.

The router `broadcast-pool` defines that when the router is created, it should use the specified routing logic. You also need to specify the number of worker actors that are deployed along with the router, in this case, the number of workers that will be processing messages simultaneously. In the following code, you create a router at the /LoadGenerator route and specify that it should create 10 workers. The terminology used in Akka.NET for the workers in a router is `routes`, and that terminology is used in the router definition:

```
akka.actor.deployment {
  /LoadGenerator {
    router = broadcast-pool
```

```
    nr-of-instances = 10
  }
}
```

It's not enough to define the router in HOCON; you also need to deploy it in the actor system. To do that, you create the `Props` for the given actor you want to deploy, as you saw in chapter 5.

One use for the broadcast router is as a tool for load-testing services, because with it you can execute a number of requests to the service simultaneously. You create a load-testing actor and the `Props` to deploy it. Once you've got the basic actor `Props`, you need to specify the router to use. You use the `WithRouter` method to achieve this and create a new `Props` object containing the extra routing information. In this case, because the routing information is referenced in the configuration, you need to tell Akka.NET that it should look in the configuration file for the specified definition, by passing an instance of the `FromConfig` class. Akka.NET looks up the definition based on the address to which the router is being deployed:

```
var loadTestingProps =
    Props.Create<LoadTestingActor>()
        .WithRouter(FromConfig.Instance);
```

It's also possible to create the router entirely in code without using a configuration file. When creating the `Props` for the actor and specifying the router, you can provide an instance of the routing logic to use. In the case of the broadcast pool, you can create an instance of the `BroadcastPool` router with the number of routes to use. You then deploy that router in the same way as the configuration approach. The following code creates a router instance and uses that directly in the `Props`. The router is then deployed, with 10 routees to which it can distribute work:

```
var loadTestingProps =
    Props.Create<LoadTestingActor>()
        .WithRouter(new BroadcastPool(10));
```

A router is itself a generalized actor and exists in the actor system exactly the same as any actor that you might write. This means that an actor can send it a message, and it will forward the message to the routes dependent on the routing logic. In the broadcast example, it will distribute the message to each routee. The router can be referenced in the same way as any other actor; also, messages are sent to it same way—with the `Tell` method:

```
loadTestingActor.Tell(new LoadTestingActor.WebsiteStressTestMessage)
```

This is all that's required to instantiate a router that creates a number of routee actors to which messages are distributed. The broadcast logic is just one example of such a router, and there are many others included in Akka.NET, which we'll come to later in the chapter. But, for now, you're able to deploy a router into the actor system and send messages to routees.

7.2.2   *Pools and groups*

In the last section, when you were deploying a broadcast *router*, you saw different terminology used: rather than a BroadcastRouter, you created an instance of a BroadcastPool. The reason for this is that Akka.NET supports two different types of routers: pools and groups. Although they both use the same logic to route messages to their routees, they differ in the way that routees are managed.

When you created a BroadcastPool, you defined the number of routees to which it should distribute messages. The router creates the specified number of routees as its children and then passes messages to them. This means that, when you're using a pool-based router, the router itself is responsible for supervision of the routees. The supervision of the workers adheres to one supervision strategy, which is to escalate all exceptions to the parent actor. If the parent then decides to restart the router, it will restart all of its routees as well. This makes pools an ideal solution for when you're only interested in having a basic set of workers that can respond to messages.

In contrast to this, if you're using a group, you need to explicitly specify the routees that the router must forward messages to. The router expects the routees to already be deployed in the actor system at the provided paths. Because the router is no longer directly responsible for the routees it communicates with, it doesn't supervise the actors at all—that's left to the parents of the actors. You can't specify things like wildcards here either; instead, you need to specify the concrete paths to the given actors. Router groups are ideal when you have a preexisting hierarchy of actors where a selection of actors in that hierarchy should be used as routees. Router groups also work well if you want to use a granular supervisor strategy.

To use a group instead of a pool, instantiate it the same way you did with a pool. But instead of specifying the number of routees, provide a collection of routee addresses. You can configure this in HOCON or code exactly as you did with the pool setup. If you want to specify the use of a group in HOCON, you can use a snippet similar to the following:

```
akka.actor.deployment {
  /LoadGenerator {
    router = round-robin-group
    routees.paths = ["/user/loadgenerator/w1", "/user/loadgenerator/we",
    [CCA]"/user/loadgenerator/w3"]
  }
}
```

As you can see, the key difference is the use of round-robin-group as the router type, and you specify the routee paths as an array of strings.

You can then create an instance of it in the actor system, exactly as you did before, by specifying that the router used in the Props should be taken from HOCON. It's important to note that when the router gets created, it doesn't validate that the actors exist at the paths provided. If there are no actors available at those paths, when the router attempts to deliver messages, they will instead be delivered to the deadLetters actor and logged as such:

```
var loadTestingProps =
    Props.Create<LoadTestingActor>()
        .WithRouter(FromConfig.Instance);
```

You can also choose to create the entire router group in code. But instead of creating the `BroadcastPool` actor, you create an instance of the `BroadcastGroup` object, and you specify the paths of the routees:

```
var loadTestingProps =
    Props.Create<LoadTestingActor>()
        .WithRouter(new BroadcastGroup("/user/loadgenerator/w1",
                                       "/user/loadgenerator/w2",
                                       "/user/loadgenerator/w3"));
```

There's one other difference between pools and groups that we've not yet covered. Because pools are responsible for all the workers that are able to receive messages, they can spawn new instances on demand to react to load and message backlog. The pool can do this thanks to autoscaling, whereby you specify the minimum and maximum numbers of workers that should be used. You specify autoscaling by providing a resizer when you create the pool, either in configuration or in code. With configuration, you add a resizer configuration element to the router configuration, where you specify three values: that it should be enabled; the lower bound, which is the minimum number of workers; and the upper bound, which is the maximum number of workers. You can see in the following example that you initially deploy the router with 5 actors, but you can scale the number of children actors to a value between 1 and 10:

```
akka.actor.deployment{
    /LoadGenerator [
    router = round-robin-pool
    nr-of-instances = 5
    resizer {
      enabled = on
      lower-bound = 1
      upper-bound = 10
    }
      }
    }
```

You can also specify autoscaling in code when you create the router by providing an instance of a resizer. The `DefaultResizer` is a simple autoscaler that uses message pressure as its reason for scaling. You can create a `RoundRobinPool` with 5 workers by default, with the ability to scale between 1 and 10 worker actors:

```
var smsGateway =
    Props.Create<SmsGatewayActor>()
        .WithRouter(new RoundRobinPool(10, new DefaultResizer(5, 50)));
```

Although pools and routers share all the routing logic, and the distribution of messages works in the same way, they do have some interesting differences that can help you build scalable architectures. Notably, autoresizing pools allow you to build architectures that are not only scalable but also elastic, ensuring that you only ever use and pay for the scale you need, while retaining the ability to rapidly scale up and down as required.

> **Router performance**
>
> Although you use routers in the exact same way as actors, and from an external point of view they appear to be nothing more than actors, internally they're optimized for message throughput. Because routers are responsible for distributing a large number of messages, it's important that they don't become bottlenecks, slowing the application down. As such, the core routing logic isn't encoded in the actor itself but is instead stored in the actor reference returned for the given router. This ensures that the router's mailbox is bypassed entirely, which decreases latency and ensures that a router's mailbox doesn't overflow due to high throughput.

7.2.3   *Wrapping up*

Routers provide an incredibly simple means of distributing messages among a large collection of workers, allowing you to effectively scale applications to react quickly to demands imposed on them. You've seen how simple a broadcast router makes it to write an application that distributes a given message to every routee associated with a router. We'll look at other Akka.NET routers later in this chapter.

7.3   *Routing strategies*

Using Akka.NET routers, you can distribute a single message to a number of routees associated with a router. But this router only allows you to broadcast a message to all of the intended targets. In certain circumstances, this proves to be beneficial, such as when you want to parallelize workloads. The example you've seen is of a distributed load-testing system. In that case, you wanted to perform as many operations simultaneously as possible.

In line with the Manifesto, you want to build applications that are responsive even under a heavy load. When considering scaling techniques, you saw that the most appropriate choice for rapid scalability is scaling out. You can use this approach to distribute messages to many targets without creating a bottleneck on a single actor. But so far, we haven't addressed increasing the throughput of message queues. Akka.NET provides a number of implementations of routing logic that distribute messages through the router to its routees. Routers allow for a wide variety of behaviors, thus allowing you to build applications that remain responsive even under intense load.

Throughout the rest of this chapter, we'll look at the routers included with Akka.NET and the advantages they provide. In each case, we'll look at how you can deploy a pool implementation in code using classes. We'll also look at how you can configure the router using HOCON, but for this approach, we'll only look at the configuration section, along with what its values mean. In all cases, when using the HOCON configuration approach for routers, the router itself is deployed in the exact same way as in broadcast actor configuration deployment. We're looking only at the pool-based approach, but note that all routers also support the group-based approach. By following the same pattern of simply changing the configuration value of the number of routees to the array of actor addresses, you can create a group instead of a pool.

7.3.1 Random routing

The simplest approach to distributing a message through a router to a single actor is to choose one of the routees randomly and then send a message to it (see figure 7.4). Assuming the random-number generator (RNG) is truly random, and given enough time, a random distribution of targets will be generated to receive the messages.

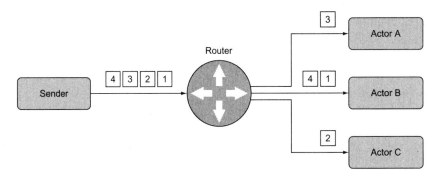

Figure 7.4   The random router selects a routee randomly for each message.

To create a random router, you provide the number of routees it should create in much the same way as with the broadcast router, the difference being that the random router only forwards the message to a single, randomly chosen route. Create an instance of the RandomPool class, which is passed to the router configuration in Props:

```
var smsGateway =
    Props.Create<SmsGatewayActor>()
        .WithRouter(new RandomPool(5));
```

The router can also be configured using HOCON, and the configuration is mostly the same as the broadcast pool, with the exception that you specify the name for the round-robin pool. In the following example, you supply the number of routees to be created by the router pool:

```
akka.actor.deployment {
    /smsgateway {
        router = random-pool
        nr-of-instances = 5
    }
}
```

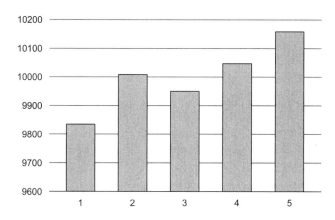

Figure 7.5 The random router may not evenly distribute messages to every routee.

After deployment, you can see the effect this has on message distribution. In figure 7.5, you can see the number of messages each of the five routees receives when you send a total of 10,000 messages. Although all the routees receive a *similar* number of messages, there's a difference of several hundred between the lowest number of messages processed and the highest. For small messages, this effect may be negligible, but for messages that require a lot of processing, there could be a sizeable difference in processing time between the shortest and longest queues.

The random router is an incredibly simple router that can effectively distribute messages to a number of routees, depending on the performance of the platform's RNG. But with the RNG's random output, it's possible that only one number is generated for an extended period of time, creating a bottleneck with one routee, while the other routees have empty queues.

7.3.2 Round-robin routing

Because the random router depends on the RNG's performance for random numbers, there's a possibility that the majority of messages will go to only one routee. Consequently, you need a way to ensure an even distribution of messages to all routees. For example, if you have three routees, you want to ensure that, if you have nine messages to distribute, each routee receives three messages in an even order. In figure 7.6, you can see the order of messages in the mailbox for each routee. The router sends the first message to the first routee, the second message to the second routee, and the third message to the third routee, before it cycles around and sends the fourth message to the first routee.

You can create a round-robin pool in much the same way as you created the last two routers: by specifying the number of routees to be used. When using the coding approach, you create an instance of the RoundRobinPool class, to which you provide the number of routees:

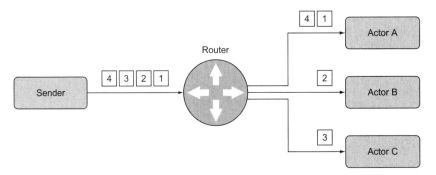

Figure 7.6   The round-robin router chooses the next routee as each message arrives and then starts again from the beginning.

```
var smsGateway =
    Props.Create<SmsGatewayActor>()
        .WithRouter(new RoundRobinPool(5));
```

You can also create the router using HOCON, by specifying the number of routees and providing the name of the router type:

```
akka.actor.deployment {
    /smsgateway {
        router = round-robin-pool
        nr-of-instances = 5
    }
}
```

The round-robin approach to message routing is simple and ensures an even distribution of messages to all routees. It's particularly effective where you have a stateless actor, which you might use to communicate with an external service, for example, and you want to scale it out to multiple instances. By using a round-robin router, you get fairly consistent throughput, assuming all routees are capable of processing a message at a similar rate.

But the round-robin is still only a best-effort router, and a number of problems are associated with it, preventing a truly even distribution. For example, if one routee is running slower than the others, its queue is likely to grow, while the others process their messages quickly, ensuring their mailboxes stay small.

7.3.3 *Smallest-mailbox router*

In Akka.NET, every actor has a mailbox, as you saw in chapter 3. When you send a message to an actor, it's appended to the end of the queue to be picked up at some point in the future by the actor's processing component. Because an actor can only process a single message at a time, if it's slow, then the message queue can grow quickly. A faster actor working in parallel with the slow one will quickly get through all of its messages and have no more work to do.

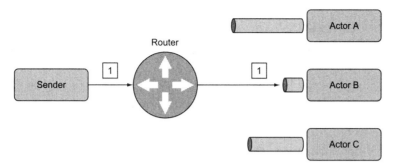

Figure 7.7   The smallest-mailbox router routes messages to the routee with the smallest mailbox queue.

To avoid having one actor sit idle while another has a long message queue, you can choose to use the smallest-mailbox router in Akka.NET. The name says it all: when a message is sent through this router, it consults the routees to see which has the smallest message queue as shown in figure 7.7. The message is sent to that actor, ensuring that actors that are processing messages quickly can receive more messages than slow-running actors.

You specify the number of routees, and the smallest-mailbox router automatically handles creating actors and processing based on mailbox size. To create the router in code, you create an instance of the `SmallestMailboxPool` class, which is provided as the router instance to the `Props` for an actor:

```
var smsGateway =
    Props.Create<SmsGatewayActor>()
        .WithRouter(new SmallestMailboxPool(5));
```

With HOCON configuration, you supply the name of the router, in this case, `smallest-mailbox-pool`, along with the number of instances to use, as you've seen before:

```
akka.actor.deployment {
    /smssender {
        router = smallest-mailbox-pool
        nr-of-instances = 5
    }
}
```

The smallest-mailbox router is particularly useful when you don't know in advance how long it's going to take to process a message. If you have a message with a payload that will lead to a lot of work, then the smallest-mailbox router is an ideal candidate for reducing the impact that the message is likely to have on subsequent messages. But it's far from a silver bullet; you don't know how long it will take to process a message until it's actually processed. As such, if you enqueue a message after a long-processing message, the enqueued message will encounter a delay.

7.3.4   *Consistent hashing*

All the routers you've seen so far have relied on selecting a random routee to process the message; but sometimes you want messages with a common trait to be sent to the same target routee. For example, you may build a key-value data store that persists its data to the filesystem. In this case, the common trait between each message is the key that identifies the item in the database.

You saw a similar scenario in chapter 3, where you had a unique means of identifying the target actor through a sensor identification string that allowed you to route new messages directly to the actor. This allowed you to have every sensor running in parallel without worrying about bottlenecks. Given these benefits, this scenario might seem to be a natural fit, allowing concurrent operations across large numbers of keys simultaneously; but it also comes with some downsides. For example, you need an instance of an actor at the provided name before you can communicate with it. When a request comes in for a given key, you must ensure, first of all, that an actor exists at that key's address. If it doesn't, then you must create an actor instance, adding a lot of overhead to every request and introducing significant latency, leading to applications becoming unresponsive. You also need to have one actor per key and store that actor in memory. Although a single actor represents very little overhead, it does start to add up on larger scales. If you're implementing a key-value store, you might see millions or even billions of keys and actors in memory.

Another difficulty is ensuring the isolation of actors. You saw that every actor should keep its state internal and not share it with other actors. Because the data you persist to disk for an actor is, by association, part of the actor's internal state, it can't share it with any other actors in the system. This can impose a lot of pressure on the filesystem, where you have one file per key and the potential for millions of very small files.

You want a single actor responsible for a select portion of the available keys, with each other actor instance responsible for a different portion of the key space. You could store each of the key space regions in a specific location, which allows the router to automatically route the message based on what a lookup table says. This approach does, however, require a lot of coordination to update a lookup table when a new key-value pair is added. Ideally, what you want is a completely stateless router that allows you to select a given routee based on the message, in a repeatable manner.

A simple approach to this is to calculate the hash of the message or a specific property in the message. This hash can be used to calculate the target routee for the message (see figure 7.8). A hash is calculated by passing the message through a hash function whose sole responsibility is to map data down to a fixed size from an arbitrary length. In Akka.NET, the hash function maps the message property from whatever its data size is, which in the case of a key-value data store will be a string for the key with variable length, down to a fixed length, which is the number of routees available to the router.

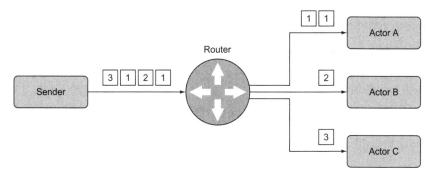

Figure 7.8 The consistent-hashing router directs every message with the same properties to the same actor.

This forms the basis of the consistent-hashing router in Akka.NET, which computes a hash for the message and uses it to decide which routee to send the message to. You can create a consistent-hashing router in code by creating an instance of the ConsistentHashingPool class. Specify the number of routees to use:

```
var smsGateway =
    Props.Create<SmsGatewayActor>()
        .WithRouter(new ConsistentHashingPool(5));
```

It's important to choose the correct property on your message so that all messages with that property in common end up reaching the correct target. You have three possible options for how to manage that in Akka.NET. The least intrusive way for both the routees and the message is to create a hash-mapping delegate when you create the router. This takes in the message and returns the property of it to use as the thing to hash. If you've got a message defined as in the following code snippet for your key-value data store, when you create the actor instance, you can supply a hash-mapping delegate by using the WithHashMapping method on the router, which supplies a new router with the mapping applied. In the following code, you have a common interface for all of the database-related operations, which allows you to easily retrieve the key out of the key-value pair:

```
var consistentHashingPool = new ConsistentHashingPool(5)
    .WithHashMapping(x =>
    {
        if (x is IDatabaseMessage)
            return ((IDatabaseMessage)x).Key;
        return x;
    });
```

Since all of your messages use a common interface, you could also use the IConsistentHashable interface, which allows you to specify what the hash key should be. The router then checks to see whether the message implements this interface, and if it does, it uses this interface to retrieve the hash key. This approach requires you to edit all the messages to rely on an underlying implementation detail, and so it may not be a valid option, depending on where the messages originate from.

```
public class Get : IConsistentHashable
{
    readonly string _key;
    public string Key { get { return _key; } }

    public object ConsistentHashKey { get { return _key; } }

    public Get(string key)
    {
        _key = key;
    }
}
```

The final option is to wrap all the messages you send to the router in an envelope that provides the internal message along with the hash. The router uses the hash to direct the message before forwarding the original message stripped out of the envelope. To use the envelope, you create an instance of `ConsistentHashableEnvelope` with the message and the hash key to use:

```
var message = new Get("Anthony");
var envelope = new ConsistentHashableEnvelope(message, message.Key);
database.Tell(envelope);
```

You're then able to calculate a hash for a message and choose the routee to which the message goes. With the hash function, you have a known fixed size for the possible output values; for example, it might generate a number in the range between 0 and 255, inclusive. You then create a circle and place these possible values around the edge of it, using the same hash function used for mapping keys to also map the node identifiers onto the ring. So, given that you create a router with three routees that act as nodes in the consistent-hashing router, you can position them onto the ring. Figure 7.9 shows an example of placing a node on the ring. That node is responsible for all of the hash values encountered, moving clockwise around the ring until reaching the next node.

Although consistent hashing helps you to choose a target for a message, it also has some disadvantages. Due to hashing each node, some nodes will inevitably be responsible for more keys than others, leading to the potential for increased load on one of the routees. To counter this problem, the consistent-hashing router allows you to specify the number of virtual nodes per routee. So, rather than having 5 routees with 1 node each, you can create 5 routees with, for example, 10 nodes each. This provides a total of 50 nodes around the ring, which promotes a more even distribution of keys around the nodes. It's important to note that the new nodes are entirely virtual and are only for the purpose of calculation; you still have only 5 routees created at any time. By default, Akka.NET uses a value of 10 for the virtual-nodes factor; but should you want to, you can supply a different value in the constructor when you create the router. Here, you use a virtual-nodes factor of 20:

```
var databaseProps = Props.Create<DatabaseActor>()
                        .WithRouter(new ConsistentHashingPool(5)
                            .WithVirtualNodesFactor(20));
```

You can create the router using HOCON configuration rather than storing these values in code. The values you need are the router name, the number of routees to use, and the virtual-nodes factor. You still need to handle how to retrieve the hashing property using code, adopting any of the techniques you saw previously.

```
akka.actor.deployment {
    /services/cache {
        router = consistent-hashing-pool
        nr-of-instances = 5
        virtual-nodes-factor = 20
    }
}
```

Although the router pool also supports automatic resizing in the same way as all the other routers, you need to be more careful when using it. In the example, you stored a state in the actor, with the file containing all of the key-value pairs also stored in that node. If you were to add another node, then it would affect which node was queried for a given key. This change would then leave you in a situation where historical data can't be retrieved from the routees. Autoresizing with the router is therefore only useful if the routees are completely stateless. If the routees are stateful, then autoresizing and the consistent-hashing router should be avoided.

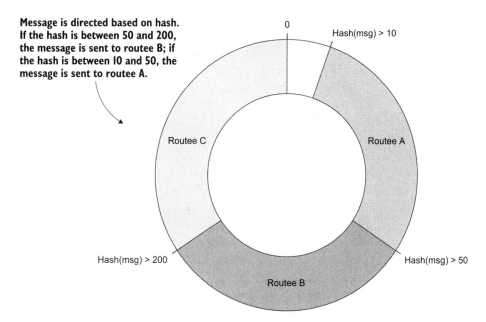

Figure 7.9 In a consistent-hashing router, routees are placed around a ring, and each routee is responsible for a portion of the ring.

Consistent-hashing routers are a great means of ensuring an even distribution of keys to all routees. The consistent-hashing approach to stateful distribution has proven to be useful in a number of large projects, including distributed NoSQL databases, such as Amazon's DynamoDB and Basho's Riak, as well as the internals of some big data–processing tools, such as Hadoop's MapReduce. In Akka.NET, you can ensure that the router distributes messages with a common trait to the same actor consistently with minimal overhead required and no coordination in the router.

7.3.5   *Scatter-gather first-completed*

None of the routers up to this point have prevented you from returning data from them, but they're designed more for scenarios where you dispatch work to be completed without a result returned. But sometimes you want a request-response model to ensure that you're able to get data out of a service. With the request-response approach, you aim for low latency between sending a message and returning a value in response.

With a single-destination router such as the round-robin router, if your system chooses a routee with a long queue, it will suffer a long delay in reaching the processing stage. But choosing a short queue that has a number of large messages also results in long latencies. The easiest way to ensure the shortest possible latency is by sending the request to all candidates capable of processing the message. Whichever one gets to the message first sends a response back to the requesting actor. To model this, you could use the broadcast router to send the message to all routees.

But then there's the problem of *all* of the routees replying to the requesting actor. The first result to arrive provides the shortest possible latency. You want the requesting actor to ignore all other messages and not have them fill its message queue.

Akka.NET provides a router designed specifically for this purpose: the *scatter-gather, first-completed router*. It distributes a message to all routees and waits for the first result, which it sends to the requesting actor, ignoring all subsequent response messages (see figure 7.10). This ensures the shortest possible latency from the collection of routees, while also preventing the requester from being flooded with the same response multiple times. If, however, no reply is received from the routees in a given timespan, then it sends a `Failure` message back to the requesting actor to notify it of the timeout.

One example of this router is a database with a number of replicas, where each routee is responsible for communicating with a single replica. When you want to retrieve a value from the database, you query the actor that executes the request. You get the response from the first replica that replies, and return that to the requesting actor. This allows you to use a database with the lowest latency.

Because you're dealing with actors that have independent configurations, you'll create a group router this time, using the `ScatterGatherFirstCompletedGroup` class. You can specify the maximum timeout before a `Failure` response is sent back to the requesting actor. In this case, specify that if it doesn't receive a response in 200 ms from one of the database servers, the router sends a timeout failure:

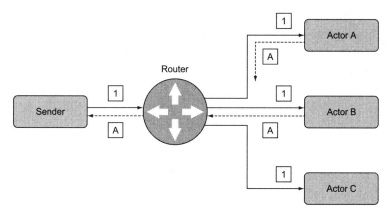

Figure 7.10 The scatter-gather, first-completed router broadcasts the message to every routee and then returns the first response.

```
var databaseReplicas =
    new ScatterGatherFirstCompletedGroup(
        TimeSpan.FromSeconds(0.2),
        databaseMaster,
        databaseReplica1,
        databaseReplica2);
```

You can create the same scatter-gather, first-completed router using HOCON. Specify the type of router to create, as well as the standard number of routees. Also specify the timeout period with time units. In the following example, you specify a timeout of 0.2 seconds. You can also use other suffixes to represent other units of time, such as minutes and milliseconds.

```
akka.actor.deployment {
    /services/database {
        router = scatter-gather-group
        routees.paths =
["/database/master",
        "/database/replica1",
        "/database/replica2"]
        in = 0.2 seconds
    }
}
```

The scatter-gather, first-completed router is incredibly useful, particularly in cases where you want to minimize the latency of request-response message passing. Despite the fact that you distribute the work to many routees, you only need to worry about a single message being returned from the router. This makes it ideal for using with the ask-based approach to receiving a message response you saw in chapter 3.

7.3.6   *Tail-chopping router*

In asynchronous systems, sometimes one actor processes a message slower than another actor does. This can happen from several causes ranging from hardware, to OSs, to transient issues that external services experience. Although these slowdowns are relatively infrequent, they pass the issue on to the user and create latency. A graph of the latencies across a large number of requests typically looks somewhat like figure 7.11. A small number of requests executes and returns almost instantaneously, with the majority of requests falling around the median latency, before you finally see a long tail of high latency.

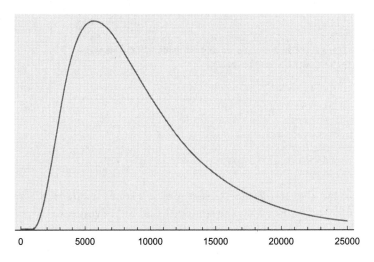

Figure 7.11   Typically, request-response latencies follow a bell curve with the majority of responses having a common time, and with some faster and some slower.

To ensure that all users enjoy a responsive application, you need to minimize the effects of long-tail latencies by preventing the seemingly random slowdowns that system components experience. The scatter-gather, tail-chopping router t first-completed router helps make this possible, thanks to distributing messages to all routees. If one routee experiences a slowdown, that doesn't cause a significant degradation of service, because another routee picks up the message and processes it. If it processes the message more quickly than the first routee, then its response is forwarded to the requester. But this results in a significant amount of redundant work, potentially leading to problems further down the line. Using the scatter-gather approach means assuming the worst possible scenario will occur: the first routee to respond will take longer than you can tolerate. But this is unlikely to be the case, because most responses complete within an acceptable time period. The aim is to shorten the tail of the graph, which is frequently less than 1% of the total requests.

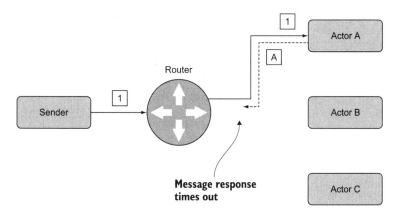

Figure 7.12   The tail-chopping router first sends a request to a random routee and starts a timer, awaiting a response before the timer expires.

This is the aim of the tail-chopping router: to significantly shorten the tail of the graph. It does this by combining a number of components. The router first selects a routee at random to send the message to, but if it doesn't receive a response before a timeout, it sends the message to another routee and awaits a response (see figure 7.12). When it receives a response, it forwards the message to the requester and ignores all subsequent responses (see figure 7.13). But if it doesn't receive a response before a timeout, it sends a `Failure` message to the requester. The tail-chopping router works on the premise that there's a high probability that one of the other routees can process the message faster than the routees chosen so far.

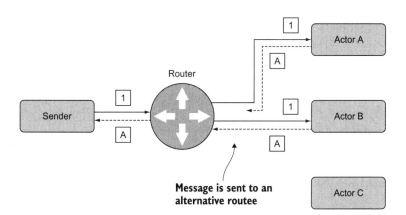

Figure 7.13   If no response is received, a second routee is chosen at random and the timer is reset; when a message is eventually received, it's forwarded to the requester.

The tail-chopping router requires a little more configuration than the other routers you've seen so far in this chapter. You can create a tail-chopping router by creating an instance of the `TailChoppingPool`. As with the other routers, specify the number of routees to use, and much like the scatter-gather router, specify the failure timeout. You also need to specify the time to wait, the *interval*, before contacting the next routee. The following example shows a tail-chopping router with 5 routees and a timeout of 1.5 seconds. It also defines forwarding the message to a second routee after 200 ms without a response:

```
var searchApiProps =
    Props.Create<SearchAPIActor>()
        .WithRouter(
            new TailChoppingPool(
                5,
                TimeSpan.FromSeconds(1.5),
                TimeSpan.FromSeconds(0.2)));
```

You can also create this router with HOCON configuration, where you follow a pattern similar to the scatter-gather router. Many of the configuration variables used are the same, notably, the number of routees and the maximum timeout, but you can also supply a `tail-chopping-router.interval` to specify the time between multiple routee calls:

```
akka.actor.deployment {
    /services/search {
        router = tail-chopping-pool
        nr-of-instances = 5
        in = 1.5 seconds
        tail-chopping-router.interval = 200 milliseconds
    }
}
```

Using the tail-chopping router to perform redundant work when you believe you can get a quicker response from another target than the current one has been effective in a number of distributed NoSQL databases for reducing the tail end of response latencies. Because Akka.NET's routers are simple, they're easy to implement in your applications for decreasing user wait time. There are downsides to using them, though: you're aware of the expected latency of the target routees, but without any idea of what that latency will be, it's likely that any configuration values supplied for the interval period will not be effective at reducing the latency tail.

7.3.7 *Wrapping up*

Although it may seem like Akka.NET supplies an abundance of routers, many of them are tailored to a specific set of situations and designed to ensure that your applications stay responsive even when faced with increased load. All the routers that Akka.NET provides are also able to use the resizer functionality once the application experiences a certain sustained level of load.

> **Broadcast support in routers**
>
> Early in this chapter, you saw the broadcast router, which allows you to rapidly send a message to all routees. This means of message distribution is also supported in all the other routers. The consistent-hashing router introduced the concept of message envelopes to retrieve the hash key for a message, but there's another envelope supported by all the routers you've seen here. If you wrap a message in a `BroadcasttEnvelope` before sending it to a router, then it will automatically distribute the message to all routees. This allows you to easily transmit data to all of the routees of a given router.

7.4 Case study: Scaling, throughput, advertising systems

Advertising has become a core component of millions of websites and has also become either the primary or sole source of revenue for many of them. At the heart of web advertising is a vast bidding war being fought between hundreds of advertising agencies, all trying to show their clients' ads on the most appropriate web pages for the right audiences. All of this needs to happen in milliseconds if an agency wants to be competitive in an industry worth billions of dollars every year.

Given the number of web pages that display ads and the number of people who visit those web pages, advertising agencies have to process a huge number of requests per second. They also have to cope with inevitable spikes in traffic. Given this need for low-latency, high-throughput services, Akka.NET provides an ideal base upon which to build advertising systems. But it's more than simple scalability that's required; an advertising system must also respond to traffic spikes.

In this chapter, you've seen how to use routers to distribute work across a number of actors. Routers can simplify and automate the process of scaling the number of actors. Given that many actors working in parallel can process more work, such an advertising system can handle more page views and send more bids quickly, providing a competitive advantage.

Figure 7.14 shows how to hide actors behind routers that can deploy more actors on demand and shut down actors after a period of low usage. Each actor is responsible for receiving input containing information related to the visiting user, which includes data such as their IP address, location, anonymized ID, and plenty more. The actor then works out whether a bid should be made. When the originating website sends a request for an ad, it's converted into a message, and then it's sent to the router. The router then chooses an actor to process the message. At the same time, the router is computing metrics and calculating the number of messages that are flowing through itself, which it then uses as a means of working out whether more actors are needed to achieve the required throughput.

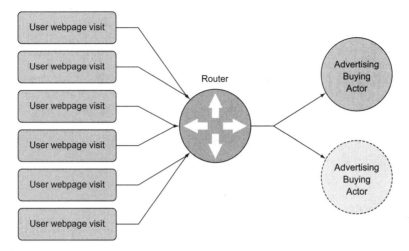

Figure 7.14   A router allows you to receive a huge number of messages, in this case when users visit a web page to see an ad, and allows you to split those messages across multiple actors, thus increasing throughput.

In cases where you need to react on demand to unpredictable usage, routers allow you to scale the number of actors to receive and process messages. By parallelizing processing, you can easily increase throughput while also reducing response times.

Summary

In this chapter, you learned

- How to increase application throughput by scaling out the number of workers processing messages
- How Akka.NET uses pools to respond to the load demands of the application by scaling up and down as required
- How Akka.NET allows you to manage routees with a group router
- How to choose different routing methodologies to suit the task at hand

Composing actor systems

One of the key objectives of the Reactive Manifesto is to ensure a responsive UX, regardless of what happens in the application, by using reactive principles. This means designing to address two problems: failures internal to the actor system and increased load on actors in the system. You've seen how the features of the Akka.NET framework handle both of these scenarios.

Failures can be handled by a combination of actor hierarchies and the supervision system. With the hierarchy, you can isolate failures to a single actor and recover with a supervision strategy handled by its parent. You've also seen that handling increased system load depends on increased message throughput. You can address this with Akka.NET's routers, which evenly distribute messages to a number of actors that perform as a single actor. Routers can scale the number of routees dynamically according to the load, so you can elastically scale by providing either more or less compute power.

Although these features help you create applications that are fault tolerant and scalable, so far they've only run on a single machine, which limits their capabilities. In our consideration of fault tolerance, we've discussed recovering from the failure of small, isolated actors running in the context of larger applications. But, as you saw in chapter 2, many things can lead to more catastrophic failure for your application. Besides failures that you handle at the application level, you also encounter issues relating to hardware failure that shut down the entire application. Hardware failures are a relatively infrequent occurrence, but you must also consider all the layers of abstraction between the hardware and the application that could result in failure. For example, if you're connecting to a server from a client, due to network connectivity issues, the server may be unreachable; alternatively, a process running on the server may end up killing the process that's running the actor system. In these cases, the problems lie outside the bounds of the actor system and so need more planning to resolve.

In chapters 2 and 3, we explored the notion that actors are cheap and that you can create millions of them per gigabyte of memory, but you need to consider the downsides of doing this. Notably, the CPU only has a limited number of cores, limiting the number of operations that can run concurrently. Although you can upgrade to a CPU with more cores or better threading capabilities, you still hit a limit on the number of processes that can run simultaneously. This creates a bottleneck where actors are waiting for available resources on the CPU; what's required is to increase the concurrency capabilities of the CPU.

To address these problems, you need to combine multiple machines so that you can either reduce the likelihood of downtime caused by machine-level crashes or distribute workloads more evenly in order to further increase the potential throughput of the actor system. Akka.NET is built with ease of distribution in mind so that it can scale out across multiple machines as well as multiple cores. You saw in chapter 1 that in fault-tolerant and scalable solutions, applications aren't tied to the physical location of an actor. Instead, they rely on location transparency that results from the message-passing architecture of Akka.NET. With location transparency, you only care about a loosely coupled address pointing to the actor's mailbox, and you let the messaging system calculate how that message should be delivered. This affords you the freedom to move actors not only between threads or cores on a single machine but also between processors on distant machines (see figure 8.1)—even if they happen to be located on the opposite side of the world.

Using actors facilitates developing applications that scale across machines. You saw in chapter 3 that actors encapsulate all their state internally, thus preventing other actors from directly accessing their stored data. Other actors communicate with an actor by sending it a message to retrieve its stored data. So you can safely relocate an actor without worrying about implicit connections between actors. Because all communication is handled through messages, it's left to the messaging system to direct them to the correct targets.

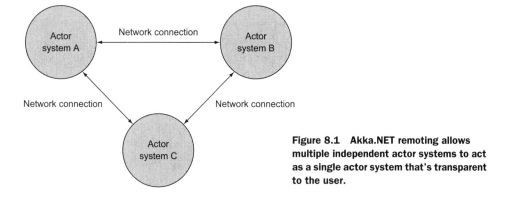

Figure 8.1 Akka.NET remoting allows multiple independent actor systems to act as a single actor system that's transparent to the user.

8.1 Introducing Akka.NET remoting

If you want to avoid the problems you're likely to encounter with an application running on just one machine, you need to distribute your application across multiple machines. This will provide a consistent level of service in the event that one machine has difficulties, or you reach the concurrency limits of a single machine. You can connect two machines together through a network and enable communication between them. But network programming entails a number of complexities, leading to complications for applications that communicate through a network.

Networks come with a number of considerations. They can be unreliable: there's no guarantee that a message will reach its intended target. Increased latency caused by the sheer distance between two machines must be accounted for. Further difficulties arise, such as determining whether a process on a remote machine is executing correctly or has failed.

Akka.NET provides a number of remoting features designed to allow multiple actor systems to communicate without you having to worry too much about these issues. These systems can exist on either a single machine or multiple machines, with communication through a variety of protocols, such as TCP or UDP, and with pluggable support for alternative transports tailored to the specific problem at hand.

You saw in chapter 3 that one of the biggest benefits of a message-passing architecture is the freedom to relocate actors on a machine. You're not tied down to a single reference for an actor; instead, you let the Akka.NET runtime relocate actors to different threads or different locations in memory. Akka.Remote takes this notion of location transparency to its limit by letting you develop applications that don't need to concern themselves with knowledge of the underlying network. In fact, with Akka.Remote, you can run your applications without the need for any code changes at all. Instead, you can simply modify the configuration of an application and immediately have it scaled out across multiple machines.

In Akka.Remote, all the machines run identical actor systems, and these actor systems are connected. All systems can run the same code without changes to individual applications in the deployment. This means that no single actor system acts as a server with others connecting to it; instead, all actor systems operate as peers, allowing for truly distributed applications with no single point of failure.

With actor systems acting as peers, you can build applications that are truly indifferent to the environment in which they're running or hosting actors. No code changes are needed to run a single application across multiple machines; the application can be driven entirely by configuration. This is enforced, to a point, through the limited API that's available for developing networked applications. You only have two ways to directly influence a remote deployment: the usage of Props, and the address system of actors, both of which we'll discuss later in this chapter.

In the internals of the remoting API, everything that could lead to problems across a network is considered and anticipated. In this chapter, you'll see how to use the remoting functionality provided by Akka.NET to distribute your applications across a network with minimal changes to code.

Akka.Remote usage

Akka.Remote is designed for situations in which the two connected machines have the same level of privileges, and it doesn't provide support for running specific roles on only one machine. The design isn't intended for use in cases where a client application is connecting directly with an actor system. You'll see examples of how to address that in a later chapter when we discuss how to expose the actor system to the outside world.

8.2 Preparing to use remoting

You can prepare your system for remoting by following the steps outlined in this section.

8.2.1 Installing Akka.Remote

The remoting capabilities of Akka.NET are shipped outside of the core distribution, so before you can use it, you need to install the library. The library is shipped through NuGet; to install it, you add the Akka.Remote project. After installing the library, you configure it so that it's able to receive connections from other actor systems.

8.2.2 Configuring remoting for a project

Before you can use the remoting functionality, you need to provide a number of key configuration parameters to the actor system. You do this with the HOCON configuration you saw in chapter 5. At the least, you specify the following information in the configuration file:

```
akka {
 actor {
  provider = "Akka.Remote.RemoteActorRefProvider, Akka.Remote"
```

```
  }
  remote {
   helios.tcp {
    port = 8080
    hostname = localhost
   }
  }
}
```

In this configuration, you make two major additions. The first is the change to the actor provider responsible for how the Akka.NET library retrieves its `IActorRef` instances and how it performs all the routing to the defined target. Here, you supply the class name for the `RemoteActorRefProvider`, which is able to retrieve references to actors running on remote machines. You also configure the network transport, which is responsible for communication between actor systems. In this case, you use a TCP socket and configure it to listen on the supplied address, and a port that's currently not being used. If you want any random unused port, you can choose to use port 0, and the OS will choose one at random.

This is all that's required to allow other actor systems to connect to this actor system instance, but you'll also need multiple actor systems configured to run with remoting enabled. The examples you'll see in this chapter have two actor systems communicating with each other. To manage this, you'll alter the listening port and the address, if the actor systems are running on different machines. You can use a number of different approaches to this, as you saw in chapter 5, but for now, you'll use two independent files with different configurations. In the following example, you set up a second actor system that listens on a different port while running on the same machine. This allows you to run across multiple actor systems throughout the rest of the chapter.

```
akka {
  actor {
   provider = "Akka.Remote.RemoteActorRefProvider, Akka.Remote"
  }
  remote {
   helios.tcp {
    port = 8081
    hostname = localhost
   }
  }
}
```

Although you now have two actor systems with remoting configured, no connections are made between them until one of the applications needs to communicate with the other. Connections are made lazily on demand as the actor system needs them. To test the remote actor systems, you run multiple instances of the application, each with a different configuration file. While testing, you can supply the configuration file as a parameter to the application and load it on demand, as in the following example:

```
Chapter8.exe node1
```

With the configuration loaded from the command line, you pass the path to the file as a parameter to the application. This means that if you refer to the configuration files as `node1.conf` and `node2.conf`, you can run two instances of the application by running the following commands in the directory containing the executables and configuration files:

```
Chapter8.exe node1
Chapter8.exe node2
```

In a production environment, you're unlikely to supply the configuration file path through the command line, and instead will use the fallback configuration options you saw in chapter 5 with HOCON. But because you'll run multiple instances in the same environment in the examples in this chapter, you'll use different configuration files to allow for completely isolated configurations.

8.3   *Communicating with remote actors*

Now that you have two actor systems configured to listen on incoming network connections, you can create applications that communicate by sending messages between these instances. Because connections in Akka.NET are created lazily, despite a network being available, there isn't yet a connection between the actor systems you created. In this section, you'll start to use the many Akka.NET features you've seen throughout the book, but spread across multiple actor systems.

Remote actor system addresses

You saw in chapter 3 that all actors in an actor system are identified by an address. The address is used by the framework to route messages to the correct actor instance in memory. So far, all the actors you've encountered have used a simple scheme for representing their address, such as the address shown in figure 8.2. The address is a URI with three key pieces of information: the scheme, which in this case is the string akka; the actor system name, which is whatever name you provide when you create the actor system; and the path to the actor, which is used to traverse the actor hierarchy to search for the specific child actor.

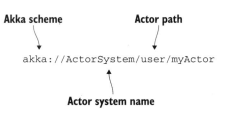

Figure 8.2   A typical actor system address

When using multiple actor systems, you need to encode additional information in the address to identify the machine that's hosting the actor system. Because remoting has support for a number of networking protocols, you need to ensure that the system understands how to communicate with the remote actor system. An example of a remote address is shown in figure 8.3.

The first change is the different scheme being used. You supply akka as before, but you also postfix it with the protocol used; in this case, the value `tcp` is added to signify that the connection method is TCP. You might see other values in this space to represent other communication protocols, such as UDP. After the actor system name, you

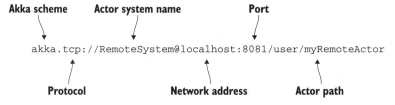

Figure 8.3   A typical remote system address

specify the address that's hosting it. This has two components, the IP address or the hostname of the remote machine, and the port that the remote system is listening on.

If you need to address an individual actor on a running system, this is the simplest way of doing so, but it doesn't favor location transparency, because you're tightly coupling your machine's location to your codebase. Given the widespread use of the cloud for deploying code, this may prove to be problematic due to the potential for frequent IP address changes with autoscaling architectures. In the rest of this section, we'll look at how to abstract locations away from code and drive the logic through configuration.

8.3.1   Sending messages to remote actors

So far, you've seen how to send messages to actors in one of two ways: by using a direct reference to an actor with `IActorRef`, or by sending a message to a given address. You can follow the same process even when dealing with remote actor instances.

You have to target a remote actor instance through the address format you saw in the previous section, making sure to include the remote actor system name and target machine. You can then create an actor selection using this address and use it as you would have at any stage previously. In the following example, you send a message to an actor running on a different machine:

```
var remoteActor =
    remoteActorSystem.ActorSelection(
        "akka.tcp://RemoteSystem@localhost:8081/user/remoteActor");
remoteActor.Tell("Hello remote actor");
```

When an actor on a remote machine receives a message, it replies in the same way that you've seen. Akka.Remote then deals with handling remote senders and serializing them so you can address them in the usual way. You can perform request-response queries against remote actors by using Ask. But because a network connection links remote actors, there's the possibility of message loss and of Ask not receiving a response, causing it to block indefinitely. So you specify a timeout period, after which the call will throw an exception. The following code says that a response from a remote actor is expected, but if that doesn't happen within 20 seconds, an exception is thrown:

```
var response =
    await remoteActor.Ask<string>("Anthony", TimeSpan.FromSeconds(20.0));
```

Akka.Remote and message ordering

When you dealt with a single in-process actor system, it was guaranteed that all messages would arrive in the correct order, but when you introduce a network connection, you lose that guarantee. In the case where two independent actor systems both send a message to the same actor, there's no guarantee that the two messages will arrive in the order in which they were sent. This is due to the latency constraints that a network imposes, which may fluctuate over time. Akka.Remote provides a guarantee that messages sent between a pair of actors will be delivered in the correct order. For example, in a pair of actors, A and B, if actor A sends messages to actor B, they will always arrive in the correct order. But if actor C also sends a message to actor B, it may not arrive in the order in which it was sent.

This setup for accessing known actors on a remote machine is ideal for dealing with an external service. For example, in a web application, you may have one actor system running as a payment service responsible for aggregating customer charges, and a second actor system responsible for running the core application logic. In the context of the example in chapter 2, the home with water-level detection, the billing system would be responsible for computing the cost based on the number of sensors a customer has running per month, or the amount of data the application is processing, and the core application logic would be responsible for running the sensor's processing.

Sometimes you want more processing power for a single server with as little overhead as possible. In this case, you should avoid being constrained to a single machine and instead scale out across more machines. You want to avoid coupling this configuration to your codebase because that means the infrastructure deployment is locked into the binary of the application. You may need to scale quickly to cope with a significant load spike. In these situations, you need to be able to provision a new machine and have it usable as an additional resource.

Akka.Remote allows you to specify through configuration that entire sections of the actor deployment hierarchy should be deployed onto a remote machine. These remote sections are addressed in the same way as if they were local. In figure 8.4, you can see an actor hierarchy in which a child actor of a parent actor is running on a different machine.

This takes the notion of location transparency to the limit, because you can develop applications without having to consider remote deployments, yet configure them to run on different machines. Because the remoting capabilities of Akka.NET are driven by configuration rather than an API, you can change the infrastructure of the application with a change to the configuration rather than requiring a full rebuild when you want to scale out. In the following example, you specify in the configuration that the actor system at the address specified should host the stated section of the hierarchy. The following code specifies that the services branch of the actor system should run on a remote actor system:

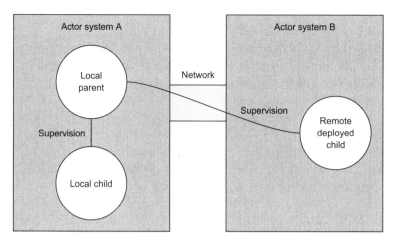

Figure 8.4 Akka.NET remoting allows you to deploy child actors remotely while also allowing for all the features of local deployment, such as supervision.

```
akka.actor.deployment {
    /services {
        remote = "akka.tcp://RemoteSystem@localhost8081"
    }
}
```

This configuration change lets you develop your actor system as though it's all running on a single machine. In the following example, you select an actor below the services actor, which looks identical to any of the previous actor selection examples in chapter 3; but due to the configuration change you just made, it calls to a remote actor system:

```
var remoteActor = actorSystem.ActorSelection("services/cache");
```

Using this mindset when developing applications, you can embrace location transparency and focus on the core aims of the application without worrying about the details of where actors in the hierarchy exist. This allows you to significantly scale out the actor system to overcome the limits you might encounter on a single machine.

8.3.2 Remote deployment of actors

If you want to scale out with actors on remote machines, you first need to get those actors running on the remote machines. Akka.Remote allows an actor system to deploy actors on a remote actor system.

There are two key ways to deal with remoting in Akka.NET: connect to existing long-running actor systems, or treat other machines as an extension of your computing resources. The remote deployment feature works for both ways, but with one constraint: you must have the same types deployed across both machines. The remote machine needs to have knowledge of the actor that it's going to deploy. In many cases, this means creating an assembly containing the actor definitions and message definitions, which is then shared between the machines.

In the first scenario, where you're dealing with an existing long-running actor system, you can deploy an actor into its system when a key event happens. For example, in the case of the web application and billing system, you may sign up a new user to the service, meaning that a new actor relating to their account needs to be created. You could either send a message to an actor on the remote system that it should create a new actor, or you can create it and deploy it on the remote system yourself. You'll see throughout this chapter some of the advantages to this approach.

When deploying into a remote actor system, you follow the same process as when you deploy actors into a local actor system. You first create the `Props` that define the proposed actor. As you saw in chapter 5, the `Props` specify how an actor should be created. In this case, you specify the type of the new actor as well as any constructor arguments. The constructor arguments must be serializable, because they'll be sent over the network to the remote system. You also need to specify how the actor should be deployed. When you don't supply a deployer, the default uses the local deployment, so deploying into a remote system requires configuration. You create a new `Props` object by calling `WithDeploy` with the chosen `Deploy` instance, in this case, `RemoteDeploy`. This takes the address of the remote machine. When you use this in combination with `ActorOf`, you receive an actor reference to an actor deployed on a remote actor system that you can communicate with as you would with any local actor.

```
var remoteDeploy =
    Deploy.None
        .WithScope(new RemoteScope
            (new Address("akka.tcp",
                        "RemoteSystem",
                        "localhost",
                        8081)));

var remoteProps =
    Props.Create<Cache>()
        .WithDeploy(remoteDeploy);
```

You can configure the actor system so that any actors existing at a certain address will be automatically routed onto a separate actor system. In this case, calls to deploy an actor at this address will automatically be routed to the correct machine as defined in the configuration. As before, any constructor arguments the actor takes must be serializable and sent over the network, but outside of this, nothing else needs to be done. Akka.Remote handles all of the remote deployment.

Remote deployment allows you to rapidly build systems that can scale out across multiple machines without any significant initial design. With Akka.Remote's configuration-driven remoting API, you can write actor-based applications that make the most of the computing resources they need while also providing location transparency.

8.3.3 *Wrapping up*

This section focused on how you can communicate with actors across multiple actor systems without worrying about the underlying network code, thanks to Akka.Remote. You've seen how to abstract away the network and focus on the core business logic in your applications without adding communication code.

8.4 *Elastic scale across machines*

A reactive architecture remains responsive even if the system is under a significantly increased load. In chapter 7, you saw how to use Akka.NET's routers to pool computational resources and treat that pool of resources as a single actor, leading to higher message throughput by running more than one processing stage simultaneously. This allows the processing of multiple messages concurrently while also maintaining the thread safety that Akka.NET provides. Concurrent processing makes the most of the multiple cores and threading capabilities of modern processors. But you'll still hit a limit of what you can do on one machine.

For example, many applications attempt to brute-force a solution to a problem by running the same code with different inputs. If you have millions of potential inputs, you're unlikely to have a CPU capable of running all of these actors simultaneously. You're also likely to encounter other limitations on a single machine. The work that actors are doing might be heavily reliant on memory usage, and running lots of actors simultaneously might lead to slowdowns due to a lack of available RAM. Alternatively, actors might be doing a lot of network-related work and downloading large files to disk, reaching a point where the network connection becomes a bottleneck.

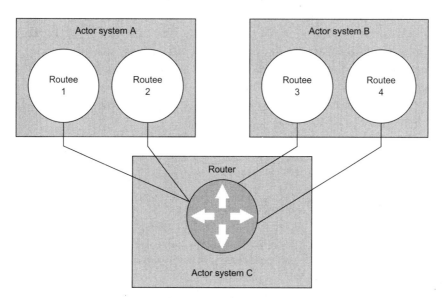

Figure 8.5 A router can be configured to use other independent actor systems as hosts for routees.

You've seen how easy Akka.NET makes it to communicate with actors running on remote machines, but it's also possible to configure routers so that they use multiple external actor systems for the routees in a pool or a group of actors (see figure 8.5, where actors systems A, B, and C are running on different machines). This combines all the benefits of routers, such as different routing strategies, high throughput, and more, with the ability of actor systems to get around the limits imposed by a single machine.

8.4.1 *Configuring a router to use multiple machines*

In chapter 7, you saw that there are two main types of routers: group routers, which deal with already deployed actor instances; and pool routers, which deploy the correct number of routees. Both router groups and pools can be used with Akka.Remote's routing strategies.

With Akka.Remote, the simplest routing technique is using group routers, which use actors that already exist and build routing capabilities on top of them. To create a group router, you provide a number of addresses that the router should treat as its routees. Because you can communicate with remote actors using the same address patterns covered previously, you can supply remote addresses to a group router and it will route messages over the network to actors on remote actor systems. In the following example, you create a new round-robin router with code to direct messages to both local actors and those running in a remote actor system:

```
var roundRobinGroup =
    new RoundRobinGroup(
        "akka.tcp://RemoteSystem@localhost:8081/user/greeter",
        "akka://LocalSystem/user/greeter");
```

But hardcoding remote network addresses into the assembly may not be the most practical solution, especially if IP addresses might change on a per-deployment basis. In these situations, it might be better to provide routees using HOCON configuration, supplying the routee paths at runtime rather than at compile time. In the following example, you configure the same round-robin group router with HOCON in the same way as in chapter 7:

```
akka.actor.deployment {
    /greeterRouter {
        router = round-robin-group
        routees.paths = [
            "akka.tcp://RemoteSystem@localhost:8081/user/greeter",
            "akka://LocalSystem/user/greeter" ]
    }
}
```

Although the group router is ideal for cases where actors already exist in the system, you may want to deploy actors as part of the router. Combining the pool router's ability to deploy routees with the remote deployment capabilities of Akka.Remote provides automatic management of routees across actor systems. When using pool routers with HOCON configuration, in addition to specifying the required information for the given router, you also need to specify the actor system addresses that the router should use to deploy routees. Here, you configure a round-robin pool to use two actor systems, one remote and one local:

```
var addresses =
    new List<Address> {
        new Address("akka", "LocalSystem"),
        Address.Parse("akka.tcp://RemoteSystem:@localhost:8081")
    };

var roundRobinPool =
    new RemoteRouterConfig(
        new RoundRobinPool(5),
        addresses);
```

You can also configure a remote router in code in the actor system, but that imposes underlying knowledge of the fact that remoting is being used, thus breaking location transparency. To use a remote router pool in code, you first create a `RemoteRouter-Config` that draws in the addresses of the actor systems, onto which you can deploy the routees along with the router pool class. For example, if you want to use code to create the same round-robin pool as the preceding example, you can write the following, which handles the remote deployment:

```
akka.actor.deployment {
    /greeterRouter {
        router = round-robin-pool
        nr-of-instances = 5
        target.nodes = [
            "akka.tcp://RemoteSystem@localhost:8081/user/greeter",
            "akka://LocalSystem/user/greeter"
        ]
    }
}
```

> **Remote router drawbacks**
>
> Although the majority of routers work well with remoting, some don't make the most of network scale-out opportunities. One example of this is the smallest-mailbox router: local routees take priority over remote routees because the router doesn't know the sizes of the remote mailboxes. In the event that you'll be scaling out a smallest-mailbox router, the round-robin router is likely to provide better service.

This approach conforms to the notion of location transparency, and applications can be scaled out onto vast numbers of actor systems with no changes needed to the assemblies themselves. Using routers allows you to parallelize and increase workloads further than you might be able to on a single machine.

8.4.2 *Wrapping up*

In this section, you've seen three ways to scale across machines. The simplest way is using group routers, which use actors that already exist and build routing capabilities on top of them. You can provide routees using HOCON configuration, supplying the routee paths at runtime. And you can configure a remote router in code, using a `RemoteRouterConfig`.

8.5 *Failure handling across machines*

Distributing work across a network provides a wide variety of benefits, but it also brings all the complexities associated with network programming, problems you never encounter when running your applications on a single machine. Machine connections are typically via Ethernet over distances ranging from a few centimeters to several kilometers and even thousands of kilometers. This distance may not seem that far, but it drastically limits the speed at which data can travel between machines and introduces latency. Although latency in itself isn't a problem, when you need lots of coordination—for example, when dealing with shared mutable state—it can lead to significant problems. Although shared mutable state is fortunately not an issue with Akka.NET thanks to the actor model, plenty of other difficulties arise.

Unfortunately, the distance between machines also poses other problems. When multiple processor cores pass data between themselves, the distance is in the range of several nanometers, giving little opportunity for data corruption. But when network connections span kilometers, there's the potential for message corruption to occur, for several reasons. It may be something as simple as someone cutting the network connection; or it may be more-complex reasons such as environmental factors influencing data flow; for example, magnetic or electromagnetic fields causing corruption, or the signal becoming attenuated or distorted over long distances.

The errors don't stop at the physical network connection; there's also a significant amount of infrastructure between the physical network connection and your application. There are routers and switches designed to ensure packets reach their intended destination, networking interfaces on the application host and the drivers that interface the hardware with the OS, and then the OS itself. These aren't likely to be perfect, and a bug in any component along the chain could cause significant propagating failures. Even if there were no bugs along the chain, you could still experience packet loss caused by network congestion. If you send too much data through a single connection, and it's unable to handle the load, it has only one option: dropping packets to prevent cascading failures.

You also need to consider the variance associated with packet latency through a network. Given the vast number of components between the application and the network connection, there's plenty of opportunity for an OS to perform an operation it deems to be more important than receiving a packet of data through the network, causing a delay in message processing. Network congestion can result in packets in the queue waiting to be processed by the OS; packets at the back of the queue will encounter delays. These potential latencies make it impossible to effectively calculate the expected latency for a given operation.

Between latency issues and packet loss, it's incredibly difficult to ensure that your distributed applications can withstand failures across a network, and to use many of the components you take for granted on a day-to-day basis. Because of latency issues, it's impossible to synchronize two independent machines with the same time. When there's packet loss, it's impossible to know the current state of a remote machine at any point in time.

When we discussed failure handling earlier in the book, you saw how to handle message loss across an unreliable channel, a must for systems that can't tolerate message loss. Akka.NET employs actor supervision, which provides isolation of errors and automated recovery from these errors. In many typical distributed applications, these are all issues you need to consider, along with how they might affect the safety and stability of the network. Fortunately, when using Akka.Remote, you can mitigate the effects of some of these failures so that you can more easily develop location-transparent applications. Thanks to features such as remote deployment and monitoring of actors, you can continue to use Akka.NET's fault-tolerance patterns, and continue to build truly responsive applications.

8.5.1 Supervisor strategies across a network

You've seen that actors aren't deployed independently, but as part of a larger hierarchy of actors with a supervision tree. Parent actors watch their children for failures, and if an error is raised, parents respond to it in the appropriate manner. Even when you deploy an actor onto a remote node as a child of a local node, you can retain this error-handling functionality so that you can build fault-tolerant applications that scale across a network.

Earlier in this chapter, you saw that you can specify an actor path to deploy an actor onto a remote actor system. If the deployed actor is the child of an actor in the local actor system, then it's supervised by a proxy actor on the remote node. In the examples you saw earlier in which you deployed an actor onto a remote node, a proxy supervisor cared for the remote actor. Figure 8.6 shows how this looks in the actor system, which remains transparent to the developer.

Using remote supervision actors creates the additional possibility of losing location transparency. You communicate with actors by means of their addresses. An address provides some context regarding the actor's deployment in the hierarchy. With remote supervision, these values diverge due to the addressing system. In figure 8.6, although the remote child actor's location in the hierarchy is directly below the parent actor system A, its *contact* address shows the *remote supervision* actor instead of actor system A. Therefore, calling `Context.Path.Parent` and `Context.Parent` on a remotely deployed actor will return different results.

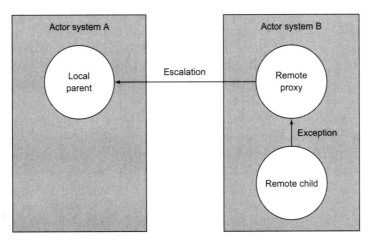

Figure 8.6   Remote children are deployed with a proxy that's responsible for supervision and handling any errors that may occur.

8.5.2   Remoting DeathWatch

You've seen that DeathWatch is used as a means of watching actors for failures, or for detecting completion when using the reaper pattern. Because Akka.Remote provides remote failure detection, you can use DeathWatch on remote actors, and also receive information about the source of failures.

You use DeathWatch to target a remote actor the same way as when you target a local actor, with `Context.Watch`. You also receive a `Terminated` message, exactly as if the remote actor was running locally, but there's even more useful information encoded in the message. In addition to the actor reference relating to the watched actor, you also receive two pieces of information designed to help diagnose the source of failure: `ExistenceConfirmed` and `AddressTerminated`. By observing the status of these properties, you can determine whether the `Terminated` message originated from the remote node or from the Akka.NET remote failure detector. If the message has the `AddressTerminated` property set to `true`, then the message means that the remote actor system is no longer responding to health checks. The `Existence-Confirmed` property helps determine whether the remote actor itself reported its failure, or if the failure resulted from an inability to resolve a reference to the actor.

In the same way you use supervision strategies across a network, you can use the DeathWatch concepts you saw earlier. You do need to be cautious when using a network connection, because there's a higher possibility of failures occurring. But by using the data you receive in the `Terminated` message, you can make better decisions about the status of a remote actor.

8.5.3 *Wrapping up*

Using a network presents opportunities for a wide range of problems to occur at various points up the technology stack. But with Akka.NET, you can use the same tooling you use with a single actor system across multiple actor systems. Failure becomes more likely as the number of running machines increases, so it's important that you consider failure early when designing networked applications. You've seen the benefits of the supervision system used in Akka.NET earlier in the book, but thanks to Akka.Remote, you can continue to create applications that are fault tolerant even when an unreliable network is involved.

8.6 *Akka.Remote security*

The remoting functionality of Akka.NET is designed to work in a peer-to-peer environment, where every connected actor system has the same level of privileges. This typically means that the actor systems are joined together on a private internal network, accessible only to the machines running the actor system instances. It's typical to see an approach similar to that shown in figure 8.7, where actor systems listen on a port that's only accessible to machines in their network, and provide gateway entry into the actor systems through an HTTP API, WebSockets, or even raw sockets.

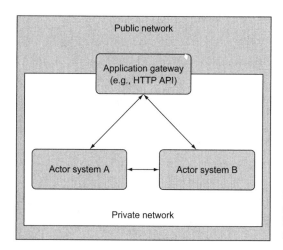

Figure 8.7 A typical Akka.NET actor system won't be exposed to the public internet and will instead stay in a private network, accessible through a gateway.

But there are still security considerations that need to be taken into account, and even more so when you open your application to the whole world. This might be the case if you have an actor system instance running on a client's machine, which needs to communicate with your hosted actor system. This could provide a means of entry into the actor system that malicious entities could exploit. Because the remoting functionality of Akka.NET is designed for use as a low-level communication layer, you need to ensure that the applications you build take security into account.

8.6.1   Limiting messages that can be sent over the network

When you send a message over the network, it's serialized into a binary representation that is then deserialized into the in-memory message. There's no validation of the original sender of the message, so it's possible for an attacker to construct a message payload with a dangerous message, which is then sent to the target actor system. Depending on the message, this could have severe consequences on the stability of the application.

An example of a dangerous message is the PoisonPill, which tells Akka.NET to shut down an actor. If this was sent over the network to the root actor supervisor at the top of the actor hierarchy, it would shut down every actor in the system immediately.

In Akka.NET, you can specify that a message type could be harmful to an actor system by making the message implement the IPossiblyHarmful interface. When Akka.Remote deserializes a message from outside the system that implements the IPossiblyHarmful interface, the message will be discarded. But if the message originates from within the same actor system, then it will be passed through to the target as intended. A number of the messages in Akka.NET implement the IPossiblyHarmful interface, notably, the PoisonPill, Kill, ReceiveTimeout, and Terminated messages. In the following example, you create a new message type that's used to delete a record from a database. This is something you don't want a client to send to the application, and it should instead only be sent from within the same actor system. To ensure this happens, the message implements the IPossiblyHarmful interface:

```
public class DeleteAccount : IPossiblyHarmful
{
    private readonly string _accountId;
    public string AccountId { get { return _accountId; } }

    public DeleteAccount(string accountId)
    {
        _accountId = accountId;
    }
}
```

Sandboxing messages to a single actor system is a good start in terms of security, as it allows you to significantly limit the impact a client can have on a running actor system, whether that client is a regular user with good intentions or a malicious user intending to compromise the system.

8.6.2   Restricting available remote actor targets

By restricting certain message types from being sent over the network, you can reduce the potential for damage to your actor system. But there are certain messages that might be harmful, but in a different context, that you do want to send over the network to remote actor systems. For example, the actor hierarchy might be laid out so that individual actors are scoped to a single customer. In this case, you don't want an unauthorized entity to be able to send a message to that customer's information, leading to a data breach or malicious attacks against that customer's data. This modeling of customer information might be like the actor hierarchy shown in figure 8.8. Here, each customer has a unique identifier in which an actor's name is based on that customer identifier. The customer actors share a common parent: the `Customers` actor.

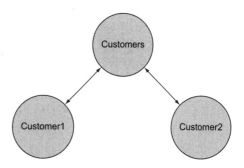

Typically, once a client has authenticated and your system has information relating to the customer account they belong to, the actor system can communicate with either the scoped customer account actor or one of its children for

Figure 8.8 An actor hierarchy may contain sensitive customer information, so you need to prevent users from retrieving data from Customer2 if the data belongs to Customer1.

specific services. But a malicious user could change the request to direct it to a different user account, and there's nothing you can do to prevent that. Instead, in Akka.NET, you can specify that only certain paths can be contacted over a network. With this technique, you can create an authorization actor whose sole responsibility is to act as a receptionist in the remote node. All messages are passed through this actor, which then performs authorization to verify that a user has the correct privileges to communicate with a given target.

You can design such a system of authorization by wrapping all messages in a custom authorization message that contains an authentication token,[1] an actor target, and a payload. When you send a message across a remote connection, wrap it in this message:

```
public class AuthenticatedMessageEnvelope
{
    private readonly object _payload;
    private readonly IActorRef _targetActor;
    private readonly string _authenticationToken;

    public object Payload { get { return _payload; } }
    public IActorRef TargetActor { get { return _targetActor; } }
    public string AuthenticationToken
        { get { return _authenticationToken; } }

    public AuthenticatedMessageEnvelope(object payload,
                                        IActorRef targetActor,
                                        string authenticationToken)
    {
```

---

[1] There are many options available for generating authentication tokens. One example is a JSON Web Token (JWT) that's created by an identity service elsewhere in the system. Such a service is out of the scope of this example, but a common choice for an identity service is the IdentityServer project (https://github.com/IdentityServer/IdentityServer4) or Azure Active Directory (https://azure.microsoft.com/en-us/services/active-directory/).

```
        _payload = payload;
        _targetActor = targetActor;
        _authenticationToken = authenticationToken;
    }
}
```

You also need to create an authorization actor in the remote actor system whose responsibility is to authorize incoming requests before forwarding messages to targets. When the authorization actor receives a message, it validates that the given token is authorized to communicate with the provided actor address. If it is, the message is forwarded to the intended destination, as shown in the sample code below. Here you use a feature for sending messages that you haven't seen yet, the Forward method. Typically, when you send a message, you use the Send method, which uses the address of the sending actor. The Forward method, however, not only sends a message, but also uses the address of the original sending actor. This means that the target doesn't know that the message was handled at an intermediary stage:

```
public class SystemReceptionist : ReceiveActor
{
    public SystemReceptionist()
    {
        Receive<AuthenticatedMessageEnvelope>(env =>
        {
            if (IsAuthorised(env.AuthenticationToken))
            {
                env.TargetActor.Forward(env.Payload);
            }
        });
    }

    private bool IsAuthorised(string authToken)
    {
        //This is only sample code
        //A production application should verify the authToken
        //And only return true if the authToken is valid
        return true;
    }
}
```

You also need to add a setting to your HOCON configuration, which specifies that the only path accessible over a remote connection is your authorization actor. Assuming you've deployed that actor at the address "/user/authorization", you can modify HOCON to only allow messages to be sent to this path over the remote connection. You modify the trusted-selection-paths element of the akka.remote configuration element and supply a list of all possible paths. In this case, you create a list containing the path to your authorization actor:

```
akka.remote {
    trusted-selection-paths = ["/user/authorization"]
}
```

Now, when someone wants to send a message over the network to the remote actor system, the message is wrapped in an envelope and sent to the authorization actor, which unwraps it, authorizes it, and sends it to the correct target. By defining which actor paths are accessible to the outside world, you effectively reduce the surface area an attacker can access. With the same techniques, you can enable authorization to prevent interference between customers.

8.6.3 Wrapping up

When you develop an application, it's imperative that you consider the security implications of any features you add. When you have an actor system that contains all of your customer data, it's vital that you effectively secure it. By using the features you've seen in this section, you can reduce the possibility that an attacker can compromise your applications.

8.7 Case study: Remoting, network applications, web server, and backend server

As application requirements and functionality grow, so do the teams who are responsible for their development. As these teams grow, they're inevitably partitioned into smaller sub-teams, with each team focusing on a specific piece of functionality in the greater application. Eventually, though, development reaches a stage where the independent teams need to work towards integrating the components to complete the product.

In this chapter, you saw how you can take multiple independent Akka.NET actor systems and connect them together, while treating the actors on remote actor systems as though they're local, all made possible by the location transparency provided by Akka.NET remoting. In figure 8.9, you can see how to connect two independent components of an enterprise application, which enables the actors on one actor system to appear in the other, and vice versa. This simplifies the integration period between components, as it treats the remote component as an extension of the original component, which is accomplished without requiring any additional tooling between the two.

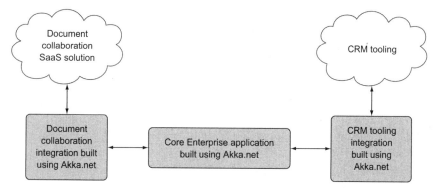

Figure 8.9 Integrations are usually complex, requiring large amounts of custom logic. By developing each integration as an individual application, you're able to dedicate resources to it, while Akka.NET remoting allows you to bring the integrations into the core application.

By using the remoting capabilities of Akka.NET, you can simplify the integration of applications created by other teams, allowing you to focus on the development of the core business logic that powers the application rather than the tedium of application integration.

Summary

In this chapter, you learned

- How to join two actor systems to compose a larger system
- How to create secure actor systems using authorization actors
- How to create scalable systems across a network

Part 3

Real-life usage

Part 3 wraps up the book by offering real-world case studies and implementations. Chapter 9 is focused on testing, from designing unit tests for functionality to verifying the functionality of distributed actor systems through multinode tests. Chapter 10 helps you integrate Akka.NET with custom protocols, focusing on sending and receiving data, integrating real-time connection mechanisms, and adding web APIs to allow communication with actor systems. Chapter 11 teaches how to add a persistent backing data store to an actor to save its state, with a focus on developing evolvable applications using Akka.Persistence and event sourcing. Chapter 12 utilizes Akka.Cluster to create elastic and scalable actor systems that span multiple machines. And, finally, chapter 13 is an end-to-end case study that will allow you to implement everything you've learned while programming one real-world production problem.

Testing Akka.NET actors

9

This chapter covers

- Designing unit tests to verify the functionality of individual actors
- Testing the interaction between multiple actors
- Verifying functionality with multinode tests

Throughout the book, you've seen that the outcome of applying the Reactive Manifesto to application design is a better UX. The services and applications you build should remain responsive even in the face of failure or scalability issues. Your goal is to provide the best possible experience to users and ensure they're happy when using your applications, but this entails more than maintaining responsiveness. You want them to use the application to its full potential without facing bugs and other issues.

An e-commerce website can experience spikes in traffic that create significant stress on services, possibly leading to failure. You can prepare for increased load to ensure that users are able to make purchases during traffic spikes. But even if you've built a system that scales up well, there still may be scenarios that prevent users from making a purchase. For example, users add items to their shopping carts before going through a checkout to complete their purchase, but if there's a bug in the logic powering the shopping cart service, the process fails, leading to frustration and lost sales.

To prevent these issues, we typically write tests that exercise the system with input data and validate that the data output from the system matches the expected values. Testing plays a key role at all stages of the software-development lifecycle, and a number of testing techniques can be used, depending on the functionality that needs to be tested.

Testing types can be generalized into one of three categories: end-to-end, behavioral, and unit tests. Each stage of testing relates to the level of depth to which you want to validate the functionality of the system.[1] Each stage goes progressively deeper into the system, starting from a black-box implementation of the system and using it as a user might (for example, through a UI or a web API), progressing down to the individual components of the system, and validating the business logic contained in each component.

Applications include areas of complex logic isolated within components. For example, a shopping cart service may have some logic that applies a discount to the items in the cart when a voucher is applied to the purchase. This sort of logic is important from a business perspective in that it acts as a way to attract new customers to the site, but you need to ensure that the discount is applied only when conditions are met, to prevent the company from losing money. You should write a number of tests that cover this logic and validate the functionality of the component. Due to the potential for many inputs to this small component, you typically have many tests to cover all possibilities. These are called *unit tests* because they test small, isolated units of functionality that are independent of the rest of the system.

As these units grow toward becoming a complete system, they interact with other independent units required for a feature. In the shopping cart example, other components may interact with the discount calculation, such as a loyalty scheme that rewards the buyer for making purchases. In this case, there are two components working together: the discount and voucher application logic, and the logic for calculating the number of loyalty points the user is due to receive for a completed transaction. You have tests to verify the functionality of the independent components, and it's also important to verify that they can operate together, and the requisite information is shared between them. These tests group together multiple components to test their integration, and thus are known as *integration tests*.

Having tested the internal functionality of the feature, you also need to verify that it integrates with all the other components of the system, such as external web services and databases. To validate this, you write more tests that treat the system as a black box with no testing of the internals, and validate that the provided outputs match the

---

[1] This book doesn't go into software testing and quality assurance in depth. This chapter provides an overview of the basics of unit testing. For a more in-depth discussion, see *The Art of Unit Testing*, 2nd edition (Manning, 2013) and *Specification by Example* (Manning, 2011).

expected outputs for a number of known inputs. Because these tests cover all aspects of the application, they're called *end-to-end tests.*

In this chapter, we'll focus on how to effectively test the internals of applications written using Akka.NET by writing unit tests and integration tests that test either single actors or multiple groups of actors responsible for communicating with each other. Although end-to-end tests are still needed to completely validate functionality, they don't require anything different from the current approaches to writing these tests.

9.1 *Introducing Akka.TestKit*

You saw back in chapter 3 how different the actor model is from the object-oriented architecture you're used to in C#, leading to a different approach to writing tests. When you write a unit test for a typical C# class, it may look something like the next example, in which you'll follow a typical three-stage approach to testing: arrange, act, and assert. You'll first arrange all the data that will be used to validate the functionality; in this case, you'll create variables to hold the input data and expected data, and create an instance of the system under test, with its dependencies. Next, you'll supply the system under test with input data and receive output from it, which supplies you with the actual value that the system has computed. Finally, you'll assert that the data retrieved from the system under test matches the data you expect. Although this test is limited, it follows a pattern you'll see in more-complex examples:

```
[Fact]
public void TheCartContainsAProductAfterAddingIt()
{
    var expectedProduct =
        new Product { Category = "Homeware",
                      Price = 3.52M,
                      SKU = "01222456" };

    var shoppingCart = new ShoppingCart();

    shoppingCart.AddItemToCart(expectedProduct);

    Assert.Contains(expectedProduct, shoppingCart.Products);
}
```

This example focuses on the data supplied as a result of calling a method, but there are many other techniques you can use to validate system functionality, including checking the object's state and validating that its new value matches the expected outcome. Sometimes, you may need to rely on introspection of the object and validate that its internal data matches some expected value.

But as you saw in chapter 3, there are two key differences between the actor model's approach to componentization and the typical object-oriented approach. In the actor model, you don't have access to the actor's internal state; and every operation in Akka.NET is designed to work asynchronously. Both present a challenge when you test components, if these components are actors.

In the discussion of the unit test example, you saw that you may need to verify that the object has updated its internal state, depending on the method being called. But in the actor model, actors encapsulate all their state and don't allow outside access to it. When you create an instance of an actor in Akka.NET, you don't even have a direct reference to the actor itself: you have an address that you send messages to. These messages are routed to the actor's location in memory. This means that when you use commonly available unit-testing tooling, you can't validate that an actor's state has been updated.

Actors communicate through message passing. In the actor system, operations happen asynchronously and will execute when the scheduler picks up a message. This means that the unit-testing technique used in the example won't work, and instead you have a scheduler route messages to the relevant processing logic. Finally, you need to consider the effect that time may have on your tests. When you're validating logic, the environment in which the tests are running may be an important factor in determining whether tests will pass or fail as a result of timing inconsistencies.

The Akka.TestKit package provides effective tooling to help ease the problems we've discussed. The testing tooling isn't designed to completely replace your existing test tools, but is designed to work alongside them so that your existing tooling is able to test all actors or compositions of actors. A number of adapters are available that allow Akka.TestKit tooling to work with many of the most common unit-testing frameworks, such as NUnit, xUnit, and MSTest. Akka.TestKit provides an implementation of `ActorSystem`, which is responsible for scheduling execution and routing messages and is designed to handle the difficulties discussed in this section.

We'll explore features that can help you more effectively test actor implementations: spawning test actors that allow you to introspect an actor reference and see its internal state, and running tests on a single thread, thus preventing race conditions. Throughout the rest of this chapter, we'll explore some of the other functionality provided by Akka.TestKit and how you can test typical scenarios as you develop actor applications with Akka.NET.

Installing Akka.TestKit

Akka.TestKit is installed in the same way as you installed previous packages, through NuGet. A number of Akka.TestKit packages are available that contain adapters to interoperate with numerous supported unit-testing frameworks. It's important to include Akka.TestKit; otherwise, certain functionality won't be available, such as asserting certain behavior.

9.2   Unit testing actors

You've seen two concepts relating to testing actors: unit testing your actors to verify their functionality when sending them a message, and integration testing your actors by verifying that message-passing components work together and messages are sent correctly. In this section, we'll look how to use Akka.TestKit to verify the behaviors associated with actors. Throughout this section, you'll use the xUnit test runner, but the same concepts apply to other adapters; the only changes you'll need to make will relate to, for example, asserts that depend on the chosen testing framework. The reasoning for using the xUnit runner will become apparent later in the chapter when we look at other testing methodologies in Akka.NET.

This section focuses on unit testing actors, particularly when you want to test their internal business logic and validate that they correctly respond to messages. To do this in a deterministic manner, Akka.TestKit can spawn new actors and run them through a single-threaded scheduler that executes all the actors synchronously, thus avoiding the issue of how time might affect your tests. Throughout this section, you'll learn more about the benefits these features bring.

9.2.1 *Spawning test actors*

Throughout the book, you've seen that actors should be designed to operate on the smallest unit of concurrency possible for that component. This is likely to contain some amount of business logic as part of the application, which needs to be verified as correct. In the shopping cart example in the previous section, you might have one shopping cart per user session as they browse the e-commerce site. You might choose to represent them as an actor instance per cart. This means that you're going to have some logic involved when performing operations such as adding new items to the cart. In this case, you need to validate that the item is in the cart after it's been added. You might also have an option to apply a discount code that leads to an updated price for the items in the cart.

As you aim to provide a great UX, you want to ensure that these pieces of functionality work smoothly. To prove that they work as expected, you create an actor and send it messages similar to those that it might receive in real-world usage. Akka.TestKit allows you to spawn a new form of an actor reference. So far, you've seen local actor references and remote actor references; now, you'll spawn test-actor references, which are specialized for use in testing, as shown in figure 9.1.

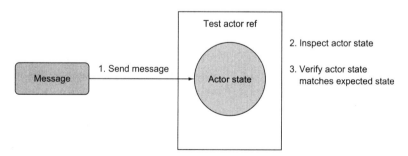

Figure 9.1 Test-actor references allow you to inspect actor state to verify an actor behaves as expected when it receives a message.

For example, if you have an actor for the checkout, you need to write a test to validate that when it receives a message telling it to add a given quantity of an item, the checkout updates correctly to reflect that. You can retrieve a test actor by creating an instance of `TestActorRef`, as in the following example. `TestActorRef` requires no backing actor system through which messages are routed; instead, the receive-handler method of the actor is called when you send it a message:

```
var testActorSystem = ActorSystem.Create("test");
var actor =
    new TestActorRef<ShoppingCartActor>(
        testActorSystem,
        Props.Create<ShoppingCartActor>());
```

`TestActorRef` is designed to be a lightweight tool for testing the internal logic of receive handlers; you can write tests that exercise an actor's logic and run the tests without the overhead of an actor system. You can quickly run tests on actors to validate that the functionality remains consistent even when you may end up refactoring the internal logic. But `TestActorRef` is synchronous in nature, limiting its testing potential. For example, some actor types rely on asynchronous communication to operate. Although the actors you've seen so far won't have problems, the actors you'll see in later chapters will prevent you from using synchronous tests.

9.2.2   *Validating internal data*

In the example already considered of unit testing an actor, the assertion was that its internal state was updated after it received a message. But the actor model guarantees that you can't see the internal state, providing a level of safety by preventing concurrency issues. One difference between `TestActorRef` and the other actor references you've seen so far is the ability to retrieve the `actor` instance that the reference is pointing to. This allows you to access fields and properties stored in the `actor` instance. Accessing an actor is simply a matter of calling the `UnderlyingActor` property on `TestActorRef`. This returns an instance of the `actor` object and allows you to use it as a regular instance and access data or call methods on it. In the following example, you retrieve the underlying `actor` instance for the shopping cart `actor` reference you created earlier:

```
var underlyingActor = actor.UnderlyingActor;
```

By having access to the underlying `actor` instance, you can perform assertions on the internal state and validate that the state has correctly updated. In the next example, you see a test that sends a message to the actor reference and then validates that the actor's state has been updated to the correct number of items. Thanks to the synchronous nature of `TestActorRef`, you can access the state immediately after sending the message. If you were writing tests in an asynchronous manner, then you would have to implement some means of periodically checking whether the state has been updated, leading to a certain amount of nondeterminism, which is not what you want when writing test code.

```
[Fact]
public void TheCartAcceptsAProduct()
{
    var testProduct =
        new Product
        {
            Category = "Homeware",
            Price = 9.99M,
            SKU = "0122224678"
        };
    var testActorSystem = ActorSystem.Create("test");
    var actor =
        new TestActorRef<ShoppingCartActor>(
            testActorSystem,
            Props.Create<ShoppingCartActor>());
    var underlyingActor = actor.UnderlyingActor;

    actor.Tell(new AddProductToCart(testProduct, 1));

    Assert.Contains(testProduct, underlyingActor.Products);
}
```

As this example shows, you can use your preferred unit-testing framework, meaning you can write any unit test in a process similar to how you currently write tests. You can work in the way that best suits the task at hand, whether that's using tests to validate existing functionality, or writing tests first and then developing features.

9.2.3 *Testing FSMs*

In chapter 4, you saw the importance of finite state machines (FSMs) and how they enable you to more easily develop actors handling multiple states. You also saw the specific FSMActor type, which allows you to develop more-complex FSMs than you might typically manage using switchable behaviors. If you want to test these actors, Akka.TestKit provides a test actor designed to allow the validation of the actor's current state:

```
var testActorSystem = ActorSystem.Create("test");
var actor = new TestFSMRef<TurnstileActor, ITurnstileState,
    ITurnstileData>(testActorSystem, Props.Create<TurnstileActor>())
```

In a way similar to how you generate the regular TestActorRef, you create TestFSM-Ref, passing in your FSMActor to test. In chapter 4, you created an FSM, which you used to control access through a turnstile barrier. Using the FSM test tooling in Akka.TestKit, you can create a test that's responsible for validating the transitions in that FSM. For example, to ensure that the barrier doesn't shut if you send it two messages of the same type in a short period of time, you can create a TestFSMRef with your TicketBarrierActor and start sending it messages.

Having sent the actor a message, you can access extended properties in the FSM. TestFSMRef provides two core properties, StateName, which is used to uniquely identify the possible states, and StateData, which is where the states can pass data between states. With these properties, you can validate that your internal logic is functioning correctly when you send a message to the actor. In the following example, you'll send the TestFSMRef the same message twice and validate that the state remains Unlocked:

```
var expectedState = Unlocked.Instance;
var testActorSystem = ActorSystem.Create("test");
var actor = new TestFSMRef<TurnstileActor,
    ITurnstileState,ITurnstileData>testActorSystem,
    Props.Create<TurnstileActor>());

actor.Tell(new TicketValidated());
actor.Tell(new TicketValidated());

Assert.Equal(expectedState, actor.StateName);
```

Being able to see the internal state of the FSM in the actor is a powerful means of testing the complex state machines you may deal with when you create a greater number of more involved actors with many states. It provides significant benefits over the simpler receive-handler approach with its limited potential for validating the current receive handler.

9.2.4   Wrapping up

Because many of your actors will feature some internal business logic, the TestActor-Ref unit tests allow for significantly lower overhead. This ensures that you can write sufficient tests to validate that the internal logic of your actors works as expected.

9.3   Integration testing actors

Although it's important to test the logic of each actor in the system independently to validate their functionality, you also need to test how actors interact with each other. Due to the asynchronous nature of the message-passing architecture, you can't rely on the synchronous testing framework you saw previously; you need to work with a dedicated asynchronous testing framework. Akka.TestKit provides such a tool to spin up a lightweight test-actor system with an increased number of inspection points to assert that your actors are communicating correctly. In this section, you'll see how to write tests to validate that when an actor receives a message, it sends the message to the correct target.

9.3.1   Creating test specifications

To write an integration test, you need to create a specification that provides tools you can use to validate messages sent through the actor system. With Akka.TestKit, you have a test-actor system that allows you to spawn an actor just as you would with a normal actor system, and you have tools to validate successful message passing. We'll explore these features in more depth throughout the rest of the chapter.

To create a specification, create a class that inherits from the TestKit class in Akka.TestKit. Any tests you write that use the actor system should inherit from this class. Tests are then specified by creating methods that are marked with the test attribute for your unit-testing framework of choice. For example, in the case of xUnit, which you'll use throughout this chapter, you need to mark your test methods with the `Fact` attribute. The following example shows how to define a simple test. Once the project containing the test code is compiled, the test runner for your unit-testing tool will detect the tests and run them:

```
public class ShoppingCartIntegrationTesting : TestKit
{
    [Fact]
    public void PricingEngineComputesCorrectPriceForAShoppingCart()
    {

    }
}
```

Once you have the test infrastructure in place, you can write some tests. First, you need an actor system to spawn an actor. The Akka specification class provides an actor system through the `Sys` property on the base class. This actor system works in the same way as the actor systems you've seen, and allows you to perform common operations such as spawning actors with `Props`.

```
var pricingActor = Sys.ActorOf<PricingActor>();
var shoppingCartActor =
    Sys.ActorOf(Props.Create<ShoppingCartActor>(pricingActor));
```

Having spawned a test actor, you can use it to send messages and communicate with other actors. Throughout the rest of this section, you'll see how to verify the messages the test actor sends.

9.3.2 *Asserting message responses*

When your test actor sends a message, its processing logic will be invoked by the host actor system, and you can observe its external effects. Typically, you expect to receive a message in response to your test actor's message, as shown in figure 9.2. In the case of the shopping cart actor, you may want to show the total cost on a web page. This means the actor needs to communicate with the shopping cart actor and retrieve the total. Your test actor can send a message that asks for the total and have the shopping cart actor respond to this message by sending a message back.

You need to test that the target actor is correctly operating in its environment by communicating back to the requesting actor. As part of the integration testing, you don't get to see the internals of the target actor; instead, you have a black-box system, meaning you can only observe the system's inputs and outputs. As part of the specification you wrote earlier, in addition to the test-actor system, you also have methods that are used to set expectations of what messages should be received before a timeout. If the test actor sends a `GetCartOverview` message, it expects a `CartOverview` message in response. To verify this with Akka.TestKit, use the `ExpectMsg` method on the object. You also need to specify a timeout. If TestKit receives the supplied message, then the test passes. Otherwise, the test fails, and the test runner will pick it up. In the

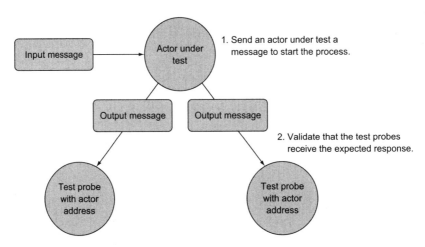

Figure 9.2 Test probes allow you to verify that actors are receiving the correct messages in response to their requests.

following example, you assert that when the test actor sends a request to calculate the shopping cart total, the shopping cart actor returns a response that matches what you expect. In this case, after having sent two messages to store a product in the shopping cart, the total should come to 19.98:

```
var product =
    new Product
    {
        Category = "Homeware",
        Price = 9.99M,
        SKU = "1231214643"
    };

shoppingCartActor.Tell(new AddProductToCart(product, 2));
shoppingCartActor.Tell(new GetCartOverview());

ExpectMsg(new CartOverview(1, 19.98M));
```

As you build complex actor systems, you're likely to see different patterns of communication between actors. TestKit provides a number of alternative assertions you can make on received messages. The previous example expected a message that was the same as the one provided, but sometimes you need to validate that the received message is of a given type, and you don't care about its internals. This is useful in cases where you can't deterministically compute the value in the sent message, but you do want to validate the existence of this message. For example, you may not care about computing the total for the shopping cart and may instead simply want to check that you receive a response. To do this, you use the generic form of ExpectMsg, which takes in the type as a generic parameter.

You also can use a predicate to validate properties of the message. For example, it may contain a timestamp and a value, and if equality is implemented to include the timestamp, then you can't get the granularity required to ensure that the important properties of the message match the expected values. If the message both matches the supplied type and passes the predicate, then the test passes; otherwise, it fails.

```
ExpectMsg<CartOverview>();

    ExpectMsg<CartOverview> (msg =>
    {
        Assert.Equal (1, msg.ItemsCount);
    }0;
```

You might also expect many messages to be sent by the actor under test, for example, where it presents a stream of information to a calling actor in the case of a subscription. Alternatively, there may be a second actor performing some other action, also causing the actor under test to send more than one message. In either of these cases, you can specify that an actor should receive all of the messages supplied. This allows you to send multiple messages and perform multiple assertions simultaneously:

```
ExpectMsgAllOf<CartOverview>(
    new CartOverview(1, 19.98M),
    new CartOverview(1, 9.99M));
```

There may also be times when you want to ensure that you receive one message within a set of messages. For example, you may be expecting a pseudorandom response that then opens up the option of receiving one message in a set range of messages:

```
ExpectMsgAnyOf<CartOverview>(
    new CartOverview(1, 9.99M),
    new CartOverview(2, 14.98M));
```

The final assertion you're likely to make is that your test actor shouldn't receive a message at all in a given time period. For example, you saw in chapter 8 how to require authorization to access certain resources; if the test actor fails to provide credentials as it sends a request, no response is expected. This is handled through `ExpectNoMsg`, along with a timeout:

```
ExpectNoMsg(TimeSpan.FromMilliseconds(2000.0));
```

These simple assertions cover most of the complex test cases you're likely to encounter as you write integration tests for multiple actors by testing for message effects.

9.3.3 *Time-based testing*

Although the tests so far have simply asserted that your actor system can return a number of messages in a set period of time, you're also likely to encounter scenarios where you have a fixed time in which you need a set number of things to happen. For example, it may be the case that an Akka.NET actor system sits in a much larger API that provides a service-level agreement that all operations will complete in a set period of time. In these cases, you need to ensure that the tests you write can either validate that these agreements are reachable or demonstrate that code changes are needed to bring the actual times in line with the expected times. You're likely to be making more than one call to a number of different actors, each responsible for a small component of the application. For example, in the e-commerce example, you have the simple shopping cart, but you'll also have to deal with product-listing services, product-recommendation services, search services, and potentially many more, which together create the shopping experience (see figure 9.3).

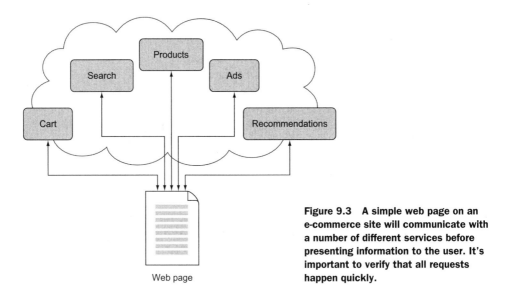

Figure 9.3   **A simple web page on an e-commerce site will communicate with a number of different services before presenting information to the user. It's important to verify that all requests happen quickly.**

It's important to know the impact that a large number of components will have on system responsiveness. For this purpose, TestKit provides an In block with a timeout for completing a number of steps. If the steps time out, the test fails, but if all the steps complete, the test passes. In the following example, you'll integrate with some of the external services we considered earlier to build a response to present to the user. In this case, you'll specify that a message sent to the shopping cart will produce a response in 2 seconds:

```
In(TimeSpan.FromSeconds(2.0), () =>
{
    var product =
        new Product
        {
            Category = "Homeware",
            Price = 9.99M,
            SKU = "1231214643"
        };

    shoppingCartActor.Tell(new AddProductToCart(product, 2));
    shoppingCartActor.Tell(new GetCartOverview());

    ExpectMsg<CartOverview>();
});
```

Many of the tests in the previous section have some degree of time sensitivity. Although these tests may succeed when run locally on a powerful development machine, if they're run on a build server, they may time out due to a lack of available resources. To counter this, you can use dilated time spans instead of regular time spans, and provide a scaling factor in the actor system's test configuration. With dilated time, the scale factor is pulled in from the configuration, and the timeout for each test component is updated. This allows for short timeouts on tests when running locally, as well as longer timeouts for build services that are shared with many other test runners.

```
In(Dilated(TimeSpan.FromSeconds(2.0)), () =>
```

Once again, thanks to Akka.NET's tooling, you can build products and services that customers enjoy using. In this case, you can accurately test the timing of communications between actors and validate a responsive UX, in line with the Manifesto.

9.3.4   *Test probes*

You've seen how to assert that the sending actor of a message receives a reply from a target actor, but you also want to validate that an actor under test sends the *correct* messages on to other targets. For example, you may need to validate that an actor forwards a message to another actor, or you may want to validate that for a given code path, an actor sends a new message to a target (see figure 9.4).

In order to validate that alternative targets are able to receive messages, Akka.NET provides the notion of *test probes*. Test probes are `IActorRefs` that you can use to verify

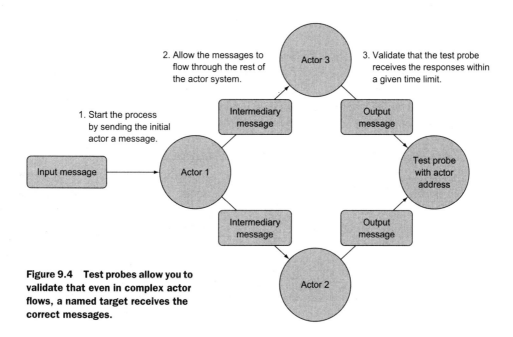

Figure 9.4   Test probes allow you to validate that even in complex actor flows, a named target receives the correct messages.

message reception, similar to the previous example, where you verified the requesting actor. To create a test probe actor, call the `CreateTestProbe` method, which returns a test probe. To integrate the test probe with other actors, you need access to the `IActorRef`, which can be accessed using the `Ref` property on the test probe:

```
var testProbe = CreateTestProbe();
```

From here, you can pass the test probe actor to other actors as a dependency and allow them to communicate with it. The actor under test has no knowledge that it's communicating with a test actor, thus ensuring that the test environment is as close to the production environment as possible:

```
var testProbeRef = testProbe.Ref;
var cartActor =
    Sys.ActorOf(Props.Create<ShoppingCartActor>(testProbeRef));
```

Now you can perform assertions on the test probe to validate that it has received messages as expected. You have access to all the assertions you saw at the start of this section, allowing you to assert receiving the correct message, message type, collection of messages, or no messages at all. But you're not actually testing that it's the original sender that's receiving the message; instead, you're testing an external actor:

```
cartActor.Tell(new GetCartOverview());
testProbe.ExpectMsg<ComputeCartTotal>();
```

Test probes are a powerful construct, allowing you to create more in-depth tests that cover large portions of the actor system hierarchy and ensure that actors in your system are correctly integrated and communicating. By using test probes, you can continue with black-box testing of the system, even when the black box relies on external actors.

9.3.5 *Wrapping up*

Many actors can be tested independently and proven to operate correctly on their own, but in a real-world system, there will be significant interaction between actors. As such, it's important that you test a subset of your system to validate that the individual behaviors will cooperate in a production system without performance problems, such as messages timing out.

9.4 *Testing distributed applications with MultiNode TestKit*

So far, the tests you've seen have focused on testing actors that all run in the same actor system, but you should also test their functionality across a network. You saw in chapter 8 how to link two actor systems together with Akka.Remote and have them communicate over a network. You also saw how much potential for failure there is once you start to communicate over an unreliable channel such as a network. There's potential for messages to arrive later than planned, in a corrupted state, out of the original sent order, or even not at all. These scenarios could lead to failure of the application or of core components in the system. You want to ensure that critical core components aren't degraded as a result of such failures. In this section, we'll look at how to inject failures at the transport level between two applications to more effectively test applications that are distributed over a network channel and ensure they maintain resiliency even in the event of uncontrollable failures.

In the discussion on failure scenarios in chapter 6, you saw that unreliable channels are one such problem, and you also saw a possible solution. Although having a theoretical problem-solving plan is useful, you can *prove* that your plan works by testing it using the MultiNode TestKit. Testing across the network provides another means of ensuring that applications and systems work in edge cases. An example of where this level of testing is useful is distributed database design, where developers need to ensure that data remains consistent and error free even when faced with unanticipated bugs. You may not be writing databases yourself, but you do need to verify certain aspects of the systems you write, such as their ability to return valid data for 99.9% of requests, a requirement that may typically be included in a service level agreement. High availability must be a core tenet of your system's design. This means having redundant services in place to cope with failure and appropriate routing to deal with failures in the code. These tasks are an important part of any high-availability service and should be tested to ensure that they work and will handle network failure.

In addition to the testing components you've seen so far, Akka.NET provides the MultiNode TestKit, a simple way of starting up multiple connected actor systems all running on the same machine, but communicating as though they were scattered across a network. Using assertions similar to those you saw earlier, you can verify that your actors continue to operate despite network difficulties. The examples you've seen so far on integration testing have focused on the xUnit test kit. This is because the MultiNode TestKit is an extension of the xUnit test kit, meaning that you must use xUnit as your testing library.

The MultiNode TestKit consists of two key components that form the basis of the tests you write: the *test conductor* and the *specifications*. The test conductor is responsible for orchestrating the work done under the hood by the test runner. This means that it provides support for tasks such as running functions on individual machines, providing barriers to allow tests to operate at the same pace, automating the process of finding the addresses for each of the actor systems, and acting as a centralized location where you can inject failures into the network layer deterministically. The specifications are designed to describe the details of the test, providing a means of telling the test conductor what operations it should perform on each independent actor system that's being tested. Throughout the rest of this section, we'll look at how to use these components to test the network resiliency of the actor systems you write and how they work in the presence of unreliability.

9.4.1 MultiNode specs

We'll first look at MultiNode TestKit test specifications. A specification (typically shortened to *spec*) provides a means of describing the structure of a test, including deploying actors across multiple actor systems, entering barriers, and inducing failures into the network, as well as using assertions, such as validating message reception.

Although the specifications are similar to those used in integration testing, there are some notable differences, which will become clear as you write spec files in this section. A test specification has three main sections: the *common configuration* shared between the actor systems under test, the *specification* detailing the operations that the test should perform, and *specific configuration modifications* that may be needed on a per-actor-system basis. In this section, we'll look at how to write a specification designed to demonstrate a simple ping-pong between multiple actors on separate actor systems, and what happens when they lose network connection.

When writing a multinode test, your first task is to create a configuration that will be shared by all actor systems, by creating a subclass of `MultiNodeConfig`. Here, you can create any HOCON configuration that your test needs and specify the names of the actor systems to use. In the following example, you tell the test conductor to use two actor systems, referred to as *roles* in the MultiNode TestKit. To add some configuration shared by all actor systems, assign it to `CommonConfigurationProperty`. In the following example, you use the provided debugging configuration, which provides enhanced logging to aid with debugging across all your actor systems:

```
public class MultiNodeGuaranteedMessagingConfig : MultiNodeConfig
{
    private readonly RoleName _first;
    private readonly RoleName _second;

    public RoleName First { get { return _first; } }
    public RoleName Second { get { return _second; } }

    public MultiNodeGuaranteedMessagingConfig()
    {
        _first = Role("first");
        _second = Role("second");

        CommonConfig = DebugConfig(true);
    }
}
```

The next step is to create the actual test that will be executed on each of the actor systems. The test is created as an abstract class that inherits from `MultiNodeSpec`. You'll soon see why it's abstract. You also need to pass your configuration object up the class hierarchy to `MultiNodeSpec`:

```
public class MultiNodeGuaranteedMessagingSpec : MultiNodeSpec
{
    private readonly MultiNodeGuaranteedMessagingConfig _config;

    public MultiNodeGuaranteedMessagingSpec()
        : this(new MultiNodeGuaranteedMessagingConfig())
        { }

    public MultiNodeGuaranteedMessagingSpec(
        MultiNodeGuaranteedMessagingConfig config)
            : base(config)
    {
```

```
        _config = config;
    }

    protected override int InitialParticipantsValueFactory
        { get { return Roles.Count; } }
}
```

Having created a test container, next you'll write test methods in the class that will be run on every node. Add the `MultiNodeFact` attribute, which the test runner will pick up, to specify that the method is a test. In your test method, you can perform any of the assertions you saw when looking at integration tests, including a validation of having received the correct message, or no message at all. You can even create a Test-Probe, as you saw earlier, to complement your suite of integration tests with large-scale tests covering a greater area of potential problems:

```
[MultiNodeFact]
public void MessageShouldBeResentIfNoAcknowledgement()
{
    var pricingActor = Sys.ActorOf(Props.Create<PricingActor>());
}
```

Lastly, you'll create a subclass of `MultiNodeSpec` for each of the nodes participating in the test. In this case, you've been using two nodes, so you need to create two classes that inherit from your custom abstract `MultiNodeSpec`. When you specify it should run this test, the test conductor will pick up one class per node in which to run it:

```
public class MultiNodeGuaranteedMessagingSpec1 :
    MultiNodeGuaranteedMessagingSpec
{ }

public class MultiNodeGuaranteedMessagingSpec2 :
    MultiNodeGuaranteedMessagingSpec
{ }
```

Now you can call the Akka.NET MultiNode TestKit runner, passing in a path to the DLL containing the tests, as well as the name of a single spec, if you want to run only one test instead of all tests in the DLL. The test runner is supplied as part of the NuGet package, but it's copied to the output directory of the project with the tests, meaning it's as simple as running the following example. It initializes a number of external processes, each of which is running its own independent deployment of the actor system:

```
Akka.MultiNodeTestRunner.exe Chapter9.dll
```

This is the bare minimum needed to set up a new test designed to span multiple actor systems. Throughout the rest of this section, we'll look at the other tools available in the MultiNode TestKit that allow for more-powerful tests.

9.4.2 *Testing individual actor systems*

When you created your test in the previous section, you specified a test method that's invoked by the test runner whenever the test is run. But there's currently no differentiation between which actor systems run which code. As it stands, every actor system will execute the exact same code. This proves to be a problem, as you don't want all the actor systems to start doing the same thing. You want them to have different responsibilities. As you saw in chapter 8, a number of different architectural styles can be used when you're developing applications that run across a network.

You can limit the execution of certain functions to selected machines. This means that you can specify, for example, that the first machine should deploy an actor that the second one is able to communicate with. In chapter 8, you saw an example of a billing system on one actor system that would be used by other actor systems. In this case, only one actor system should contain the billing actor.

As part of a multinode test, you can call the RunOn method to limit the scope of the function to a selection of machines. In the following example, you specify that the test runner should only run the test actor on the node that you called First. When this test is executed by the test runner, it will only execute the function if the role it's currently running on matches the role you've specified it should run on:

```
RunOn(() =>
{
    var pricingActor = Sys.ActorOf(Props.Create<PricingActor>());
}, _config.First);
```

By limiting the execution of your function to an individual node, you can build complex tests that more accurately represent the deployment and release scenarios in a production environment. You can design tests for catching bugs relating to the system infrastructure rather than just the code.

9.4.3   *Barriers*

When you run test code on different actor systems, you introduce the possibility of a race condition in your tests. For example, consider the scenario where node A deploys an actor into its own actor system, and node B makes a call to that recently deployed actor. Because node B requires that node A has already spawned an actor, if the actor deployment takes an extended period of time, then the test may fail because it's unable to find the deployed actor. You need to allow time for preconditions to be met before you proceed with the remainder of the test. As a test is run, it can enter a barrier coordinated by the test conductor. Upon entering the barrier, the current test run will block until every other node participating in the current test has also entered the same barrier.

Entering a barrier is achieved through a call to the EnterBarrier method, which requires a name for the barrier. The name is used to ensure that all the nodes in the actor system are at the same stage and have entered the barrier. Once EnterBarrier is called, no other test steps run, and test execution pauses. In the following example, the second node doesn't need to do any test setup and instead waits for the first node to complete its deployment of a new actor. Here, the barrier is called "Deployment-Complete". Assuming every node has also entered the barrier with the same name, you can proceed to the next section of the test, which in this case is for node B to send a message to node A:

```
EnterBarrier("DeploymentComplete");
```

Barriers are a quick and easy way to ensure that the distributed tests you write operate together and work at the same pace, forestalling race conditions and random test failures in your multinode tests.

9.4.4   *Testing for network failure*

You saw in chapter 8 that a network powering Akka.Remote can at times be unreliable, leading to plenty of opportunities for the systems you write to become unreliable. Testing applications that span a network can often be a difficult or laborious process requiring a number of tools, and can even be dependent on the OS you use. But because the test conductor powers all of the network routing for the remoting layer of Akka.NET, you can modify the network connection by communicating with the test conductor. This means that from the test conductor sitting outside the remote system, you can inject failures at different layers of the application.

The test conductor allows you to perform a number of network changes designed to simulate some of the networking difficulties encountered in a production environment. When using the test conductor, you can simulate a node crash and kill a test runner, add throttling to the network channel to slow messages down, and drop messages completely (see figure 9.5). These are all similar to issues that you might encounter when you deploy your applications into a multi-tenanted cloud environment, for instance. Nodes might automatically close for OS updates; messages might be throttled if a neighboring VM starts a large downloading operation; or messages might disappear en route through a network path.

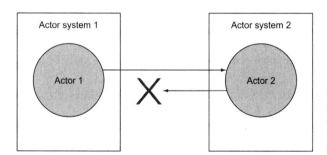

Figure 9.5   When using the test conductor, you can drop messages sent over a network connection to simulate the effects of a network interruption.

To enable these features of the test conductor, set the `TestTransport` property of `MultiNodeConfig` to `true`. This will cause the remoting layer to use the fault-injecting transports instead of the usual network transports. In this example, you set up the configuration to allow you to test the transport:

```
public MultiNodeGuaranteedMessagingConfig()
{
```

```
TestTransport = true;

_first = Role("first");
_second = Role("second");

CommonConfig = DebugConfig(true);
}
```

Now you can start communicating with the test conductor and injecting failures into the networking layer. The simplest failure is to ignore all the data traveling between two nodes, a feature known as *blackholing* in Akka.NET. You restrict the messages sent between nodes and drop them, either in both directions or in the receive or send direction. Call the `Blackhole` method on the `TestConductor` property, specifying the source role, target role, and the direction of message loss. In the following example, you specify that the transport should drop any messages traveling between the source and the target:

```
TestConductor.Blackhole(_config.First,
                _config.Second,
                ThrottleTransportAdapter.Direction.Both);
```

Sometimes, you need to restrict messages to a certain number per second. For example, your actor system may be communicating over a low-bandwidth connection, such as a 2G or 3G mobile connection or a slow broadband connection. In these cases, you need to validate that you're not sending so much data that it gives the impression that a remote node is unable to communicate with you. You can set `TestConductor` to only allow through a certain number of messages per second, calculated by the total size sent over the network. For example, you may have a limitation of 500 Kbps of bandwidth. By using the test conductor, you can limit the communication between two nodes to 500 Kbps. In the following example, you specify that the communication between node 1 and node 2 should be limited to that of a slow 3G mobile connection, in this case, roughly 0.5 Mbps:

```
TestConductor.Throttle(_config.First,
                _config.Second,
                ThrottleTransportAdapter.Direction.Both,
            0.5f);
```

Finally, you may want to make a node disappear entirely, mapping to cases where machines shut down suddenly without the opportunity for finalization, such as in the event of a hardware failure, the host OS restarting, or even the host runtime encountering an unrecoverable error. To emulate this, you can tell the test conductor to shut down that node. This will remove the node from all the connected nodes' lists, ensuring that any other barriers are passable:

```
TestConductor.Shutdown(_config.First);
```

These three basic cases—transport, bandwidth, and crash—cover the majority of the issues that you're likely to encounter that involve the networking layer. By testing them, you can ensure that systems are able to endure network difficulties in a production environment. The test conductor proves to be a very valuable tool in gaining assurance that your systems are truly resilient and able to stand up to even the harshest environments.

9.4.5 *Wrapping up*

The MultiNode TestKit is an incredibly powerful tool that allows you to test your applications in complicated integrations. Although many test environments replicate production environments, they're unlikely to see the same sorts of issues you might encounter; but the MultiNode TestKit used as part of Akka.NET allows you to simulate some of the most obscure issues possible, issues that you may even overlook during the testing stage of development, but that could have catastrophic outcomes if ignored.

9.5 *Case study: Testing, test-driven development, unit testing*

For most software developers, unit testing and integration testing play key roles in the development process, providing an automatable means of verifying that an application correctly follows behavioral specifications. By using the Akka.NET test kit outlined in this chapter, you can define tests that work together with your existing tests as part of your development process. Figure 9.6 shows how to structure a typical solution that uses multiple projects. A *production project* contains the definitions of your actors. This will be the project that's deployed into the production environment and is responsible for performing the business logic. In addition, a *test project* contains a number of unit and integration tests. When changes are made to the production project, the test project is run through a test runner, and if any tests fail, then it can be assumed that the change has broken your application logic.

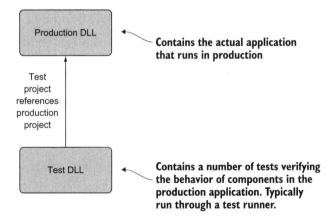

Figure 9.6   A typical test project structure is simple but offers the opportunity to easily reproduce a known test case to check for potential regressions.

With the Akka.NET test kit, you can use the common test-driven development practices that have become widespread in other areas of .NET software development. You can integrate the test kit with other test runners as part of an automated system that prevents the deployment of potentially bug-ridden code into a production environment.

Summary

In this chapter, you learned

- How to design a unit test that tests the functionality of a single actor
- How to develop integration tests that verify that multiple actors work together
- How to test distributed applications using the MultiNode Testkit

Integrating Akka.NET

This chapter covers

- Designing custom protocols to receive and send data
- Integrating with real-time connection mechanisms
- Adding a web API frontend for web application communication

All the examples you've seen in the book so far have contained actors in actor systems and haven't exposed them to the world. As you build actor applications, you want to make their data available for consumption by various technologies, of which there are many. The data in your actor systems might be sent to IoT devices to enable command-and-control-style scenarios; mobile apps and games for refreshing information on user devices, video game consoles for multiscreen gamer experiences; other cloud services responsible for other utilities; or websites (figure 10.1). In all these cases, you need to present the information stored in your actor system in the appropriate manner for each service.

In chapter 8, you saw that with Akka.Remote you can expose actor systems over the internet by allowing them to listen on a specific port and accept incoming communication from other actor systems. This has some key benefits, most notably its simplicity, but it leaves you in a difficult position, because the recommended

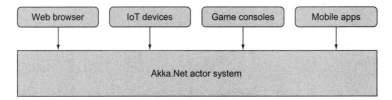

Figure 10.1   An Akka.NET actor system may need to receive input from a number of different devices, all using different technologies.

security practice is to only allow access to Akka.NET actor systems from behind a fire-wall, preventing system exposure to the internet. But there's another reason why you're unlikely to allow communication through actor systems. In all the cases we've seen where you want to integrate with an actor system, your current client platform of choice may not be capable of running an Akka.NET actor system.

Let's consider the example of an IoT device, typically, a low-powered hardware designed for energy efficiency to conserve battery life. Akka.NET isn't optimized for low-powered devices as it needs a full CLR virtual machine to execute the .NET appli-cation. This is a lot of overhead to execute on something that's low powered. You also need to consider transport and integration with third-party tooling. In the world of IoT, MQTT has become a standard for device communication. If you use Akka.NET with its remoting capabilities, you potentially exclude your device from communicat-ing with other manufacturers' devices.

You also need to consider the supporting libraries on client machines. Although some machines may be more powerful and able to support a fully functioning virtual machine, you may be unable to run Akka.NET due to security permissions on the cli-ent's device. For example, an iOS mobile device won't allow you to run a just-in-time compiler; you have to run an ahead-of-time compiler. This means that you're not able to run a full virtual machine in your application; you need special tools to ensure the abilities of VM tooling.

Another consideration is the languages used to access an actor system. Akka.NET actor systems can communicate only with other Akka.NET actor systems: the client application must be written in C# or F#. This is often impossible. One example is video game development, which often uses low-level languages such as C and C++ to make the most of the hardware and get the best performance. Using C or C++, game developers wouldn't be able to communicate with an Akka.NET backend system.

Finally, you should ensure that the tools you're using to interoperate with other systems are appropriate given historical and likely future tooling. An example of this is the use of HTTP in web browsers. As backend servers are changing to a more reactive model, HTTP communication between the user's web browser and backend servers has become fairly standardized. As the internet community increasingly uses web applications to deliver content to users, you need to support access to data in a way that is both consumable and manageable.

Your actor systems must be consumable by a wide range of devices and their particular protocols and technologies. You need to consider how to design actor systems capable of generating responses in milliseconds that can communicate with other systems, applications, and devices.

In this chapter, you'll see how to integrate a new Akka.NET application with protocols and technologies you're likely to encounter in a preexisting .NET application. This allows you to put incredibly simple integrations in place that permit access from many different devices. You'll see how to create actor systems that can be accessed through HTTP using your preferred web framework; in this case, you'll use ASP.NET, but you can follow the same guidelines with alternatives such as NancyFx, ServiceStack, Suave, and many others. You'll also see how to create reactive services that run on the web by integrating with web sockets, using SignalR. Finally, you'll see how to integrate low-level TCP socket connections into your application so you can build protocols on top of the socket connections.

10.1 Integrating with ASP.NET

Over the past twenty years, the web has changed significantly. Originally intended for sharing research materials between academics, it's evolved into a tool that people rely on for communication, entertainment, and so much more. Web browsers have changed accordingly and have grown so much in functionality that it's now possible to create applications that are delivered through the internet to the user's web browser, thanks to the power of HTML, CSS, and JavaScript.

In contrast with the changes that users can see in the frontends of today's applications, the backends have followed the same protocol of HTTP communication. The HTTP specification has seen some minor changes but has, for the most part, stayed consistent. This level of consistency and standardization presents some clear benefits for those looking to integrate their application over a network. Most devices provide either support for a web browser or, at the very least, a set of tools for making requests to an HTTP API. This level of availability has led to HTTP becoming the transport of choice for many applications.

In the .NET ecosystem, a wide variety of web servers are designed for writing applications that communicate with clients over HTTP. In addition to the Microsoft-supported ASP.NET web framework, other options from the wider community include NancyFx, ServiceStack, and Suave. All have their respective merits and all can be used with Akka.NET; in this section, we'll look at Microsoft's widely used ASP.NET framework. Integration with ASP.NET builds on one of the concepts you saw back in chapter 3: you can send a message to an actor and then wait for a response, with the Ask method. The techniques used in this section are also applicable to the other frameworks, and the examples can be ported to them.

Assuming you have an application already set up[1] and configured with the basic features required to build an ASP.NET website, you can add all the components required to use Akka.NET. As before, you need to add the references to the prerequisite components of Akka.NET; for the most basic Akka.NET application, this means installing the Akka package from NuGet exactly as you did in chapter 3.

Before you can use Akka.NET, your application needs an actor system set up and configured to run. You saw in chapter 3 that you should only have a single actor system, containing all of your actors, deployed for each application. To make an actor system available across your entire application and ensure that the actor system runs for the lifetime of your application, you can use one of two approaches:

- *Global.asax*—You can initialize your actor system in the Global.asax file and make it accessible to all parts of the application with a static property. By using the Global.asax file, you can also register to certain events raised by the ASP.NET framework or IIS host. For example, you can listen to events that send notifications that the application will soon be shut down or restarted. This allows you to shut down the actor system and save the state of the actors in preparation for the event.
- *Startup.cs*—In addition to an IIS host for your application, you can use one of the OWIN-compatible hosts, allowing you to change the server quickly and easily. This removes the possibility of using the Global.asax file, which is tied to IIS. But as an alternative, you can store data in the OWIN environment, which is then accessible from anywhere in the application.

In this example, you'll use the Startup.cs option for its simplicity and cross-platform capabilities. OWIN is a simple contract that .NET web servers can implement that allows applications to be moved between different hosting technologies with minimal effort. For example, an application that uses OWIN middleware can be targeted at a self-hosted version for local development and then deployed onto an IIS instance when in a production deployment.

OWIN works as a pipeline in which each component has a subsequent operation that's executed, until it gets to the end of the chain, upon which a result is passed back along the chain. This means that if you want to use your actor system further down the chain, you need to ensure that you've initialized it at the very start of the queue. To add an element to the OWIN pipeline, call the `Use` method on the `IAppBuilder` provided in the `Configuration` method. `Use` takes a function as a parameter that takes the environment and the next element in the chain and returns a task. You'll create an actor system in this function and store it in the environment, where you can access it from any step in the chain that follows it. In the following example, you store the actor system in the environment dictionary under the key `akka.actorsystem`. Follow

---

[1]   This book focuses on features relating to Akka.NET and as such doesn't go in depth into features related to ASP.NET. For information on ASP.NET, including getting-started tutorials, documentation, and more, visit http://asp.net or refer to Jeffrey Palermo et al., *ASP.NET in Action* (Manning, 2012).

the same process for creating an actor system as if you were creating it in a console application, which includes loading the configuration from a file:

```
public class Startup
{
    public void Configuration(IAppBuilder appBuilder)
    {
        var actorSystem = ActorSystem.Create("webapi");

        appBuilder.Use((ctx, next) =>
        {
            ctx.Environment["akka.actorsystem"] = actorSystem;
            return next();
        });
    }
}
```

If you have an element that follows the actor system creation, you can access the actor system stored in the environment. If your pipeline looks as follows, then anything in the web API step can access the actor system by using the OWIN environment:

```
appBuilder.Use((ctx, next) =>
{
    ctx.Environment["akka.actorsystem"] = actorSystem;
    return next();
}).UseWebApi(config);
```

If you add a controller to your project, you can retrieve the actor system by using the OWIN extension methods. Now that you have a reference to the actor system, you can interact with it just as you would if it was a console application. Even though it will be accessed by multiple threads, you're still safe to interact with the actor system due to Akka.NET's guarantee that each actor will only process one message at a time. But actors operate concurrently, making them ideal for web applications where you might have multiple users with multiple web browsers or applications trying to modify the data stored on the web server concurrently.

You can now start to work with the actor system in your controller. For example, if you want to pull data out of the actor system as part of a get request, you can select an actor path and send it a message with Ask, awaiting the response. Because Ask returns a task and operates asynchronously, you can use asynchronous controller support alongside it. In the following example, you request data from one of the actors in the system by sending it a message and awaiting a response with Ask:

```
public class GreeterController : ApiController
{
    [HttpGet]
    [Route("hello/{name}")]
    public async Task<string> GetGreeting(string name)
    {
        var owinCtx = Request.GetOwinContext();
        var actorSystem = owinCtx.Get<ActorSystem>("akka.actorsystem");
        var greeter = actorSystem.ActorSelection("/user/greeter");
        var greeting = await greeter.Ask<string>(name);
```

```
        return greeting;
    }
}
```

As you can see, this integration is incredibly simple, especially in small services, but there are some issues that you might encounter if your web service becomes popular. You saw in chapter 7 that the best option for scaling is to create more instances of something, rather than scaling up your existing infrastructure. As it stands, every time you add a new web server, you'll add a new actor system as well, each of which is independent. Fortunately, you saw in chapter 8 how to combine multiple actor systems together, thanks to Akka.Remote. You can set up your actor system as a service that other servers can connect to. Each web server in your example has a lightweight actor system containing no actors, which you use to communicate with the shared actor system. Your architecture looks like figure 10.2, where each web server shares a centralized actor system. All of this is possible using the features you saw in chapter 8.

By combining your actor system with a web API, you can access it from the vast majority of devices and systems. Anything that can access your web API or website can communicate with your actor system. You also get the benefit of the vast array of existing middleware for OWIN, ASP.NET, and other web frameworks, using prebuilt and thoroughly tested options and thus reducing the time spent developing components such as security.

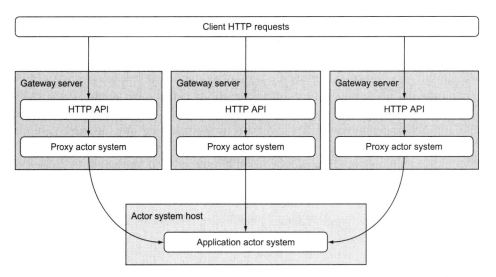

Figure 10.2 When developing a load-balanced web application, you can keep the frontends stateless by having a common actor system that the frontends all communicate with.

10.2 Integrating with SignalR

Integrating your actor system into your existing applications through a web service affords some key benefits, such as the ability to access it from almost any device. As a means of data interchange, it's relatively static, allowing clients a single-point-in-time snapshot of their data. But in an age where data flows rapidly and users want immediately responsive systems, you must periodically check whether the service has some updated data for the user. In line with the Reactive Manifesto, you want to write responsive applications and services, and that means systems that can react nearly instantaneously to changes in the environment.

Instead of waiting for the user to refresh the web page, your system would be more responsive if you quickly push changes to the client without them interacting with the application at all. Although this may not have been possible 20 years ago, the habits of users have greatly changed, inducing further changes in web browsers. One example of change is using web sockets, which provide a bidirectional persistent channel of communication between the user's web browser and the web server. Due to the persistent nature of communication, your application can push new messages to the client as soon as they arrive on the server, causing an update to the UI or notifying the user of new information.

An example is when you render charts that are plotting the data being aggregated by your system in real time. In this situation, you can push new readings to the UI, which can append them to the end of the graph, providing live visualizations of the current state. In this scenario, your actor system may receive data from IoT devices that it then acts on, performing calculations continuously and predicting the future direction of readings, which it then presents to the user.

In .NET, SignalR is the library commonly used for providing WebSocket support to web applications, including a number of abstractions over the top of the low-level WebSocket protocol. The library also offers a number of fallback mechanisms in the event that the user's web browser doesn't support WebSockets. The two abstractions provided by SignalR are *persistent connections* and *hubs*, each of which has their own valid use case:

- *Hubs*—Hubs are a means of performing remote procedure calls either from a JavaScript client to a .NET server or from a .NET server to a JavaScript client.
- *Persistent connections*—Persistent connections are sockets over which you can transfer data to clients by pushing messages through a connection on the server side.

Throughout this section, we'll look at how to use SignalR in an Akka.NET application to provide a constant stream of information to clients by using persistent connections. Although it's still possible to use hubs, persistent connections more closely match the messaging and usage patterns of an Akka.NET application. In order to use SignalR in your web application, you need to add a reference to the Microsoft.AspNet.SignalR NuGet package in the same way you added a reference to the Akka.NET libraries.

10.2.1 *Communicating through an actor*

SignalR provides a fairly advanced level of abstraction over the WebSocket protocol, allowing you to focus on the business logic rather than on accepting connections and passing data through them. But wrapping your SignalR abstraction in an actor provides benefits, the biggest being preventing concurrency bugs when clients connect and disconnect and send messages. As the SignalR connection is likely to be used in an ASP.NET application hosted on an IIS server or in a console application, a number of threads can be used to handle incoming connections. This creates the potential for data races or other concurrency problems. By wrapping your connection in an actor, you can head off these issues, as well as completely integrate your WebSocket connection with your actor system, thus benefiting from Akka.NET's remoting, routing, and supervision.

You'll first define some basic classes that represent the messages your persistent-connections actor can process. The messages fall into one of two categories: commands that tell the actor to do something (in this case, you tell the actor to send a message with the SendMessage command); and events that inform the actor that something has happened, such as the UserConnected, UserDisconnected, and MessageReceived messages in the following code. This is in line with what you've seen in other chapters where you've created messages to send to actors. You can add a number of properties that reflect the information you want to store on a per-connection basis. For example, when your persistent-connections actor receives a message, it can track the connection that sent the message; or, when a new connection is received by the server, it identifies the username of the connection and the connection identifier.

```
public class ClientDisconnected
{
    private readonly string _connectionId;

    public string ConnectionId { get { return _connectionId; } }

    public ClientDisconnected(string connectionId)
    {
        _connectionId = connectionId;
    }
}

public class ClientConnected
{
    private readonly string _connectionId;

    public string ConnectionId { get { return _connectionId; } }

    public ClientConnected(string connectionId)
    {
        _connectionId = connectionId;
    }
}

public class MessageReceived
{
    private readonly string _connectionId;
```

```
    private readonly string _data;

    public string ConnectionId { get { return _connectionId; } }
    public string Data { get { return _data; } }

    public MessageReceived(string connectionId, string data)
    {
        _connectionId = connectionId;
        _data = data;
    }
}

public class SendMessage
{
    private readonly string _connectionId;
    private readonly string _data;

    public string ConnectionId { get { return _connectionId; } }
    public string Data { get { return _data; } }

    public SendMessage(string connectionId, string data)
    {
        _connectionId = connectionId;
        _data = data;
    }
}
```

Having defined your messages, you can create a ReceiveActor that responds to them and reacts appropriately. The actor can maintain any state you want, and it will be safe from potential race conditions across all threads in the thread pool. You may want to store a unique user identifier along with the request so that you can address all of the persistent connections for a given user, thus allowing you to push messages to all of their web browser sessions.

```
public class WebsocketActor : ReceiveActor
{
    public WebsocketActor()
    {
        Receive<MessageReceived>(msg =>
        {
            //Application specific functionality
            //for receiving messages
        });

        Receive<ClientConnected>(client =>
        {
            //Application specific functionality
            //to handle client connects
        });

        Receive<ClientDisconnected>(client =>
        {
            //Application specific functionality
            //to handle client disconnects
        });
    }
}
```

You now have an actor that sends messages through a WebSocket connection so that browsers can receive push-based messages through the web server from the actor system in a web browser.

10.2.2 *Connecting to the user's web browser*

You currently have a ReceiveActor, WebsocketActor, that can handle events raised by the SignalR library, as well as handlers that allow it to push data to clients, but you have no means of sending data to clients. You need to create a SignalR connection that will allow your WebsocketActor to interact with WebSockets.

You'll create a class that inherits from SignalR's PersistentConnection class. In the following example, you create a class that overrides the default behavior when your WebsocketActor receives a message, a client connects, or a client disconnects. When one of these events happens, the method is invoked:

```
public class GraphingConnection : PersistentConnection
{
    protected override Task OnReceived(
        IRequest request,
        string connectionId,
        string data)
    {
        return base.OnReceived(request, connectionId, data);
    }

    protected override Task OnConnected(
        IRequest request,
        string connectionId)
    {
        return base.OnConnected(request, connectionId);
    }

    protected override Task OnDisconnected(
        IRequest request,
        string connectionId,
        bool stopCalled)
    {
        return base.OnDisconnected(request, connectionId, stopCalled);
    }
}
```

Having created a persistent connection class, you need to host it in the application. This functionality is provided by OWIN, as you saw in the previous section. To register the persistent connection, add a MapSignalR call into your OWIN startup class following the actor system initialization. The following example shows what the OWIN startup looks like when you have an Akka.NET actor system, SignalR, and MVC in the same project:

```
public class Startup
{
    public void Configuration(IAppBuilder appBuilder)
    {
```

```
var actorSystem = ActorSystem.Create("webapi");

appBuilder.Use((ctx, next) =>
{
    ctx.Environment["akka.actorsystem"] = actorSystem;
    return next();
}).MapSignalR<GraphingConnection>("graph");
    }
}
```

I mentioned at the start of the previous section that one reason to wrap your connection in an actor is to ensure that your application isn't susceptible to race conditions. SignalR creates a single instance of the persistent connection, but it gets executed as part of a thread pool provided by the application host, which could potentially lead to concurrent invocations of the methods on this class. To counter this, you can forward all the events to the persistent-connections actor you created earlier. Before you can send a message to it, you first need to be able to reference the actor system. By configuring SignalR after you configure the actor system in the OWIN startup, you can access it from the OWIN environment, a dictionary of strings and objects relating to the request, following the same pattern you saw in the previous section. The actor can access the OWIN environment using the `Environment` property on the incoming request on each method it overrides. Having retrieved the actor system, your actor can interact with it and send it messages. In the following example, having received a message, the actor first wraps the message in an envelope along with the connection identifier and then sends it to the persistent-connections actor, responsible for the SignalR connection:

```
protected override Task OnReceived(
    IRequest request,
    string connectionId,
    string data)
{
    var actorSystem =
        (ActorSystem)request.Environment["akka.actorsystem"];
    var websocketActor =
        actorSystem.ActorSelection("/user/messagingConnection");
    websocketActor.Tell(new MessageReceived(connectionId, data));
    return base.OnReceived(request, connectionId, data);
}
```

In addition to handling events from the connection, the persistent-connections actor handles commands that need to be processed and forwarded through the connection. In the following example, you can see how to retrieve `PersistentConnections` from the actor so you can send messages to a given client identifier in response to a `SendMessage` command:

```
var connection =
    GlobalHost
        .ConnectionManager
        .GetConnectionContext<GraphingConnection>();
```

```
Receive<SendMessage>(msg =>
{
    connection.Connection.Send(msg.ConnectionId, msg.Data);
});
```

By wrapping a lot of the behavior in the derived `PersistentConnection` class, you can remove the possibility of race conditions, thus reducing the potential number of bugs.

10.2.3 *Wrapping up*

With WebSockets, you can create end-to-end reactive web applications so users can receive updates in their frontend UI immediately after the event has been triggered in the backend system. With SignalR, you can build web applications where users can visualize and manipulate data in your actor system incredibly easily. Combining SignalR with Akka.NET allows users to see their application changing and responding to events in real time. They can act on the information they're presented with as soon as it happens without waiting for a refresh.

10.3 *Custom integrations with akka.io*

Besides the cases we've discussed, many other systems and devices may want to connect to your actor systems and send messages. HTTP has clear benefits in its uptake and support across a vast number of devices, but it proves to be fairly heavyweight due to its reliance on text rather than a simple binary protocol. In some environments, this amount of overhead could lead to difficulties. For example, in an IoT scenario where you're sending data through a cellular modem, you need to minimize the amount of data to bring down costs and avoid data loss. But you shouldn't just limit your view to IoT scenarios where there are direct benefits. If you're interoperating with other custom-developed solutions, you may see significantly reduced latencies as a result of using a simpler protocol, leading to a more responsive application, which is in line with the aims of the Manifesto.

In custom integrations, you want to provide a low-level connection to your actor system so you can operate on a socket level rather than going through a complex pipeline of operations to get a request from a user. You want your actor system to receive a message every time the socket receives a message and allow an actor to process the message instead of relying on complex code surrounding sockets, which can be difficult to correctly set up. Custom integrations allow you to quickly write tooling that relies on basic or less popular protocols. For example, by using the low-level socket APIs in Akka.NET, you can easily create implementations like DNS servers, monitoring servers, and mail servers, or implement your own protocol tailored to the requirements of your application.

Throughout this section, we'll look at how to use `akka.io` to create a socket server designed to communicate with a common metrics collection protocol known as *StatsD*. StatsD is an API that can receive counters, gauges, and timers sent to it over a network from either TCP or UDP. With this kind of low-level protocol in your actor system, you can use all the benefits Akka.NET provides, such as message routing, fault tolerance, and on-demand scaling. These features ensure that your system can react instantly to any load or failure encountered when receiving metrics, making `akka.io` an incredibly valuable tool for debugging that requires a certain degree of resiliency, even in the face of failure, in order to provide the information you need to understand the causes of failure.

The simple StatsD protocol consists of two core concepts: buckets and values. A bucket is a means of representing a metric you want to collect; for example, you may create a bucket called `UserService.Login.Latency` as a way of representing all the latencies observed when users log in through the user service. Of the number of valid metric types, in this section we'll focus on three: counters, gauges, and timers. Counters are used for basic counting tasks; some examples of metrics you may want to count include the number of requests for a web service, the number of times your system fails to retrieve a value from a cache and needs to talk to a database, and the number of times an exception was thrown. Gauges are for already averaged data. This might include things such as system load or average latency; these are things that are likely to be set once every second and don't fluctuate. Timers are used to specify the amount of time an operation took to complete; for example, the latency involved when executing a query against a database or the time it takes between a request being received from the user and a response being sent back to the user.

The StatsD implementation requires a line of text to be sent to the socket as part of a single packet sent over the network, the basic structure of which is shown in the following example. It includes the bucket name, a value for it, and the type of metric it is. You provide a string for each component. These can be anything for the bucket name and value, and then the final part matches a string representation of each of the metric types. This can be sent over either a TCP or UDP socket, depending on what the server is configured to listen on.

```
<metricname>:<value>|<type>
UserService.RequestCount:50|c
```

Having created an implementation of the protocol in Akka.NET, you can dispatch the received metrics to anywhere else in your actor system to perform tasks such as data storage, stats aggregation, and notifications. But we'll focus on the actual task of ingestion and how you can map incoming packets over to messages that can be used in the context of your actor system.

10.3.1 Creating a listening socket

`akka.io` provides support for a number of different scenarios based on factors such as whether your system should be listening for incoming packets or sending packets over the socket, as well as the socket protocol it should be listening on. Although TCP and UDP support is provided as pluggable transport in the Akka.NET distribution, you can also create your own transport mechanism to reflect other networking technologies. For example, you may want to create an `akka.io` transport that can communicate over a pipe rather than a socket, or use a socket with a different transport protocol than UDP or TCP, such as SPDY. In this example, you'll use the TCP socket for one thing only: listening for incoming messages.

Before your actor system can receive messages over a socket, you need to tell the OS that you want any messages received on a certain port to be forwarded to your application. You'll use the `TcpManager`, which handles all of the bind operations to get the OS to route TCP packets to the application. The `TcpManager` is made available through an extension method on the actor system itself and is accessed through the TCP extension method on the system. In the following example, you get the reference to the `TcpManager`, which then allows the actor system to bind to a specific port:

```
public class StatsDServer : ReceiveActor
{
    public StatsDServer()
    {
        var tcpManager = Context.System.Tcp();
    }
}
```

The typical approach to building socket servers with `akka.io` is to have a server actor that's responsible for port binding, as well as handling incoming connection requests from the socket, before passing the network connection to another actor, which deals with the specifics of that one connection. Figure 10.3 demonstrates how to design such a system. A server actor deals with incoming messages from the `TcpManager` relating to the status of the connection. This includes binding success or failure messages, incoming connection requests, and socket errors. The server actor has a number of children that are spawned on a per-connection basis. As you saw in chapter 3, actors are a very cheap abstraction, so you can create millions of them in a single application.

The first component of figure 10.3 is the server actor, which is responsible for communication with the `TcpManager`. The server actor tells the `TcpManager` where to send

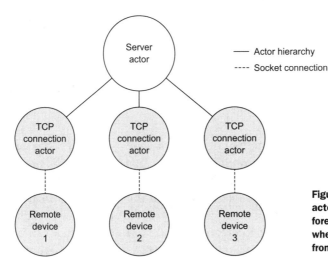

Figure 10.3 `akka.io` creates an actor per network connection, forestalling concurrency problems when the system receives messages from multiple senders simultaneously.

all new incoming connections. It sends the `TcpManager` a `Bind` message with a refer-ence to the actor that should receive new messages, as well as the incoming endpoint on which to listen for packets. In the following example, you create a TCP-connection actor that's responsible for server-related responsibilities, and send a message to the `TcpManager` telling it that this new actor should receive incoming connection requests:

```
tcpManager.Tell(new Tcp.Bind(Self, new IPEndPoint(IPAddress.Any, 8080)));
```

With this accomplished, your new TCP-connection actor needs to receive incoming messages containing incoming connections. A new actor typically receives two mes-sages during initialization: `Bound` and `Connected`. `Bound` is sent when the socket lis-tener has been established and is able to start receiving incoming connections. The `Bound` message contains the socket address that the OS is listening on. When a new connection is established with the TCP listener, a new actor is spawned in the actor system, which is responsible for handling all of the low-level socket tasks, such as mes-sage serialization, buffering, and any other tasks. This actor sends a message to the server actor, informing it that a new connection is available. Then the server actor can register an actor that should receive the deserialized messages from this connection. You could choose to register them in the server actor, but in the following example, you create a new actor that's responsible for that single connection. This decision allows you to process more packets in parallel while also getting all the benefits of sin-gle actors, including finite state machines, which may be useful for complex situations that use involved handshake protocols. In the following example, you spawn a new communication actor that's responsible for each incoming connection and for responding to incoming messages:

```
Receive<Tcp.Bound>(bound =>
{
    Console.WriteLine("The connection was bound to port 8080");
});

Receive<Tcp.Connected>(connected =>
{
    var connectionActor =
        Context.ActorOf(Props.Create(() => new StatsDServerChannel()));
    Sender.Tell(new Tcp.Register(connectionActor));
});
```

Having created an actor hierarchy with one actor per connection, the actor system can process incoming information from each actor. When a TCP-connection actor receives an incoming packet, `akka.io` first reassembles the complete TCP message, which may have been split across several packets, before sending it, wrapped in a `Received` message, to the actor registered to the given connection. You can then access the bytes transferred over the network through the `Data` property of the `Received` message. From here, you can convert it into an appropriate format. This may include leaving the message in a binary format, converting it into a text format, or deserializing into an object graph with tools such as Google's Protocol Buffers or other binary-serialization tooling. In this case, you convert the message to an ASCII string, because this matches the specification as laid out by StatsD. In the following example, you can convert the received `ByteString` into a parsable string and take the appropriate action:

```
Receive<Tcp.Received>(packet =>
{
    var statsDData = packet.Data.DecodeString();
    HandleStatsDData(statsDData);
});
```

With metrics data in your actor system, you can use other Akka.NET features to better understand the data. You may want to create an actor for each bucket that will be responsible for aggregating the incoming data and creating alerts based on that data; you may want to ingest it into other systems or databases for easier metrics analysis or visualization.

10.3.2 *Sending data through akka.io*

Having created a socket that is capable of listening, you may want to open a connection to a socket listening at a remote endpoint. You may want to create a low-level socket implementation, but because you have `akka.io`, you can bring your client socket connection into the actor system, following many of the same principles you saw when you created a socket capable of listening for incoming data. You can follow many of the same ideas, but as one client is only able to connect to one server, you can simplify it further.

When you created a server, the first step was to bind it to a socket so your actor system could receive incoming messages, but when developing a client designed to consume a socket, your system must connect to the remote endpoint before it can send data. To connect to a remote socket, your server retrieves a reference to the `Tcp-Manager`, which is responsible for handling all of the low-level socket management, and sends it a `Connect` message. In the following example, you create an actor that's responsible for communicating with the server. It does this by sending a message to the `TcpManager` actor, with the endpoint that the server is listening on. The endpoint consists of two key pieces of information: the IP address of the remote host and the port on which it's listening.

```
var serverEndpoint =
    new IPEndPoint(
        IPAddress.Parse("127.0.0.1"),
        8080);
tcpManager.Tell(new Tcp.Connect(serverEndpoint));
```

A new connection is created, and the actor that's requesting a connection is informed of whether the connection was successful or not. If the connection was unsuccessful, it receives a `CommandFailed` message with a string representation of the issue. But if the connection was successful, then the requesting actor receives a message with both the remote endpoint for communicating and the local endpoint the connection was opened on, and it can start the communication with the server. Every message the sender wants to pass is forwarded through the socket. In the following example, you can see how to use the switchable behavior functionality of an actor to communicate with the server by having a different behavior for connected and unconnected states. The actor can receive a variety of messages relating to either the connection itself or other actors in the system who want to communicate with the socket.

```
Receive<Tcp.Connected>(msg =>
{
    Sender.Tell(new Tcp.Register(Self));
    Become(Connected(Sender));
});

Receive<Tcp.CommandFailed>(msg =>
{
    Console.WriteLine("Failed to connect to remote endpoint");
});
```

Now that you have a client connection through your server endpoint, your actor system can start communicating with a remote server. You've already seen the StatsD protocol, and you'll now see how to communicate with a server running the protocol. With a client in your actor system that communicates with the StatsD server, the server can ingest metrics with little effort. This means that you can persist metrics such as the time taken to process certain message types or the number of messages an actor has processed. The following example shows how your actor system can receive messages and send them through the socket: it sends a `Tcp.Write` message to a coordinating actor, with a `ByteString` that contains the message data. You can create a `ByteString` from other `ByteStrings`, an array, or a string, meaning that you can easily serialize the ASCII strings required by the StatsD protocol. But there may be other situations in which your actor system receives a message from the socket: an IO error if the network connection was physically cut; a peer reset error if the other party quickly quit the application without first closing the connection; or if the remote party normally disconnects. In these cases, the coordinating actor sends a message relating to the cause of the problem. For example, if a peer reset occurs, a `Tcp.PeerReset` message is sent; or if a network error occurs, a `Tcp.IOError` is sent. Your actor system can handle these errors and respond appropriately. For example, it may cache incoming messages until it can reconnect, and then send them once the connection has been reestablished. In this case, you write a message to the log that the connection was reset:

```
private Action Connected(IActorRef connection)
{
    return () =>
    {
        Receive<string>(msg =>
        {
            var write = Tcp.Write.Create(ByteString.FromString(msg));
            connection.Tell(write);
        });
    };
}
```

Although the example here focuses on connecting to an Akka.NET socket server, the implementation that you've created can connect to any StatsD servers that use TCP, because you're not constrained to connecting to other actor systems. You're also not limited to using the StatsD protocol, and you can implement clients for any protocol sent over a network. For example, you could just as easily create a client that interoperates with an SMTP server to send and receive emails, or a DNS server providing IP addresses for domain names.

10.3.3 *Wrapping up*

In this section, you created a socket connection on both a server actor system and a client actor system, allowing communication between the two. Although you could have used the Akka.Remote features you saw in chapter 8, this would have limited your system to connecting with other Akka.NET actor systems, but akka.io allows input on a common protocol, in this instance StatsD, so other clients can connect and publish metrics. You can use other technologies where appropriate, for example, shell scripts when you want to monitor OS-level metrics, or use clients available in other languages such as Java or Ruby, allowing you to receive metrics from any system in your system architecture.

By using akka.io, you quickly and easily set up a high-performance, low-level socket connection for receiving messages sent from applications outside of the actor system, with minimal overhead, low latency, and immediate availability. This level of abstraction helps to remove many of the complexities of networked applications. By having a well-known, easy-to-use API, your system can receive messages from the network in a performant manner without deep technical knowledge of the OS kernel and how it handles packets received from the network.

10.4 *Case study: IO, integration, IoT applications*

Increasingly, IoT devices are used in hostile environments where you don't have many of the conveniences of a traditional software project. For example, when designing systems, you expect high-speed broadband connections between client and server. But as you seek data from remote environments, you're likely to encounter low speed, low bandwidth, and high latency from operating over older cellular connections. You must choose the correct protocol for transferring data over the network. In typical scenarios, you might choose HTTP, but in hostile environments, you'll use a low-level protocol, specialized for the task at hand, focusing on minimizing the packet size.

You can use the IO components of Akka.NET to use actors for simplifying the acquisition of data from a network socket and immediately processing it with your actor system. From here, you can decompress or deserialize the contents of the network packet and push it to other actors in the system. This allows you to perform complex logic on actors that process the messages as .NET objects.

As an example, one of the tasks relating to IoT workflows is receiving time-series data and performing complex event processing on it to understand historical data and predict future trends. In figure 10.4, a number of IoT devices are deployed in a field on a farm. These devices monitor the moisture of soil and weather data over time, which they periodically upload to an Akka.NET system in the cloud. This system aggregates the data from multiple devices and calculates predictions based on the current data and historical data to ascertain whether irrigation should be switched on. Given that these devices are deployed in rural locations outside of major population centers, it's likely that the only internet connection available will be through a cellular connection, probably 2G or EDGE. As such, you'll have to use a protocol that prioritizes small packet sizes because of the high cost of cellular data and the low bandwidth available. Figure 10.4 shows how you can create an actor that receives data from a network socket and passes it to an actor dedicated to processing the event data from each device. Other actors can aggregate data from clusters of devices, if necessary.

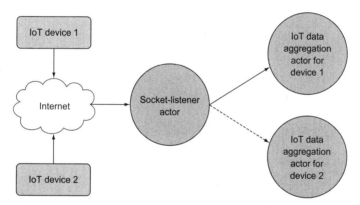

Figure 10.4   IoT applications operating in hostile environments may be subject to bandwidth constraints. By opening a direct socket into your actor system, you have the opportunity to create a custom protocol relevant to the circumstances.

Using the IO components of Akka.NET, you can simplify the ingestion of data from a network source that might not have a preexisting network client. Despite the complexities typically associated with low-level socket programming, the IO components in Akka.NET allow you to treat a socket as another actor.

Summary

In this chapter, you learned

- How Akka.NET can be combined with other tools, such as a web API and SignalR, to build reactive applications
- How to use `akka.io` to treat sockets as first-class components of an actor system

11

Storing actor state with Akka.Persistence

This chapter covers

- Adding a persistent backing data store to an actor to save its state
- The concepts behind event sourcing
- Creating evolvable applications using Akka.Persistence and event sourcing

Throughout the book so far, you've developed a wide variety of actors designed to operate in a number of different scenarios—both small, isolated actors and larger systems such as e-commerce applications. All these actors share a common trait: they exist as an abstraction over the top of application memory. Although actors incorporate desirable attributes such as message queues, processing, and state, the primary purpose of an actor system is to support concurrent workloads and reduce the surface area on which concurrency bugs can occur.

For every actor you've created so far, the actor's state has been ephemeral, and if the actor shuts down, upon restart it returns to the state it had when it was created. But sometimes you need an actor to be more resilient and return to the last state it had before it shut down. Actors in Akka.NET can be shut down for a wide range of reasons: you might need to relocate the actor onto a different actor system because you're running low on resources; you might take the approach of failing fast and letting Akka.NET restart the actor in the event of an error; or you might need to shut the application down when you want to upgrade it, which will cause all of the actors in the actor system to shut down.

In all of these instances, you need to have systems in place so that you can re-create an actor's state as and when required. Let's consider the example of the shopping cart of previous chapters. An actor represents the user's shopping cart and stores references to items in the actor's state; you want to ensure that the user continues to see those items in their cart as they move around the website. If your system experiences a failure that crashes the entire application, when it restarts, you want the user to see all their items in their shopping cart. From a business perspective, if a user spent a lot of time browsing the website adding items to their cart and then lost them, their irritation may result in taking their business elsewhere.

This presents a challenge: you must enable tasks related to saving and recovering an actor's internal state. You need to move the shopping cart actor's internal state into a persistent storage system such as a database or a filesystem. You also need to be able to re-create the actor's internal state from the persisted state. Fortunately, the Akka.Persistence tool lets you write actors that can persist state and recover it from a variety of file stores, ranging from SQL and NoSQL databases to flat files in a filesystem; you also have the ability to plug in alternative data stores. In this chapter, we'll look at how to write applications in which actors can store and recover state, thanks to Akka.Persistence.

11.1 *Understanding event sourcing*

Before you start using Akka.Persistence, it's important to understand how state is persisted to the data store. An actor's state is an abstraction over some location in the computer's RAM. In many applications, you persist this location in memory to a database table, with an object relational mapper (ORM). This pattern, known as the *active record pattern* (see figure 11.1), has become a common approach due to its simplicity, but it presents a number of problems: notably, object-relational impedance mismatch, whereby objects in memory don't map directly onto database tables.

Figure 11.1 The active record pattern relies on mapping an in-memory object into an object in a data store that mutations are then saved to.

You can therefore consider the internal state to be nothing more than an initial state along with a number of changes in the form of events. Although this might sound relatively obscure, this idea forms the basis for systems that are hundreds of years old. For example, with accounting records, rather than record the total money in the account at a point in time, you instead maintain a log of all the transactions that have taken place against that account. This includes all debits from the account to their destination, and the credits into the account from their origin. This provides vastly improved traceability and auditing capabilities than what you would achieve with the active record approach, in which you have a line representing the amount of money in the account. You can also rebuild the state, in this case representing the total money in the account, by reapplying every event onto the starting state.

This conceptual model isn't limited to the accounting world, and a number of systems in software development also rely on these ideas: for example, a Git source-control repository. It has an initial state (an empty directory) along with a number of changes to files in that directory. You might add files to the directory as you develop an application, make changes to files to add new functionality, or remove files entirely. Every time you commit a change to the repository, you have a point-in-time snapshot of the state. This model of persisting changes is significantly more lightweight for source-control systems, as you may need to rebuild the state at a snapshot point. Although you could store the whole repository's contents at each snapshot point, it would rapidly expand to become a huge file.

The active record pattern isn't limited to source-control technology; you can apply the model to the applications you write. Let's reconsider the shopping cart example. The shopping cart has an internal state: the items contained in it as a result of the user adding and removing items. By persisting these events, you can rebuild them into the current list of items. Figure 11.2 shows how to represent a shopping cart actor as a process over time during which events are applied to the state, resulting in a new state. As you scan from left to right, you can see how events are applied, starting with an empty shopping cart and then adding a television; then, adding a laptop and removing the television. At each stage along the way, you can see the state of the shopping cart. This provides significantly enhanced observability of system changes, as well as the ability to audit historical changes, if needed. As you have an ordered list of all the changes that exist in your application, you can pass the list to another actor, and as the new actor replays the events, each event will produce a state equal to the original one. When using active record systems, you don't get this level of historical detail and so can't correct historical errors as easily, resulting in invalid data.

This model, known as *event sourcing*, sits at the heart of Akka.Persistence and provides the basis for persisting and recovering actor state as part of a larger actor system. Throughout the rest of this chapter, we'll look at how to use Akka.Persistence to create actors that follow the event-sourcing model.

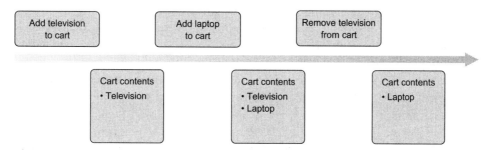

Figure 11.2   You can think of a shopping cart's state as the result of applying events to it from an initial state.

11.2   Using Akka.Persistence

To use Akka.Persistence, you first need to install the library files; again, the library is provided through NuGet and can be installed from the Akka.Persistence package. Having installed the library, you can begin writing actors based on the actor types provided by Akka.Persistence.

11.2.1   Writing persistent actors

The `PersistentActor`, a variation of the actors you've seen, lies at the heart of Akka .Persistence. You've used `ReceiveActor` to write actors as handlers matched to message types, and the specialized `FSMActor` to create a finite state machine. `PersistentActor` is another specialized actor with a specific use: persistence. To create an actor that has a backing store, you define an actor that inherits from the `PersistentActor` class and implement the required methods on it. The following example shows how to define a shopping cart actor responsible for storing items a user adds to their shopping cart. The actor has a number of additional methods as part of the contract:

```
using Akka.Persistence;

public class ShoppingCartActor : PersistentActor
{
    public override string PersistenceId { get { throw new
    NotImplementedException(); } }

    protected override bool ReceiveCommand(object message)
    {
            throw new NotImplementedException();
    }
    protected override bool ReceiveRecover(object message)
    {
        throw new NotImplementedException();
    }
}
```

The first requirement is a persistence ID, the value that Akka.Persistence uses as its means of identification when it persists state into a database. It's important that the persistence ID is unique on a per-actor basis; otherwise, you may muddle state and events between two distinct actors, leading to unexpected behavior. You can choose an ID based on the actor's location in the actor hierarchy, or the actor's name if the name is unique. In the following example, you give the actor a persistence ID of `"shoppingcart"` because the application will have only one shopping cart. In a production environment, you'll have many shopping cart actors, and you'll need to uniquely identify each one. This may be either a generated GUID or an integer representing it. The persistence ID is also used to recover the state for the actor, so it's important to use a deterministically generated identifier. This might mean having a parent actor responsible for persisting all the actors that exist below it.

```
public override string PersistenceId { get { return "shoppingcart"; } }
```

This shopping cart actor also implements the `ReceiveCommand` method. `Receive-Command` is analogous to the `Receive` method that you implemented earlier in some actor instances. Notice that this method is called `ReceiveCommand` and not `ReceiveEvent`, despite the fact that Akka.Persistence embodies the concept of *event* sourcing. The reasoning behind this is the distinction between *commands* and *events* in event sourcing. Although the two seem similar, there's a subtle difference between them:

- *Commands*—Commands are directives telling an actor to do something. In the case of the shopping cart, you'll pass it the command `AddItem`. Commands are named in an imperative manner: they direct the target to do something.
- *Events*—Events are the outcomes of commands. If the shopping cart is told to add an item, then the direct outcome of that command is an `ItemAdded` event. Events are named in the past tense: they're the result of a completed action.

This might seem unnecessary, but consider what happens if an actor has to perform some additional actions while it's working. In the shopping cart example, it doesn't need to do anything beyond adding/deleting items in its internal state, but in a more complex example, it will probably need to perform more operations. For example, it may need to post a message onto a message queue for an external system to process. If the actor were to post that message onto the queue every time it processes an event, then it might enqueue the same message multiple times because of reprocessing the event every time it recovers its state. By splitting sourcing into commands and events, you can more easily handle the outcome of actions.

The following code example shows the code that needs to be added to an actor that receives commands and emits events as a result. It receives the command `AddItem` containing an item identifier representing a stock number, as well as the number of items to add. The actor matches on the incoming message and performs the appropriate action. In this case, it creates the `ItemAdded` event, which contains the stock number as well as the total number of items to add. After creating the event, the actor persists it by calling the `Persist` method with an event and a handler. Upon calling `Persist`, the message is written into what Akka.NET calls a *journal*. The journal is an ordered log of all events for a given persistence ID. The handler is executed when the event is successfully stored, and is where the internal state of the actor is modified. In this case, you add the items to a dictionary of all of the stored items.

```
class AddItem
{
    public string ItemId { get; }
    public int ItemCount { get; }

    public AddItem(string itemId, int itemCount)
    {
        ItemId = itemId;
        ItemCount = itemCount;
    }
}

class ItemAdded
{
    public string ItemId { get; }
    public int ItemCount { get; }

    public ItemAdded(string itemId, int itemCount)
    {
        ItemId = itemId;
        ItemCount = itemCount;
    }
}

protected override bool ReceiveCommand(object message)
{
    if (message is AddItem)
    {
        var msg = (AddItem)message;
        var itemAddedEvent = new ItemAdded(msg.ItemId, msg.ItemCount);
        Persist(itemAddedEvent, HandleEvent);
        return true;
    }
    return false;
}

private void HandleEvent(object @event)
{
    if (@event is ItemAdded)
    {
        var evt = (ItemAdded)@event;
        if (_items.ContainsKey(evt.ItemId))
        {
            var currentCount = _items[evt.ItemId];
            var newCount = currentCount + evt.ItemCount;
            _items[evt.ItemId] = newCount;
        }
        else
        {
            _items[evt.ItemId] = evt.ItemCount;
        }
    }
}
```

A note on stashing

You saw in chapter 4 how to create a message stash for your actors. With Akka
.Persistence, the actor already has a stash defined, which it uses to store incoming
messages when a persist operation is already in progress. This can interfere with
some of the methods that shut down an actor. For example, you saw how to shut
down an actor by sending it a `PoisonPill` message, but this message is handled by
the actor *system*, meaning that the `PoisonPill` will be handled even if there are
other messages currently in the stash awaiting processing. The way to handle this
problem is to create a dedicated message used for handling shutdown in persistent
actors, for which the command calls `Context.Stop`. You can see an example of how
you might handle that in the following code:

```
class Shutdown { }

protected override bool ReceiveCommand(object message)
{
    if(message is Shutdown)
    {
        Context.Stop(Self);
        return true;
    }
}
```

Now that you have a system in place for handling commands, generating events, and
persisting those events, you need a way to handle those events if the application is
recovering from a failure. You can do so by implementing the `ReceiveRecover`
method, which receives events from an event journal after an actor is restarted.
During recovery, commands received by the actor are stashed so that they're handled
after the state has fully recovered. This gives you the ability to modify the state in line
with what you saw previously when modifying the state in a command handler, in the
example preceding this sidebar.

Now, whenever you create a new instance of this actor type, `PersistentActor`
checks the event journal to see whether events have already been persisted. If they
have, the persisted events are sent to the actor to be handled through the `Receive-`
`Recover` method. In this method, the actor can match on the event and update the
state, depending on the type of event received. The following example shows matching on the event type and updating the state exactly as when you wrote command
handlers:

```
protected override bool ReceiveRecover(object message)
{
    if(message is ItemAdded)
    {
        HandleEvent(message);
        return true;
    }
    return false;
}
```

During the actor's lifecycle, you can check what state the actor is in: recovery mode and receiving persisted events, or regular operational mode and receiving commands from other actors. `IsRecovering` tells you the actor is still recovering, and `IsRecovery-Complete` tells you the actor can process commands received the usual way.

```
if(this.IsRecovering)
{
    //Perform specific logic for when the actor is in the
    recovering state
}
else if(this.IsRecoveryComplete)
{
    //Perform specific logic for when the actor has finished
    recovering it's state
}
```

You can proactively determine the status of recovery with the `RecoveryCompleted` event, which is sent to the `ReceiveRecover` method when the system has successfully processed all incoming events. For this, you create a further match case that handles the `RecoveryCompleted` event:

```
protected override bool ReceiveRecover(object message)
{
    if(message is RecoveryCompleted)
    {
        //Perform specific actions once the actor state has been
        recovered
    }
    if(message is ItemAdded)
    {
        HandleEvent(message);
        return true;
    }
    return false;
}
```

As you can see, some additional concepts are involved when you use Akka .Persistence actors, but not many changes are required to create an actor that can persist all of its changes to a database and then recover that state upon a restart.

11.2.2 Configuring a journal

In the previous section, you saw how events are persisted to a data store, or, in Akka.Persistence parlance, a journal. This journal can be a SQL or NoSQL database or another option, but, by default, Akka.NET persists events to a short-term data-storage structure in memory, which is deleted if the application is closed. If you want to change this setting, you need to modify the HOCON configuration in a manner similar to what you saw in chapter 5.

Various plugins are provided for persisting journal events, but in this example, you'll look at how to store them in a Microsoft SQL Server–supported journal. To use this journal, you first install actors to communicate with it, by installing the Akka .Persistence.SQLServer package from NuGet.

Now, you need to configure the journal for communication by adding it to your HOCON configuration file. You follow the same process of creating a configuration file and using it as you did in chapter 5, but you modify it to add settings for Akka .Persistence. The following example shows how to specify SQL Server as the journal to use and how to connect to it by specifying the connection string. You create a dedicated configuration section in the Akka.Persistence settings for the journal, where you specify the journal to use, which is a location in the configuration file. The specified location contains two pieces of information: the class to use as the persistence journal (in this case, the SqlServerJournal class) and the connection string to the database for persisting state.

```
akka {
    persistence {
        journal {
            # SQL Server journal plugin.
            sql-server {
                # Class name of the plugin.
                class = "Akka.Persistence.SqlServer.Journal.SqlServerJournal,
    Akka.Persistence.SqlServer"

                # Dispatcher for the plugin actor.
                plugin-dispatcher = "akka.actor.default-dispatcher"

                # The connection to the SQL server database which will store
    the persisted events.
                connection-string = "<SQL Server Connection string>"
            }
        }

        snapshot-store {
            sql-server {
                # Class name of the plugin.
                class =
    "Akka.Persistence.SqlServer.Snapshot.SqlServerSnapshotStore,
    Akka.Persistence.SqlServer"

                # Dispatcher for the plugin actor.
                plugin-dispatcher = ""akka.actor.default-dispatcher""

                # The connection to the SQL server database which will store
    the persisted snapshots.
                connection-string = ""
            }
        }
    }
}
```

In this example, you used SQL Server as the data-store journal, but you can choose from a wide variety of plugins, including Postgres, Azure Table Storage, Azure Blob Storage, and others. In addition, the Akka.NET community has created many plugins for various databases. You can also create custom journals in the event that one doesn't already exist for your data store of choice, but that's beyond the scope of this book.

11.2.3 Wrapping up

In this section, you've seen how to build actors backed by a journal that stores events, and how to specify your journal of choice. In the rest of this chapter, we'll dive deeper into some of the more advanced features of Akka.NET that give you better performance from data, and different overviews of data.

11.3 Akka.Persistence performance tuning

Although the performance of Akka.Persistence is just as good as the active record approach in most situations, sometimes you'll want to increase the message throughput of persistent actors. In this section, you'll see a couple of approaches that can help you to make the most of the library and continue to use it in cases where you might otherwise be strained.

11.3.1 Snapshot stores

Although event-sourced applications provide plenty of advantages, there are also downsides, one of which is how much time it can take to recover internal state. As the state is computed by applying events in the order they were persisted, when a huge number of events are persisted, it will take longer and longer to recover the state.

Consider the example of an indecisive customer using their shopping cart. Because your system stores every change to the actor's state, if a customer repeatedly adds and removes items from their cart, a large number of events can quickly build up. If many items are involved, as might be the case for a grocery store cart, this could lead to a lot of events. As more events are added, it takes more time to retrieve them all from the data store, and they must be applied sequentially.

A situation like this could make it difficult to maintain a reactive Akka.Persistence application. You saw in the previous section how the actor stashes incoming messages while it's in the process of recovering state. This presents a problem if an actor needs to recover state frequently, for example, if it fails frequently. If an actor takes seconds to recover state as a result of many events, then it's unable to respond to messages from other actors until it has completed its recovery. If you're building applications that require low latency to ensure responsiveness, then having operations block for several seconds isn't ideal.

With Akka.Persistence, you can use a snapshot store, which stores snapshots of actor state at specific points in time, allowing an actor to replay states from those points. You can see an example of this in figure 11.3. Rather than recovering every event from the beginning of the actor's lifecycle, the actor can choose the latest snapshot and replay events from that point on.

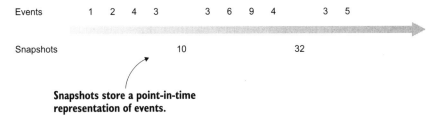

Figure 11.3   Snapshots allow you to limit the number of events that must be replayed every time a persistent actor needs to recover its internal state.

To store a snapshot in a persistent actor, you call the `SaveSnapshot` message with whatever you want as the state. In the shopping cart example, you would choose to store your dictionary of items and item counts. But you don't want to store a snapshot after every event, because there's no garbage collection of historical snapshots; they accumulate in the database. Instead, you should save a snapshot either after a certain number of events have been emitted or after a certain period of time has elapsed since the last message. In the following example, you keep track of how many messages have been handled since the last stored snapshot, and if a maximum is exceeded, then you persist a new snapshot. In contrast to event persistence, snapshots are persisted asynchronously, so other messages can be processed while snapshots are persisted. This is because snapshots are designed as an optimization technique rather than a primary storage mechanism.

```
private int _eventsProcessed = 0;

private void HandleEvent(object @event)
{
    if (@event is ItemAdded)
    {
        //Event logic
        _eventsProcessed++;
    }
    if(_eventsProcessed > 10)
    {
        SaveSnapshot(_items);
        _eventsProcessed = 0;
    }
    return false;
}
```

Having saved a snapshot, you need to recover the actor's state from the snapshot itself instead of replaying events from the beginning of the actor's lifecycle. For the recovery stage, you need a new type of message. If a snapshot exists for the persistence ID of an actor, the message first retrieves the latest snapshot and the event associated with the snapshot. These are presented to the actor as part of a `SnapshotOffer` message. The actor can access the state persisted through the `Snapshot` property on the

message. The following example shows how to set the actor's state from the received
`SnapshotOffer` message:

```
protected override bool ReceiveRecover(object message)
{
    if(message is SnapshotOffer)
    {
        var snapshot = (SnapshotOffer)message;
        _items = (Dictionary<string, int>)snapshot.Snapshot;
        return true;
    }

    if(message is ItemAdded)
    {
        HandleEvent(message);
        return true;
    }
    return false;
}
```

After the snapshot offer has been received, the persistent actor is then sent events that
follow the sequence number of the snapshot, if any. This means that it can continue
receiving events to recover to the latest state.

Snapshots allow you to reduce the time it takes to recover to the latest state by
maintaining history at a specific point in time. But it's important to understand that
they exist as an optimization technique rather than as a basis for storage.

11.3.2 *Async write journals*

You saw in the previous section how, by using the `Persist` method on a persistent
actor, you can supply an event and a callback that then persists an event and executes
the callback on completion. You also saw how the actor stashes incoming messages
until the write on the last event has completed, ensuring the operation remains consistent. This technique is ideal for most situations, because you get good-enough performance, but in some situations, any form of blocking causes the response time to
grow rapidly; for example, when large numbers of writes go through the system at one
time. In these cases, blocking can cause the queue of incoming messages to rapidly
grow, causing system failure.

To handle this situation, Akka.NET supplies the `PersistAsync` method, which
sends a request to the write journal containing the event to write. You once again supply an action for when the write request completes, but the main difference from
`Persist` is that when you use the `PersistAsync` method, while the write request is in
flight, the actor can process the next message in its mailbox. This does, however,
necessitate a relaxed consistency guarantee. In synchronous persistence, the application will only handle the next message if it was able to successfully write the last event
to the journal. If the write failed for any reason, such as a database being unavailable,
then the next message isn't processed. But when using asynchronous persistence, an
actor continues to process messages without any guarantee that the state has been

written. This makes it ideal when you're receiving vast amounts of data, some of which you can afford to lose. One example of this is writing and aggregating log or metrics data. In these cases, you ideally want to record all the data for later use, but losing several minutes of data is acceptable if it means the system doesn't fail.

You can see an example of using `PersistAsync` in the next example, where you write an event asynchronously to the event journal. The rest of the actor stays the same, and you change the call to `Persist` to a call to `PersistAsync`:

```
protected override bool ReceiveCommand(object message)
{
    if (message is AddItem)
    {
        var msg = (AddItem)message;
        var itemAddedEvent = new ItemAdded(msg.ItemId, msg.ItemCount);
        PersistAsync(itemAddedEvent, HandleEvent);
        return true;
    }
    return false;
}
```

`PersistAsync` rapidly increases message throughput for an actor by allowing the actor to process other messages while waiting on writes to complete. Be mindful of the potential effect this could have on the actor, and if consistency is a core requirement of the actor, then other alternatives should be investigated before choosing asynchronous write journals.

11.3.3 *Wrapping up*

When an actor needs to recover state frequently, you can use a snapshot store, which allows an actor to replay states from specific points in time. Snapshots allow you to recover to the latest state by maintaining history at a specific point in time. When your system is processing a large numbers of writes, waiting on persistence can cause blocking as the queue of incoming messages grows. The `PersistAsync` method allows an actor to handle the next message instead of waiting for the previous one to be persisted.

11.4 *Akka.Persistence performance tuning*

Akka.Persistence is incredibly fast in its own right, but under certain circumstances, the default configuration is unfortunately not as fast as an active-record approach. You can counter this with a number of provided features. You've seen how using snapshot stores helps decrease recovery time for an actor restart. You've also seen how to relax the consistency of your actors by using asynchronous write journals, allowing them to handle more write operations on events in less time.

11.4.1 *At-least-once delivery*

You 1113.290 saw in chapter 6 that there are a number of ways an actor can counter problems. In the wake of errors, supervisors and supervision strategies can restore actors. If message-passing fails in an asynchronous messaging application, you can

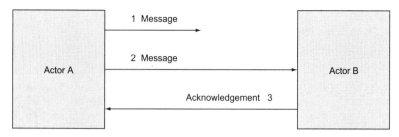

Figure 11.4 An at-least-once delivery actor system continuously resends a message to a target actor until it eventually receives an acknowledgement in reply.

build an actor responsible for receiving acknowledgements from the target to guarantee message processing. If an actor fails to receive an acknowledgement in response to a message, it resends the message until an acknowledgement is returned.

This is known as at-least-once messaging, because the message is delivered repeatedly until its processing is confirmed (see figure 11.4). This is contrary to the typical Akka.NET approach to messaging whereby you send at most one message, and it acts in a fire-and-forget manner. Such an actor is satisfactory for small cases, but there are significant edge cases that can occur in asynchronous distributed systems, and such a protocol needs guarantees that it will continue to operate even in the face of adversity. Fortunately, as part of the Akka.Persistence library, Akka.NET provides a thoroughly tested and developed solution for delivering messages at least once.

The at-least-once delivery system in Akka.Persistence permits other features, such as persisting whether the target has correctly received the message in the event that the application fails and the entire actor system is shut down. This provides even stronger fault tolerance guarantees than those you saw when you developed a simple solution for blue-sky scenarios. In this section, we'll look at how to use the at-least-once delivery actor in Akka.Persistence to develop actors that can resend messages until they are successfully processed.

An actor that attempts delivery multiple times must inherit from the AtLeast-OnceDeliveryActor. This actor provides a number of additional features on top of those provided by a PersistentActor, which makes it easier for you to develop actors with different delivery semantics. In this section, we'll consider a trivial example where the actor sends a string to a remote target and waits for a response. This relates to real-life scenarios where you can't afford to lose an update, such as when deducting money from a user's account or when performing an update that must succeed. The following code shows the shell of the actor you'll create, which inherits from the AtLeastOnceDeliveryActor class:

```
class CustomDeliveryActor : AtLeastOnceDeliveryActor
{
    public override string PersistenceId { get { throw new
    NotImplementedException(); } }
```

```
protected override bool ReceiveCommand(object message)
{
    throw new NotImplementedException();
}

protected override bool ReceiveRecover(object message)
{
    throw new NotImplementedException();
}
}
```

In the same way as with the persistent actor definition, you supply a `PersistenceId` that's used to persist and recover state. Follow the same restrictions you saw when dealing with persistent actors, and ensure that the `persistenceId` is deterministic and is recoverable between actor restarts. In this case, you hardcode the `persistenceId`, but in production environments, you need to ensure that it's unique across multiple actor instances:

```
public override string PersistenceId { get { return "GuaranteedSender"; } }
```

Similar to the persistent actor, at-least-once delivery actor commands must be handled; in this case, two commands—the request to send a message to a target and the confirmation message received from the target. You'll use a fixed target that will receive all messages, and you'll operate on the basis that any strings the delivery actor receives will be treated as data to be sent to the target actor. Coming up is an example of this in which the delivery actor matches on the incoming data. If it's a string, then it creates a new `MessageSent` event, and if it receives a `Confirm` command, then it creates a `MessageConfirmed` event. You also need to handle the recovery of events in the same manner as with a persistent actor to restore state if the actor fails. In this case, the operations you perform on events are the same as with a persistent actor when you're recovering state as well as when you're emitting events. You can create a common method that both the command handler and recovery use for each of the events. The following example shows the method definitions alongside the command handler and recovery code that calls the `UpdateState` method:

```
protected override bool ReceiveCommand(object message)
{
    if(message is string)
    {
        Persist(new MessageSent((string)message), Handler);
        return true;
    }
    else if(message is Confirm)
    {
        Persist(new MessageConfirmed(((Confirm)message).DeliveryId),
    Handler);
        return false;
    }
    return false;
}
```

```
protected override bool ReceiveRecover(object message)
{
    if(message is MessageConfirmed)
    {
        Handler((MessageConfirmed)message);
        return true;
    }
    else if(message is MessageSent)
    {
        Handler((MessageSent)message);
        return true;
    }
    return false;
}
```

With your `UpdateState` shell in place, you need to implement the logic in it. This is where the delivery actor will either deliver the message or mark it as being received, depending on the event it's dealing with. If it's a `MessageSent` event, then it calls the `Deliver` method, which is provided by the `AtLeastOnceDeliveryActor`. `Deliver` takes in the path to the destination actor and a callback that's used to create the message. The `AtLeastOnceDeliveryActor` maintains a unique number sequence that represents the next message to be sent, which it uses to mark which messages have been confirmed. The delivery actor sends the sequence number to the target so the target can respond with which messages it has processed. In the following example, the delivery actor sends a `Message` wrapper that contains a string to send as well as the sequence number provided by the `AtLeastOnceDeliveryActor`. The delivery actor also needs to handle the `MessageConfirmed` event, which it created when it received a `Confirm` command from the target actor. In this case, it calls `ConfirmDelivery` with the returned sequence number from the target actor. In the following example, you can see how these components fit together in the `UpdateState` method, the shell of which you defined earlier:

```
private void Handler(MessageSent message)
{
    Deliver(_destinationActor.Path, deliveryId => new
    MessageEnvelope(deliveryId, message.Message));
}

private void Handler(MessageConfirmed confirmed)
{
    ConfirmDelivery(confirmed.DeliveryId);
}
```

With the infrastructure in place on the sending side, you also need to send a confirmation message from the target back to the delivery actor with the sequence number of the message currently being processed. Here's a small example that receives the wrapper event, prints the string to the console, and then sends an acknowledgement message to the delivery actor in response:

```
class GuaranteedPrinterActor : ReceiveActor
{
```

```
    public GuaranteedPrinterActor()
    {
        Receive<MessageEnvelope>(msg =>
        {
            Console.WriteLine("Received a message: {0}", msg.Message);
            Sender.Tell(new Confirm(msg.DeliveryId));
        });
    }
}
```

With an `AtLeastOnceDeliveryActor`, a number of properties allow you to configure certain semantics of the delivery protocol, all of which are configurable from the HOCON configuration for at-least-once delivery actor functionality. For example, by using the `MaxUnconfirmedMessages` property, you can specify how any unconfirmed messages are kept in memory while awaiting responses. If you have too many messages in flight, then any time the delivery actor calls `Deliver`, it will fail and throw a `Max-UnconfirmedMessages-ExceededException` error, allowing the actor to back off and try again later. By default, the maximum is 100,000, but it may be necessary to lower this number if you have many `AtLeastOnceDeliveryActor` instances, so as to prevent lack-of-memory errors. In the following example, the number is reduced to 1,000:

```
akka.persistence.at-least-once-delivery.max-unconfirmed-messages = 1000
```

The `AtLeastOnceDeliveryActor` also sends warnings if it fails to receive a response after sending a message a number of times. By default, that number is five times, but it is possible to increase or decrease that number by setting `warn-after-number-of-unconfirmed-attempts` in HOCON configuration. Then you can handle the `UnconfirmedWarning` messages in the command handler to choose the appropriate course of action.

```
akka.persistence.at-least-once-delivery.warn-after-number-of-unconfirmed-
    attempts = 5
```

The `AtLeastOnceDeliveryActor` periodically resends unconfirmed messages that it still has in memory. It batches these messages and sends them in one burst every time period. By default, this property is set to 10,000, but, depending on things such as the network, it may be useful to modify this by providing a value for the `redelivery-burst-limit` property in HOCON. The following example shows how to change the limit to 1,000 instead of 10,000:

```
akka.persistence.at-least-once-delivery.redelivery-burst-limit
```

The `AtLeastOnceDeliveryActor` is a powerful construct to create actors that overcome transient issues caused by network difficulties in a fault-tolerant manner. With a journal-backing store, you can even resend unconfirmed messages to target actors if the application shuts down inexplicably.

11.4.2 *Upgrade strategies for applications using event sourcing*

Over time, you're likely to encounter situations that arise due to the evolution of your application; for example, multiple versions of messages. Consider the shopping cart

V1 event schema   V2 event schema

Figure 11.5 Event adapters allow you to modify events from a journal to an actor and vice versa, enabling you to make changes to event-sourced applications while also maintaining the full event history.

example again. You represented a shopping cart item with a stock identification number and the quantity of that item in the cart. This information was stored in the event journal. But although this might have been appropriate at the time, this process for persisting stock identifiers may later lead to problems. For example, you may have chosen one format when only a few products were available for sale, but with sales growth, you may need a new stock identification method. When you change your processing logic to use the new event type, you can't recover the old events. This contradicts the reason you wanted to persist state in the first place: to recover state later.

To handle these situations, Akka.Persistence provides for event adapters (see figure 11.5) that map data types used in your code to data stored in your event journal. This separation provides a number of distinct advantages:

- *Data migrations*—This is one scenario we've already considered. When an event model changes between two versions of the application, you need to handle transitions between the data types so that you can continue to read in old data types.
- *Separation of domain and journal data models*—When you develop your application domain, you might create special classes to represent cases that should never happen in an effort to make illegal states unrepresentable. One example of this is a custom email class designed to only be created if it follows a certain pattern, or it will otherwise fail. When you then persist this data to the journal, you don't necessarily need the wrapper class, and it will inflate the amount of time and disk space taken to persist the individual event. Another situation is if you wanted to use a custom serialization technology to persist data. For example, in the case of large messages, you may want to use a technology such as Google's Protocol Buffers for compact storage of events. By creating an event adapter, you can specify that you use one representation for the data when it's in memory and another for when it's stored in the journal.
- *Journal-specific features*—Your database may support features that open up additional benefits. One example is if the database supports the persistence of JSON documents; it may be beneficial to persist journal events as JSON documents, thus getting either better performance or better future query features. By using

an event adapter, you can take the in-memory representation and convert it into the shape required by the database, and vice versa.

In this section, we'll look at how you can write an event adapter for the shopping cart. We'll assume that in version 1 of your events, you persisted the stock identification number as a string, but in the upgraded version 2, you need to map events into a new format. The new format is a new class that holds the stock identifier. The following example shows how to create an event adapter by implementing the `IEventAdapter` interface. The interface provides three methods that you need to implement.

```
public class ShoppingCartEventAdapter : IEventAdapter
{
    public IEventSequence FromJournal(object evt, string manifest)
    {
        throw new NotImplementedException();
    }

    public string Manifest(object evt)
    {
        throw new NotImplementedException();
    }

    public object ToJournal(object evt)
    {
        throw new NotImplementedException();
    }
}
```

The first method is `Manifest`, which allows you to link a manifest to an event. A *manifest* is a type hint that matches on the string for future deserialization of the event with the appropriate mechanism. This can be set to a value specific to your purposes; in this case, you just return an empty string:

```
public string Manifest(object evt)
{
    return String.Empty;
}
```

You also need to implement the `ToJournal` method, called when an event is being persisted to the event journal—in this case, after the `Persist` method has been called. Because you have old events persisted, you don't need to do anything special, and you can return the event that was passed to you (in this case, `ItemIdentifier`). This event will then be serialized and persisted into the data store. If you wanted to store an event in the data store as a Protocol Buffers–encoded byte array, this is where you would convert it into that format with the Protocol Buffers serializer.

```
public object ToJournal(object evt)
{
    if(evt is Events.V2.ItemAdded)
    {
        var newEvt = (Events.V2.ItemAdded)evt;
        return new Events.V1.ItemAdded(newEvt.ItemIdentifier.Identifier);
    }
```

```
        return evt;
    }
```

The final method you need to implement is the most important one, the `FromJournal` method, which allows you to map an event from one type into another type. In this case, you need to create a new event from the `ItemIdentifier` event. You start by defining the new event: a class containing a `StockIdentifier` property and a count, shown in the following example. You then define the mapping function by creating an instance of the new event from the old event. In the following example, you create a new instance and map all the properties into the new event. One point to note about the `FromJournal` method is that it returns an `IEventSequence` interface. This means that you can return one event, more than one event, or no events at all. In this case, you return a single event, which you store in a new event sequence.

```
public IEventSequence FromJournal(object evt, string manifest)
{
    if(evt is Events.V1.ItemAdded)
    {
        var oldEvt = (Events.V1.ItemAdded)evt;
        var newEvt = new Events.V2.ItemAdded(new
    Events.V2.StockIdentifier(oldEvt.ItemIdentifier));
        return EventSequence.Single(newEvt);
    }
    return EventSequence.Single(evt);
}
```

Finally, you also need to configure the event journal to use `IEventAdapter` when it passes events to the journal. Use the HOCON configuration for the event journal `SqlServerJournal` you chose in section 11.2.2. To specify which event adapter bindings to use, first create a mapping of the event adapter type to a name for it. In the following example, the fully qualified type name, including the namespace and assembly, is `v1`. Then set up an event binding, which maps an event type onto an adapter. In the following example, you provide an event adapter name—in this case, the `v1` string—for the version 1 event type, with namespace and assembly. Because you're also converting from `V2` to `V1` format for storage into the journal, you also need to add a type binding for the `V2` event.

```
akka.persistence.journal {
    sql-server {
        event-adapters {
            v1 = "Chapter11.ShoppingCartEventAdapter, Chapter11"
        }

        event-adapter-bindings {
            "Chapter11.Events.V1.ItemAdded, Chapter11" = v1
            "Chapter11.Events.V2.ItemAdded, Chapter11" = v1
        }
    }
}
```

Event adapters help you solve one of the primary update issues you'll encounter when developing event-sourcing applications over an extended period of time. They also make accessible the advanced features of event-journal data stores, without sacrificing the advanced features provided by Akka.Persistence.

11.4.3 Wrapping up

Under certain circumstances, the Akka.Persistence default configuration isn't as fast as an active-record approach, but you can counter this with a number of provided features. The at-least-once delivery system allows you to resend messages until they are successfully processed. Event adapters allow you to modify events from a journal to an actor and vice versa, enabling you to make changes to event-sourced applications while also maintaining the full event history.

11.5 Case study: Persistence, storage, staged upgrades

For many industries, compliance is a vital aspect of their systems. This is especially true in the world of finance, where detailed records must maintain an accurate historical representation of every action that has been taken. An example of this is in the world of automated trading, where hundreds of stock transactions happen every second. It's imperative that these companies can demonstrate to the authorities, such as the SEC in the United States or the FCA in the UK, that securities trading transactions and profits are legally valid. For example, securities commissions require documentation as a way of precluding insider trading. Similarly, the securities market offers opportunities for nefarious parties to launder money, hiding the source of income in order to evade either law enforcement or taxation.

As such, in the finance industry, businesses face regulatory audits where trades are assessed to ascertain whether they were in breach of regulations. To pass these regulatory audits, businesses must maintain a history of every single trade that has been made, rather than storing only the stocks currently held in a portfolio. In this chapter, you saw how the persistence components of Akka.NET maintain a persistent ordered history of every event that was received by an actor. This event history can be replayed to show the events that led to a state at any point in time. You can model this by creating an actor per stock portfolio, where a stock portfolio is a collection of stocks in different listed companies along with the count of stock owned in each case. Every time an actor receives a message to either buy or sell stock from the portfolio, you persist the message, meaning that you maintain a log of every transaction that was made per portfolio. This is illustrated in figure 11.6, which shows an actor—a stock portfolio—that receives messages indicating whether to buy or sell a stock. The messages could originate from automated systems or from humans, but regardless of their origin, as soon as they're received by the portfolio actor, they're persisted to a data store. From this data store, the individual trades can be replayed, allowing the portfolio to be rebuilt to any point in its history.

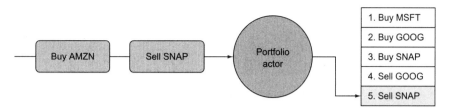

Figure 11.6   Finance applications need full audit trails in the event of investigation. Using Akka.NET persistence, you can simplify the process of maintaining an audit trail by persisting every event that the actor processes, in this case, a list of trades.

By using Akka.NET persistence, you can maintain a log representation of every event that was created by an actor. This allows you to simplify the process of audit trail creation, a feature that's a requirement in many heavily regulated industries such as finance, insurance, and healthcare.

Summary

In this chapter, you learned

- How to add a backing data store to an actor to persist changes to its state
- How to apply concepts relating to event sourcing to actors
- How to upgrade the logic contained in an event-sourcing application

Building clustered
applications with
Akka.Cluster

This chapter covers

- Creating elastically scalable actor systems across multiple machines
- Interacting with Akka.NET cluster infrastructure in an actor system
- Applying Akka.NET concepts to clustered applications

You know that a reactive application depends on systems that are responsive, regardless of system failures, failures in external dependencies, or increased load; and you've seen numerous tools and design methodologies to help you achieve that end. You've seen how to get around many of the problems relating to fault tolerance and scalability when running on a single machine through the use of Akka.Remote.

When you create applications that use Akka.Remote, you architect with the explicit intention of having to perform manual configuration changes. For example, when you had a subset of the actor deployment tree hosted on another machine, you needed to specify the exact network address for the machine that was hosting it. You had to do the same thing when you assigned routees on separate machines to develop applications that could scale out. But there was no process in place for what should happen if the machine hosting the actor system failed, leaving you with no actor system running. You'd need to constantly monitor your Akka.Remote application and be ready to update the configuration at any point during the day or night. Even if you managed to script the process of updating the actor system to point to new instances as they became available, you'd still be faced with inevitable downtime, because you'd need to reprocess configuration by restarting the actor system.

Although using Akka.Remote certainly presents some advantages over using a single machine, it doesn't yet match all the traits of reactive applications, which can automatically react to their hosting environment and remain fault tolerant in the face of failure, or scale when faced with increased or decreased load. The key part here is the *automatic* reaction to their environment. Akka.Remote's role wasn't automatic and required some degree of human intervention to manage. In an ideal situation, you'd add more machines that would become part of a single actor system distributed across multiple machines.

Akka.NET provides this functionality through the Akka.Cluster module, which builds on top of the low-level functionality provided by Akka.Remote to create a high-level overview of the networked actor system. It creates a cluster of the individual actor systems and allows you to address all the machines as though they were a single actor system. In this chapter, you'll see how to create a cluster from independent actor systems. You'll see how to deploy actors into the cluster and let Akka.Cluster transparently handle the deployment on any machine in the cluster. You'll also see some of the more advanced features available in Akka.Cluster that help you easily build applications that make the most of the resources available in these vast clusters of machines.

12.1 Introducing Akka.Cluster

Akka.Cluster builds on top of the networking abstraction provided by Akka.Remote to create a scalable, fault-tolerant cluster of machines that can represent a cluster of actor systems as a single actor system (see figure 12.1). Akka .Cluster is therefore incredibly useful for scenarios in which you need high availability guarantees that you can't achieve by using a single machine to host an actor system.

Some of Akka.Cluster's concepts can be confusing, especially considering it presents a new area of computing—*distributed* computing. It's useful to define some of the terms used throughout this chapter:

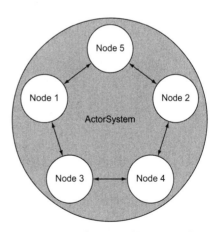

Figure 12.1 With Akka.NET 's clustering capabilities, you can treat a cluster of individual machines as a single actor system.

- *Node*—An individual actor system instance that runs as part of a larger cluster. A node runs an Akka.NET application that connects to and communicates with other nodes in the cluster.

- *Seed node*—A contact point for new nodes to join the cluster. It has all of the same responsibilities as a regular node, but it has a well-known address that new nodes can contact.

- *Cluster*—A set of individual nodes that are joined together through the membership component of Akka.Cluster. A cluster of nodes is addressable as though it was a single node rather than a collection of independent nodes.

- *Gossip protocol*—An internal component of Akka.Cluster responsible for communicating changes in cluster membership to all the other nodes in the cluster, thus creating a uniform overview of the cluster state.

- *Leader*—The node in the cluster chosen to be in charge of accepting changes to the cluster state and that is responsible for adding or removing new nodes, which are then disseminated through the gossip protocol to other nodes in the cluster. There is no leader election process; instead, the leader is chosen deterministically when the cluster is in a stable state.

- *Failure detector*—The Akka.Cluster component responsible for detecting whether a node has become unavailable, through heartbeat message failure in a given time period.

Although many of these components run internally in Akka.Cluster without human intervention, they provide the low-level tooling that directly powers many of the high-level features that you'll see throughout this chapter and that will be referenced in each section. When all these components are combined, you have an actor system representation that spans a number of machines. This presents you with the following benefits, in addition to the other benefits you get when building applications with Akka.NET running on a single node:

- *Scalable*—In order to add a new machine to the actor system cluster, you must provide the address of one of the nodes that's already running in the cluster, which allows you to instantly scale and add resources on demand.

- *Fault tolerant*—All the nodes in the cluster periodically send heartbeat messages to demonstrate their health to other nodes in the cluster. If no heartbeats are received from a node, the failure detector detects this and communicates it to the cluster. If a sufficient number of nodes agree that a node is no longer responsive, it can be removed from the cluster, and the actors hosted on that node can be deployed onto another node in the cluster.

- *Peer to peer*—All peers in an Akka.NET cluster have the same responsibilities, allowing you to create new nodes that can talk to any peer in the actor system and receive events relating to other peers in the cluster.

- *No bottleneck point*—Because Akka.Cluster creates a peer-to-peer cluster of machines, there's no single machine that coordinates all of the other actor systems. This ensures that the performance of the cluster doesn't degrade as a result of a single node in the cluster being under a heavy load.

- *No single point of failure*—Using gossip messages, all nodes in the cluster are responsible for detecting failures of other nodes and then disseminating this information to the other nodes in the cluster. No single node in the actor system is responsible for handling membership in the cluster, guaranteeing that if one node becomes unavailable, then the cluster can autonomously fix itself and continue running the application.

Before you can use Akka.Cluster, you need to install the Akka.Cluster package. As with other Akka.NET packages, it's distributed through NuGet and can be installed by running the following command in the package manager window, or by searching for Akka.Cluster in the NuGet UI:

```
Install-Package Akka.Cluster
```

After the Akka.Cluster package is installed, you need to configure your application for clustering. All the configuration for Akka.Cluster is handled with HOCON configuration in a way similar to how you configured Akka.Remote, as shown in the following example. Akka.Cluster contains three key components: configuring the actor reference provider, specifying an endpoint for Akka.Remote to listen on, and providing one or more seed nodes that you can join to when initializing the cluster. You configure the actor reference provider to use `ClusterActorRefProvider` rather than the single-node actor reference provider. This is similar to the `RemoteActorRefProvider` you used with Akka.Remote. You also specify a listen endpoint; in this case, port 8080, and you listen on localhost. Because this uses Akka.Remote under the hood, you can configure this exactly as with Akka.Remote, specifying other properties such as public hostnames if you're running the application through a load balancer. Finally, you can also add a seed node for Akka.Cluster. You specify the seed node to be the node's own address. This means that it will join itself and form a cluster of one node.

```
akka {
    actor.provider = "Akka.Cluster.ClusterActorRefProvider, Akka.Cluster"
    remote {
        helios.tcp {
            port = 8080
            hostname = localhost
        }
    }
    cluster {
        seed-nodes = ["akka.tcp://Chapter12Cluster@localhost:8080"] # address
     of seed node
    }
}
```

Now that you have a single node running, you can create a configuration for any subsequent node that uses the address configured for the first node as the seed node. Because a seed node is an address of one node that's running in the cluster, once you

have more than one node in the cluster, you can specify any of the nodes as a seed
node.

```
akka {
    actor.provider = "Akka.Cluster.ClusterActorRefProvider, Akka.Cluster"
    remote {
        helios.tcp {
            port = 8081
            hostname = localhost
        }
    }
    cluster {
        seed-nodes = ["akka.tcp://Chapter12Cluster@localhost:8080"] # address
     of seed node
    }
}
```

One of the other most useful configuration changes you can make on a per-node basis
is to specify a role for a node. Assigning a role is a way of limiting the scope of the
work that a node is responsible for. For example, consider an application that runs
some intense computational work such as financial modeling, and some IO-intensive
work such as web-page scraping. You can get better performance out of your application if you tailor the hardware to the usage. This might be by using a machine with a
faster network for web scraping, and machines with lots of CPU cores for financial
modeling. In this case, you don't want IO work happening on machines with lots of
cores. Using roles, you can scope the work you deploy, as you'll see throughout this
chapter. To assign a role to a node, you modify the cluster configuration to specify the
roles that the current node belongs to:

```
akka.cluster.roles = ["network"]
```

You can then create an actor system on each node with the configuration shown in
previous chapters. It's important to note, however, that you need to ensure that every
actor system that joins the cluster has the same name. If the names differ, then the
node wanting to join will be blocked from joining. This means that every node in the
actor system differs only by the listen address. In the following example, you create a
cluster with the name Chapter12Cluster:

```
var configFile = File.ReadAllText("chapter12.conf");
var config = ConfigurationFactory.ParseString(configFile);
var actorSystem = ActorSystem.Create("Chapter12Cluster", config);
```

Now that you have a number of machines communicating together through
Akka.Cluster, you can develop more-advanced distributed applications. In the rest of
this chapter, you'll see some of these features and how to use them in your Akka.NET
applications.

12.2 Cluster-aware routers

One of the biggest benefits of using Akka.Cluster is that you can scale out your actor system to more nodes as load on the system increases. But you want to make the most of this scalability. Chapter 7 showed that Akka.NET provides scaling support with a variety of routers, which can route messages to actors that have already been created (in group routers), or actors that are created by the Akka.NET router (in pool routers). You can even add new routees to the pool when demand is high if you use pool routers.

Chapter 8 showed how to integrate routers with Akka.Remote to specify that routees should be deployed onto other nodes if you're using pools, or to specify full addresses for group routers, referencing actors already deployed on remote actor systems. Because Akka.Cluster uses Akka.Remote as its networking layer, you can still use this technique to create routers that span nodes in the cluster, but you'll lose fault tolerance with a configuration reliant on a single node: a single point of failure.

To address this, Akka.Cluster provides the notion of *cluster-aware routers*. These are the same routers you saw in chapter 7, but they integrate with the gossip protocol used by Akka.Cluster to receive notifications of when certain events happen: for example, when new nodes join the cluster or when existing nodes are suspected of being unresponsive. In these cases, when using cluster-aware routers, you can remove routees if you suspect their host node is unavailable, or add new routees if new nodes have been added to the cluster. Cluster-aware routers let you use routers that simplify developing scalable applications while also making the most of the Akka.Cluster's scaling benefits. All the routers available in the standard Akka.NET package can be used with Akka.Cluster, but the same caveats apply as when using these routers with Akka.Remote. Although many of the routers work well across a network, the smallest-mailbox router acts effectively as a random router due to the lack of knowledge of mailbox sizes across the network.

12.2.1 Creating cluster-aware router groups

Router groups allow you to specify the paths to a selection of actors and direct messages to them. You can do the same thing with Akka.Cluster, but you can send the messages across a cluster of machines instead. The cluster-aware router groups use cluster membership to determine which of the routees specified exist on machines that live in the cluster. If the routee specified exists on a node deemed unresponsive, then messages won't be directed to that target and will instead be sent to other routees. The cluster-aware router group also uses gossip messages to react to changes in the cluster and add or remove routees to the group as their hosts are deemed either live or unresponsive.

Figure 12.2 shows a cluster-aware router and routee nodes joining a cluster. A first node joins the cluster, which alerts the router that a new potential routee is available. The router verifies that the new node has routees on it and starts routing messages to it. Later, a second node joins the cluster and the process repeats, allowing the router to add that routee to its list of available routees.

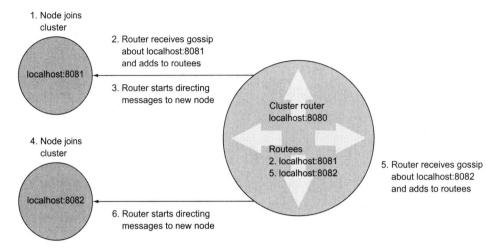

Figure 12.2   The sequence of events that occurs in the router as you add new nodes to the cluster

When you use groups of actors with cluster-aware routers, it's important that the actors exist at the paths specified as soon as possible after startup. The other nodes in the cluster will all send messages to the provided path on any node as soon as it's marked as being up in the cluster. If a routee is delayed at startup, it may lead to race conditions where messages are sent to an actor that don't yet exist.

You can create routers using either HOCON configuration, as in the following code example, or directly, using code. In the deployment section of the HOCON configuration, you can specify the router for a given path. The example also shows how to specify a cluster-aware router for a given path. You follow the same format as when developing a local router, but you also specify a number of specific properties for creating cluster versions. With a `cluster` section added to the actor deployment, the router is configured to use clustering capabilities. You enable clustering by setting the enabled property to on as well as specifying whether the routees should only be sent to those nodes that have the specified role. You can also specify not to use local routees and instead direct all messages to actors on other nodes. This is particularly beneficial in situations where you want to create a master-worker environment, where a number of masters submit work into a cluster of worker nodes. By default, Akka.Cluster limits the total number of routees to 10,000, but you can configure that number with the `nr-of-instances` property and reduce the number if it might overload an external system.

```
akka {
   actor{
      provider = "Akka.Cluster.ClusterActorRefProvider, Akka.Cluster"
      deployment {
        /workdispatcher {
           router = consistent-hashing-group # routing strategy
           routees.paths = ["/user/worker"] # path of routee on each node
```

```
        nr-of-instances = 3 # max number of total routees
        cluster {
            enabled = on
            allow-local-routees = on
        }
    }
  }
 }
}
```

You can deploy your HOCON actor configuration by specifying that the router definition should be taken from the config when you create the Props for the router. By using this definition, you can switch between systems that run locally on one node without clustering to creating a multinode-clustered environment, all by simply changing the configuration and restarting the application.

```
var worker = system.ActorOf<Worker>("worker");
var router = system.ActorOf(Props.Empty.WithRouter(FromConfig.Instance),
    "workdispatcher");
```

You can also use code to create routers instead of using HOCON. You create an instance of the ClusterRouterGroup class and supply it a router group that provides the routing logic as well as the settings that define how the router gets deployed across the cluster. In the following code example, you create the cluster-aware router using the ConsistentHashingGroup router group type, but you don't provide the internal router with any paths. These will be provided by the cluster-aware router. The cluster-router group also needs a settings object that contains all the configuration for the cluster router, specifying many of the same settings as when you used HOCON to create a router. You specify the maximum number of routees that should be used in the router, and supply a list of the routee paths that should be used, while also including the root user actor in their paths. You also specify whether to use local routes, as you did with HOCON, and whether the router should only target paths on nodes belonging to a given node.

```
var routeePaths = new List<string> { "/user/worker" };
var clusterRouterSettings = new ClusterRouterGroupSettings(3, routeePaths,
    true);
var clusterGroupProps =
    Props.Empty.WithRouter(new ClusterRouterGroup(new
    Akka.Routing.ConsistentHashingGroup("/user/worker"),
    clusterRouterSettings));
```

By using cluster-aware group routers, you can route messages to any node in the cluster while also maintaining ownership of the deployment lifecycle of those nodes. Because the router has deep integration with the cluster membership, this ensures that you don't need to manage which routees are available in the cluster at any one time.

12.2.2 Creating cluster-aware router pools

In chapter 7, you saw how to create router actors that can deploy all of their routees and scale them on demand by using router pools. You can create the same type of router actor across a cluster of nodes with Akka.Cluster. When a new node joins the cluster, the router actor is deployed onto the new node and is then added to the list of available routees. If a node becomes unresponsive, it's removed from the list of available routees.

Figure 12.3 shows new nodes that join the cluster and how these are added to the router's list of available routees. Node2 joins the cluster, triggering the notification to the router. The new routee is then deployed, and messages are routed to it. The process repeats when Node3 joins the cluster. A message is sent to the router notifying it that a new node has joined, the routee is deployed to the new remote node, and the node is added to the list of routees.

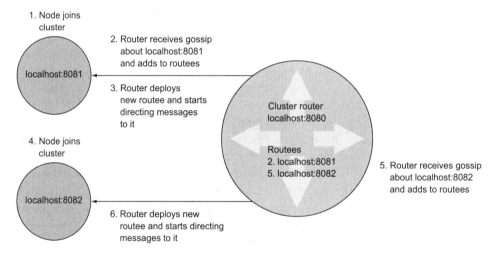

Figure 12.3   The sequence of events that occur when using a pool router and a new node is added to the cluster

Because the only real difference between group routers and pool routers is which actor maintains ownership of the lifecycle of the routees, you can use the same principles to create cluster-aware pool routers as you can to create cluster-aware group routers. You can use HOCON configuration to create a router instance, or you can create the router instance entirely in code. The following example shows how to create a pool router using HOCON configuration. The only difference is that you specify the internal router type to be a pool instead of a group, omit the routee paths, and add `max-nr-of-instances-per-node`, which specifies how many routees should be created by the pool on each node.

```
akka {
   actor{
      provider = "Akka.Cluster.ClusterActorRefProvider, Akka.Cluster"
      deployment {
        /workdispatcher {
          router = round-robin-pool # routing strategy
          max-nr-of-instances-per-node = 5
          cluster {
             enabled = on
             allow-local-routees = on
          }
        }
      }
   }
}
```

You can deploy this cluster-aware pool router by specifying that the router definition should be taken from the HOCON configuration instead of creating it in code:

```
var routerProps = Props.Empty.WithRouter(FromConfig.Instance);
```

You can also create a router pool in code, specifying a `ClusterRouterPool`. This works in a way similar to the cluster-router group in that it takes in an instance of a router to specify the internal logic as well as a settings object that contains any configuration. In the following example, you create a round-robin pool that operates across a cluster by passing `RoundRobinPool` to the cluster-aware router that doesn't have any routees. You also pass in the settings, supplying values as needed. In this case, you need the maximum number of routees per node as well as in total across the cluster, and whether to use the local node to deploy routees or which roles should host routees.

```
var clusterPoolSettings = new ClusterRouterPoolSettings(1000, 5, true);
var clusterPoolProps =
    Props.Create<Worker>().WithRouter(new ClusterRouterPool(new
      RoundRobinPool(5), clusterPoolSettings));
```

With cluster-aware pool routers, you can easily deploy actors right across a cluster that can handle messages on any node with minimal human intervention, sparing you needless worry about the intricacies of cluster development.

12.2.3 Wrapping up

With cluster-aware routers, you can easily create applications that scale across a cluster even as you add more and more instances. If you're using HOCON configuration to develop routers, then you can expand from a solution that runs locally on a single actor system to one running on a cluster of thousands of machines without code changes, which allows you instead to focus on the configuration.

12.3 Working with cluster gossip

You saw how to use cluster-aware routers to scale out across the cluster. But sometimes you need to drop down to a lower level and interact directly with a cluster itself. You can use the same Akka.NET gossip protocol notifications used in cluster-aware routers in any actors that you create yourself. In this section, you'll see how to get an overview of a cluster at a point in time, and how to react to cluster changes by registering actors for notifications from the gossip service in Akka.Cluster.

12.3.1 *Retrieving cluster state*

As you develop cluster applications, you may need to take an overview of a cluster node at a particular point in time. For example, you might be building monitoring tooling that needs to examine what a cluster is doing. You can retrieve this information directly from the actor system cluster extension:

```
Cluster cluster = Cluster.Get(Context.System);
```

Once you've retrieved the cluster extension, you can get an overview of the cluster by accessing the `State` property. This allows you to see which nodes are currently members of the cluster through the `Members` property. You can also see which of them are unreachable by inspecting the `Unreachable` set of members. If the cluster is in a stable state, you can also see which member is currently the leader by accessing the `Leader` property. Finally, you can get the set of all roles that currently exist across all nodes by using the `AllRoles` property.

12.3.2 *Handling cluster gossip messages*

In chapter 6, we noted many sources of failure for an application running on a single machine, and even more for multiple applications connected in a network. This means that when you're running an application on Akka.Cluster, you'll encounter situations where you believe a node has become unreachable. Fortunately, you don't have to worry about these details yourself because the Akka.Cluster failure detector handles heartbeat messages without needing any intervention. But you may want to receive notifications of changes in the cluster state caused by failures. You've seen one example of how this information is used when you saw how to create routers that are influenced by cluster status. There are plenty of other scenarios in which you would want to receive this information. For example, if you're storing state in actors and a node hosting one of those actors becomes unreachable, then you might need to switch to using a different node hosting a replica of the data.

In Akka.Cluster, you can register an actor you develop with the cluster extension to receive notifications of any changes that occur in the cluster. To do this, you first retrieve the cluster extension:

```
Cluster cluster = Cluster.Get(actorSystem);
```

Now you can use the `Subscribe` method to retrieve events in the cluster. When you call the `Subscribe` method, you supply a reference to the actor that is due to receive cluster messages. You also supply a value indicating how you want to receive the initial state of the cluster: either as a single snapshot with a picture of the current state of the cluster, or as a sequence of ordered events that represents the transitions the cluster has taken from its initial state to its current state. In the following example, you specify that you want the current actor to receive the current state in the form of the events that represent the current state, and then you want to receive the member events whenever there are any unreachable nodes:

```
cluster.Subscribe(Self,
    ClusterEvent.SubscriptionInitialStateMode.InitialStateAsEvents,
    typeof(ClusterEvent.UnreachableMember));
```

You can now handle these messages like any others to build up a picture of the current actor system state as soon as any changes are detected in the cluster state by the gossip service. You can write to the actor system log when a change is detected in the actor system:

```
Receive<ClusterEvent.UnreachableMember>(msg =>
{
    Context.System.Log.Info("A node was detected as being unreachable: {0}",
      msg.Member.Address);
});
```

By handling cluster events as they happen, you can proactively adjust your application to minimize the latency or maximize the availability of the application, ensuring that users get the most responsive experience possible.

12.3.3 Wrapping up

You'll rarely need to work with cluster-status APIs directly; instead, you'll build your applications on top of the abstractions that Akka.Cluster provides, one of which is cluster-aware routers, and you'll see several others in the remainder of the chapter. But you can use cluster-status APIs to build applications that are more responsive: you can redeploy actors, or you can redirect messages to handle an increased load if cluster size grows and it seems that a node failure is likely.

12.4 Cluster singleton

There are times when you don't necessarily want an instance of an actor on multiple nodes, as would happen if you were to use a router. Instead, you might want to have a single instance of an actor that's responsible for performing a certain task; for example, an actor that handles resource coordination across a cluster. You don't want a lot of actors competing with each other and overloading a resource. If you use an actor to decide which machines to deploy a VM or container image onto, you don't want multiple actors deploying multiple images, using up more resources than are available on the machine

In this case, you could deploy a single actor responsible for the task. The Akka.Cluster *cluster singleton* allows you to deploy an actor onto the cluster on a single node and migrate it when the node hosting it becomes unavailable. It's important to note, however, that using this approach and creating a single actor responsible for performing a certain task will lead to a bottleneck: all traffic must travel through this single component, degrading performance. You should consider whether alternative solutions exist that could distribute the load across a number of actors.

To create a cluster singleton, use the `ClusterSingletonManager`, which will handle the creation and deployment of the actor into the actor system on the most appropriate node. The cluster singleton will always be deployed onto the oldest node in the cluster because it's least likely to be subject to node churn, caused by adding and removing new nodes (see figure 12.4). In the event that this oldest node is removed from the cluster, the `ClusterSingletonManager` is responsible for redeploying the singleton onto whichever actor is now the oldest in the system. It's possible that during handover while the singleton is redeployed, there's no running instance of the cluster singleton.

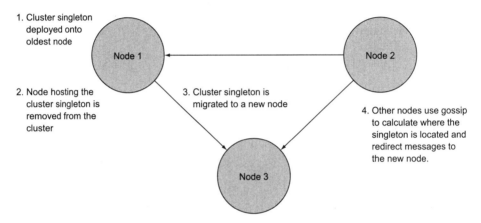

Figure 12.4 A cluster singleton is a powerful tool that permits only one instance of an actor to be deployed in a cluster.

Another consideration is what happens during a network partition if the cluster thinks it has split and so marks a node as down. The two halves of the cluster might then deploy their own cluster singleton, and you'll have two cluster singletons deployed in independent sections of the same cluster. This might lead to unexpected behavior when you need to guarantee that only one actor is ever accessing an external resource at the same time. In these cases, it's best to manually remove nodes from the cluster rather than rely on the failure detector to mark unreachable nodes as down.

You create the cluster singleton by using specialized `Props` generated by the `ClusterSingletonManager`. The following example shows how to create the `Props` for an actor called `Coordinator`. In a typical application, this actor would be responsible for coordinating certain actions across all nodes in the cluster. You create the regular `Props` that you need to create the actor, in which you can specify how to create the actor and which constructor parameters are required. The `Props` settings are passed to the `ClusterSingletonManager`. You also specify the termination message, should the singleton need to be relocated in the event that the oldest node becomes available again after a failure. In this case, you use the `PoisonPill`, but if you have more complex work before shutting down, then you may want to use a custom termination message. Finally, you also supply the settings used for handling the cluster singleton. For example, in this case, you specify that the singleton should only be deployed onto a node that belongs to the `coordinator` role.

```
//Create the Props for the actor which will be deployed on only one node in
    the cluster
var coordinatorProps = Props.Create<CoordinatorActor>();

//Create the settings for the cluster singleton manager, retrieving them from
    the actor system
//configuration and then overriding the name of the singleton
var settings =
    ClusterSingletonManagerSettings.Create(actorSystem)
    .WithSingletonName("coordinator");

//Create the Props for the cluster singleton manager by providing the props
    of the singleton and the
//settings to use for the singleton
var clusterSingletonProps =
    ClusterSingletonManager.Props(coordinatorProps, settings);
```

With these specialized `Props`, you can deploy the actor in the same way you'd deploy any other actor in your system. Here's how to use the `ActorOf` method on `actorSystem` to deploy the actor:

```
var coordinatorSingleton = actorSystem.ActorOf(clusterSingletonProps,
    "coordinatorManager");
```

Now you need to create a means of accessing the actor that has been deployed in the cluster, `CoordinatorActor`. Akka.Cluster provides the `ClusterSingletonProxy`, which acts as a message target and allows you to easily forward received messages onto the singleton's correct location in the cluster. The proxy is also registered to track the cluster state and can reroute messages to whichever node is hosting the singleton. In the following code example, you create the `Props` required for the proxy and then deploy it. When creating the `Props`, you need to specify the actor path to the singleton that you previously created, `coordinator`. Because you deployed it at the top of the actor hierarchy, the path will be `/user/coordinator`. You also need to supply any additional configuration: specify that you deployed the singleton onto nodes with a specific role. If the roles fail to match, the proxy can't accurately route messages to the correct target.

```
//Create the settings for the proxy using the configuration supplied in the
    actor system
//configuration and override the name of the singleton to match the name
    provided above when
//creating the actor for the cluster singleton manager
var coordinatorProxySettings =
    ClusterSingletonProxySettings.Create(actorSystem)
    .WithSingletonName("coordinator");

//Create the Props for the coordinator, ensuring the path matches that of the
    cluster singleton manager
```

```
//created above when deploying the cluster singleton manager
var coordinatorProxyProps =
    ClusterSingletonProxy.Props("/user/coordinatorManager",
     coordinatorProxySettings);

//Deploy the coordinator proxy to the path /user/coordinatorProxy other
    actors will then
//send messages to this address and have them  forwarded onto the singleton
    wherever it is
//deployed in the cluster
var coordinatorProxy =
    actorSystem.ActorOf(coordinatorProxyProps, "coordinatorProxy");
```

Now that you have a proxy, you can send messages to it as you would to any other actor in your system, and they'll be forwarded onto the singleton regardless of where it exists in the cluster.

```
coordinatorProxy.Tell("Hello coordinator!");
```

12.4.1 *Wrapping up*

Cluster singletons shouldn't be your first choice when developing cluster applications with Akka.Cluster, but there are certain tasks that require having only a single instance available in the cluster at any point in time, and the Akka.Cluster cluster singleton makes those tasks significantly easier. By handling migration in the event of failure, the Akka.Cluster cluster singleton ensures that you always have an instance of the actor available somewhere. Combined with the Akka.Persistence features in the previous section, the Akka.Cluster cluster singleton allows you to easily create reliable actors backed by a data store.

12.5 *Cluster sharding*

As you develop applications using Akka.NET, you naturally develop an actor hierarchy driven by the domain design, where parents and children exist. For example, you may logically group all actors related to a given user so that there's no possibility for cross-pollination between users. This presents something of a problem: unless you explicitly state that part of an actor hierarchy should be deployed onto a given remote target, an actor will be deployed locally, directly beneath its parent. But you may have too many actors deployed under a single parent on a node. This can impede message processing because CPU resources are limited, or actors may encounter issues when modifying their internal state due to insufficient memory for all actors on the node.

You can shard these actors across nodes in the cluster to balance the load and prevent a node from becoming a single point of failure or a bottleneck. You need a way to deterministically deploy actors onto alternative nodes in the cluster and redirect their messages to them. Akka.NET provides the Akka.Cluster.Sharding module, a way of partitioning child actors into shards across a cluster without requiring significant work on your part. A shard, in this case, is a horizontal partition of the actors in your actor system. Figure 12.5 shows how several actors with the same parent might be partitioned

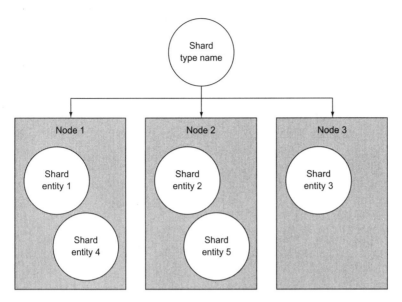

Figure 12.5 Akka cluster sharding permits the automatic partitioning of actors across multiple nodes in a cluster.

across a number of nodes. Using sharding, you can deploy more actors with a common parent than is possible on a single node.

12.5.1 Creating a new shard

Consider a situation in which you might need such sharding capabilities, as when creating an actor for storing the state of a user's shopping cart. In this scenario, hundreds of thousands of shopping carts exist on an e-commerce site, with signed-in users as well as browsing visitors. This is a problem if your application is deployed on many nodes running on commodity hardware. Although you could use machines with more RAM to host all the shopping carts, you'd pay for the extra RAM even when you only host a few shopping carts. This is an ideal scenario for Akka.Cluster.Sharding in that you can easily shard the shopping carts across multiple nodes in the cluster.

You'll define your shopping cart actor exactly as you have in the past. For this example, you'll use ReceiveActor, which means that if the cluster shuffles the actors, you'll lose any state stored in your actor. When dealing with Akka.Cluster, the recommended approach is to use persistent actors so that state can be restored if an actor is moved to another node. To keep this example focused on cluster sharding, you'll use the ReceiveActor. The definition is similar to examples you've seen before, where an actor receives a request to add a new item to the cart or retrieve the cart status.

```
public class ShoppingCartActor : ReceiveActor
{
    private List<string> _items = new List<string>();
```

```
    public ShoppingCartActor()
    {
        Receive<AddItemToCart>(msg =>
        {
            _items.Add(msg.ItemId);
        });
    }
}
```

You'll add an extra property containing the target identifier to messages you send to the shopping cart actor. The reason for this will become apparent later in the section, when you see how to direct messages to the correct shard containing the target actor. Adding the shopping cart identifier gives your messages the same properties that you've seen before, but now you also have a string containing the shopping cart identifier:

```
class AddItemToCart
{
    public string ItemId { get; }
    public string ShoppingCartId { get; }

    public AddItemToCart(string itemId, string shoppingCartId)
    {
        ItemId = itemId;
        ShoppingCartId = shoppingCartId;
    }
}
```

Before you can create a shard, you first need to create a *message extractor*. This class will be responsible for retrieving from a message the actor identifier as well as the shard on which the actor is located. The message extractor will be used by Akka .Cluster.Sharding to handle redirection of messages to the correct actor instance. To create a message extractor, create a class that implements the IMessageExtractor interface. In the code example below, you create a message extractor for shopping cart actor messages. You need to implement the three methods for retrieving the entity ID, the entity shard, and the actual message.

In retrieving the entity ID, the message extractor checks the type of message, and if it's one of the messages you defined above, then it extracts the shopping cart identifier. When dealing with shard handling, the extractor chooses an appropriate number of shards to make the most of the clustering capabilities. If it chooses too few shards, it can't make the most of all available resources when scaling out the number of instances. If it chooses too many shards, the routing struggles to find the correct node on which the shard is located.

A good rule of thumb is to use ten times more shards than the number of nodes expected in the cluster. For example, if there's a 10-node cluster, then use 100 shards. You calculate the shard for the message by using the hash code of the node identifier and then calculating the remainder when dividing by 100. Assuming the hash function is uniform, this creates a uniform distribution of actors across the cluster.

The final method you need to implement is retrieving the message, because the message contains the shopping cart identifier itself; you return the message directly. This method is useful if you're storing the message as a property in an envelope message.

```
class ShoppingCartMessageExtractor : IMessageExtractor
{
    //The EntityId method retrieves the identifier for the shopping cart to
     which
    //the message should be directed
    public string EntityId(object message)
    {
        return (message as AddItemToCart)?.ShoppingCartId;
    }

    //The EntityMessage retrieves the  content of the message which should be
     sent
    //to the target actor
    public object EntityMessage(object message)
    {
        return (message as AddItemToCart);
    }

    //The ShardId method is used to work out which shard the message should
     be directed to
    public string ShardId(object message)
    {
        var hash = (message as AddItemToCart)?.ShoppingCartId.GetHashCode();
        var shardId = hash % 100;
        return shardId.ToString();
    }
}
```

Now you need to specify how you tell Akka.NET to deploy the actors across a number of shards instead of onto a single node. To create a shard, you retrieve the cluster sharding extension, and then call the Start method, supplying the shard name to use, the Props for how to create the actor you're sharding, as well as an instance of the message extractor. The following example shows how to define a new cluster shard. Call this on every node that you want to act as a host for cluster sharding. This may be every node in the cluster or only selected nodes, such as those with a specific role.

```
//Create the Props for the actor which resides in a shard
var shoppingCartProps =
    Props.Create<ShoppingCartActor>();

//Retrieve the shard extension from the actor system
var shardingExtension =
    ClusterSharding.Get(actorSystem);

//Create the settings for the cluster sharding, retrieving them from the
//actor system config
var clusterShardingSettings =
    ClusterShardingSettings.Create(actorSystem);

//Build up a shard region which will be responsible for creating and shutting
```

```
//down actors on each individual node in the cluster
var region =
    shardingExtension.Start("shoppingCart",
                            shoppingCartProps,
                            clusterShardingSettings,
                            new ShoppingCartMessageExtractor());
```

Now you can send messages to a shard of actors, and the cluster-sharding infrastructure will direct the messages to the correct shard. You need to start cluster sharding on every node that you want to host actors in an individual shard, and run the preceding code to start cluster sharding on the startup of every node that's part of the cluster. In the next section, you'll see how to communicate directly with a shard, as well as how to create a proxy to communicate with it.

12.5.2 *Communicating with actors in a shard*

Now that you have a shard for hosting actors, you want to send messages to the correct actors in that shard. If you have a direct handle to the shard—for example, if you created it as in the previous example—then you can give it a message. In the following example, you create a message called 1 to add a new item to the shopping cart. When you send 1 to the shard coordinator, it's directed to the node actor hosting the shard. If that node actor exists, the shard coordinator sends it a message; if it doesn't already exist, the shard coordinator creates a new instance of the actor before sending it a message.

```
region.Tell(new AddItemToCart("REF2201", "1"));
```

Sometimes, you don't want a node to participate in cluster sharding but do want it to communicate with actors that exist in the shard. To handle this, you create a proxy that will handle the routing of messages to the correct shard. To create a proxy, you get the actor system extension and call the StartProxy method, supplying the name of the shard, which role it's deployed on, and the message extractor you created previously. Having created a proxy, you can send messages to it, and they'll be directed to the correct node in the actor system.

```
//Create a shard proxy which will  forward messages onto the correct shard
    which
//is hosting the actor
var shardProxy =
    shardingExtension.StartProxy("shoppingCart", null, new
    ShoppingCartMessageExtractor());
```

Now that you can communicate with an actor in a shard, you can build up actor-system applications that scale out across entire nodes with minimal effort. Akka .Cluster.Sharding also provides some other techniques that help you build applications that continue to react to their environment, which you'll see in the next section.

12.5.3 *Handling passivation in shards*

Sometimes, actors in a shard are required for a short time before they can be shut down. They might only receive messages for a five-minute period every 24 hours, for example. With Akka.Cluster.Sharding, you can use *actor passivation*, which lets you shut down an actor after a period of inactivity, and the shard coordinator can re-create the actor when it next receives a message. For example, if you have a business chat-room application, the rooms will only be used during typical working hours, 8 a.m. through 6 p.m. Outside of these times, you can shut the actor down and release computing resources that could better be used elsewhere.

To create an actor that supports passivation, you must tell the parent to shut down its child. It's important that you don't use `Context.Stop`, as this may lead to losing messages; instead, you send the parent a `Passivate` message, which shuts down the child actor after it has finished processing messages. If the parent again receives messages intended for the child actor, the parent re-creates it and starts sending it messages. The following example shows how to create a receive timeout of one hour, after which the actor receives a `ReceiveTimeout` message. From there, you can send the parent a `Passivate` message, supplying the message that should be sent to the child to shut it down.

```
public ShoppingCartActor()
{
    SetReceiveTimeout(TimeSpan.FromHours(1.0));

    Receive<ReceiveTimeout>(msg =>
    {
        Context.Parent.Tell(new Passivate(PoisonPill.Instance));
    });
}
```

Passivation is a useful concept when you have actors that you need only once every few hours. It allows you to shut down idle actors, preserving resources that other actors can use.

12.5.4 *Wrapping up*

Akka.Cluster.Sharding is an incredibly powerful tool that allows you to rapidly scale out actors across an entire cluster without needing to worry about the details relating to state. This means you can focus on the application logic without needing to worry about what should happen in the event of a node failure or other potential edge cases.

12.6 *Distributed publish-subscribe*

With Akka.Remote, you can retrieve a path to an actor on an actor system and send a message to that path. Although this approach also works in Akka.Cluster, you need to consider how Akka.NET handles the movement of actors around the cluster. During cluster sharding, the shards hosting actors can be moved around the cluster and onto different nodes. This poses a problem, particularly when dealing with paths to actors, because an actor might send a message to a path on which the receiving actor no longer exists because it has been moved elsewhere in the cluster.

Akka.Cluster provides the distributed publish-subscribe feature, which allows you to send messages to actors that have registered to receive messages on a path or on a topic. By using `DistributedPubSubMediator`, you can send messages around the cluster to any actors that are listening on a path or on a topic without having to worry about the node on which the actor is deployed.

Internally, the mediator maintains a registry of actor locations along with subscriptions, which is disseminated around the cluster in an eventually consistent manner. This means that subscriptions may not appear across all nodes, but after a few seconds, the gossip protocol used by the mediator will have disseminated any registry changes to all of the other nodes in the cluster.

In this section, you'll see the two ways in which you can use Akka.Cluster's distributed publish-subscribe to send messages to all actors interested in a particular topic or only selected actors listening on a specific path.

12.6.1 Topic messaging

Topic messaging allows you to publish a message on a named topic, and all the actors that have subscribed to that topic will receive the message (see figure 12.6). An example of this is a chat room where you want to publish a message and send it to all members. In this case, you might have one topic per chat room; for example, if you had a chat room called *general* and another called *random*, you'd create two topics named after their respective chat rooms.

You can model each chat-room user with an actor, which registers with the mediator for each chat room that the user belongs to. The following example shows an actor that receives a message to join a chat room, and it messages the mediator that it wants to receive messages sent to that chat room. The actor first retrieves the mediator from

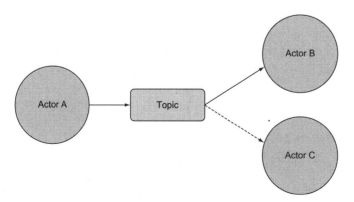

Figure 12.6 Topic messaging allows you to broadcast a message to all actors that are subscribed to a certain topic regardless of their location in the cluster.

the distributed publish-subscribe actor system extension, the entry point for all applications that need access to the mediator. Now, when it receives a `JoinChatroom` message, it sends a `Subscribe` message with the name of the topic for subscription to the mediator—in this case, the chat room name—and also the `IActorRef`, which will receive all the messages sent to that topic. In this case, you use the `Self` identifier.

```
//Create a class which holds the message which will be sent to the given
    chatroom
class ChatMessage
{
    public string Sender { get; }
    public string MessageContent { get; }

    public ChatMessage(string sender, string messageContent)
    {
        Sender = sender;
        MessageContent = messageContent;
    }
}

//Create a class which will allow an actor to join a given chatroom
class JoinChatroom
{
    public string ChatroomName { get; }
    public JoinChatroom(string chatroomName)
    {
        ChatroomName = chatroomName;
    }
}

//Create a class which represents a user which is able to join a chatroom and
    receive
//messages from that chatroom
class UserActor : ReceiveActor
{
    public UserActor()
    {
        Receive<JoinChatroom>(msg =>
        {
            //Retrieve the pub/sub extension and then subscribe to updates to
    a given topic
            var mediator = DistributedPubSub.Get(Context.System).Mediator;
            mediator.Tell(new Subscribe(msg.ChatroomName, Self));
        });

        //The pub/sub extension informs us if our subscription to the topic
    was successful
        Receive<SubscribeAck>(_ => Become(Subscribed));
    }

    public void Subscribed()
    {
        //Now that we're subscribed, you can listen out for messages which
    get published
        //to the topic
        Receive<ChatMessage>(msg =>
```

```
        {
            Console.WriteLine("Received a message from {0}: {1}", msg.Sender,
     msg.MessageContent);
        });
    }
}
```

You can create instances of this actor on any node in the cluster, and regardless of where the actor has been spawned, it will receive any messages that have been posted to the chat room. You can expand the user actor to handle a message that tells it to post a message to the chat room, in this case publishing a message onto a topic. The following example shows how to send the mediator a `Publish` message. In the message, the actor specifies the topic it wants to send the message to, in this case, the name of the chat room and the message it wants to distribute to all subscribers of the topic.

```
var mediator = DistributedPubSub.Get(actorSystem).Mediator;
mediator.Tell(new Publish("chatroom", new ChatMessage("user1", "Hello from
    user1")));
```

The topic messaging option in Akka.Cluster's distributed publish-subscribe feature fits the true definition of publish and subscribe, allowing you to easily post a message to hundreds of listeners simultaneously, regardless of their location in the cluster.

12.6.2 *Point-to-point messaging*

In addition to topic messaging, distributed publish-subscribe lets you send a message to an individual target in the actor system. Messages you send using this technique will be delivered to only one target somewhere in the cluster, but, again, you don't need to concern yourself with where that target is located. Continuing with the example of a chat room, by using point-to-point messaging, you can create private messaging: a message is sent to only one user.

In this approach, actors register with their path in the actor hierarchy. For example, an actor might have the path /user/customers/-customer1/users/user1. The following example shows how to register an actor as the only recipient of a message. Instead of using `Subscribe`, which you use with topic subscriptions, you use `Put`, which takes the `IActorRef` of the actor that's subscribing. The actor reference you send to the mediator must exist on the same local actor system as the mediator; otherwise, the subscription request will be ignored and an error will be generated.

```
public UserActor()
{
    //Register the actor to receive any messages published on the path of the
     actor
    var mediator = DistributedPubSub.Get(Context.System).Mediator;
    mediator.Tell(new Put(Self));

    Receive<SubscribeAck>(_ => Become(Subscribed));
}

//Spawn the actor at the address /user/anthony
var user =
    actorSystem.ActorOf<UserActor>("anthony");
```

You can wrap the message in a `Send` envelope along with the receiving actor's path. In this case, if you send a message with the path `/user/customers/customer1/users/user1`, the actor registered with that path receives the message. The following example shows how to format the actor path based on the username in the `Private-MessageUser` message. You send the `Send` message to the mediator, which routes it to the correct node in the actor system.

```
mediator.Tell(new Send("/user/anthony", new ChatMessage("user2", "Hello
    user1!")));
```

Note that if you have multiple actors registered with the same path, the mediator will use random-routing logic to choose which target receives the message. You specify that the mediator should use the local actor system, if a registration exists there for the path, by using the `LocalAffinity` flag in the `Send` message. The following example shows how to mark the `LocalAffinity` flag on the `Send` message when you send it to the mediator:

```
mediator.Tell(new Send("/user/anthony", new ChatMessage("user2", "Hello
    user1!"), localAffinity: true));
```

Alternatively, you could modify the routing logic that the mediator should use by editing the HOCON configuration to specify it. Here's how to modify HOCON to specify a round-robin approach to distributing the message to multiple subscribers instead of the default random approach:

```
akka.cluster.pub-sub {
  # The routing logic to use for 'Send'
  # Possible values: random, round-robin, broadcast
  routing-logic = round-robin
}
```

You might also need to broadcast a message to all subscribers in the cluster with the registered path. If you have three actors registered around the cluster with the same path and all perform the same task for redundancy purposes, you might need to broadcast a message to all subscribers, for example, to update configuration. By sending a `SendToAll` message to the mediator, you can broadcast the message to all subscribers.

```
mediator.Tell(new SendToAll("/user/downloader", new
    ConfigurationUpdate(usePersistentStorage: true)));
```

Point-to-point messaging allows you to easily send messages across a cluster to an individual target without having to worry about where exactly that target is located in the cluster. This vastly reduces the amount of state your application needs to maintain and allows you to focus on the core logic of the application.

12.6.3 Wrapping up

By using the distributed publish-subscribe functionality in Akka.NET, you can solve many of the problems you're likely to encounter when building applications across a cluster. Rather than keeping track of lots of state in your application, you can delegate it to the mediator.

12.7 *Cluster client*

Having now created an Akka.NET application that uses clustering, you've let the Akka.Cluster package deal with many of the tasks related to deployment of actors in the cluster, at nodes driven by computation and by the reactive nature of the framework. This presents you with a potential difficulty when it comes to accessing the actors stored in it from outside of the cluster. One example of this is if you have multiple independent Akka.NET clusters running separate applications. You may at some stage need to integrate the two applications together and allow communication between the two clusters. But with no known fixed hosts for actors in the cluster, this means that you can no longer follow the Akka.Remote approach to communicating with remote actors by specifying fixed well-known paths.

Akka.Cluster's `ClusterClient` allows an actor to connect to a cluster without joining it (see figure 12.7). It's important to note that the `ClusterClient` should only be used for communicating between separate actor systems and should not be used for communication internal to an actor system; the distributed publish-subscribe component should be used for internal communication.

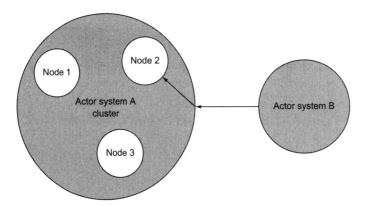

Figure 12.7   The cluster client allows communications with actors hosted in a cluster from other actors that are located on actor systems outside of the cluster.

The `ClusterClient` works by specifying one or more known contact points that you can use to connect to a cluster, much like the seed nodes you saw earlier when considering how to get new nodes to join an existing cluster. To connect to a cluster, you run the cluster receptionist component on either all the nodes in an actor system or on only those selected nodes belonging to a specific role. The first step when using the `ClusterClient` is to specify which services are accessible to actors that reside outside of the cluster. This increases the security of the cluster by ensuring that external clients can't interact with actors that may be storing sensitive data as their internal state.

The following example shows how to retrieve the cluster receptionist extension and then register an actor to be accessible to external actors by calling the Register-Service method on the cluster receptionist. In the example, you create an actor that acts as an echo service, replying to the requesting actor with whatever message it received. You could also use RegisterSubscriber, which allows listening to a specific topic, similar to distributed publish-subscribe.

```
//Create an actor which replies to the original sender with the message
//it received
class EchoActor : UntypedActor
{
    protected override void OnReceive(object message)
    {
        Sender.Tell(message);
    }
}

//Deploy the echo service to the path /user/echo
var echoService = actorSystem.ActorOf<EchoActor>("echo");

//Retrieve the cluster receptionist extension
var receptionist = ClusterClientReceptionist.Get(actorSystem);

//Register the echo service with the cluster client
receptionist.RegisterService(echoService);
```

Outside of the cluster, you configure the client application to communicate with the cluster. You first need to ensure that your actor system has a port open to allow messages to be sent in response. You also need to change actorRefProvider to use either RemoteActorRefProvider or ClusterActorRefProvider. In the client HOCON configuration, you create a port to listen on and set actorRefProvider to use Remote-ActorRefProvider:

```
Client HOCON configuration
```

Now, on the client, you create an actor that acts as a proxy to the cluster. You specify the initial contact points, which are the nodes that run the cluster receptionist and permit communication. In this case, you create two receptionist paths that the cluster client uses. If other receptionists are running in the cluster on different paths than those the client knows about, they will be sent to the client. This ensures that even in the event of a node becoming unresponsive, the ClusterClient can still communicate with the cluster through another node. On the client, you can create a Cluster-Client proxy that uses the contact points as the initial cluster receptionist points.

```
//The set of nodes which the cluster client will first  connect to in the
    cluster
var initialContacts =
    ImmutableHashSet<ActorPath>.Empty
```

```
.Add(ActorPath.Parse("akka.tcp://Chapter12Cluster@localhost:8080/system/recep
    tionist"))

.Add(ActorPath.Parse("akka.tcp://Chapter12Cluster@localhost:8081/system/recep
    tionist"));

//The settings used to configure the cluster client
var clusterClientSettings =
    ClusterClientSettings.Create(actorSystem)
    .InitialContacts(initialContacts);

//Creaste the Props used to deploy the cluster client on the local actor
    system
var clusterClientProps =
    ClusterClient.Props(clusterClientSettings);

//Deploy the cluster client into the local actor system
var clusterClient = actorSystem.ActorOf(clusterClientProps, "clusterClient");
```

You can now send messages to the cluster through the proxy and communicate in the same way you communicated through distributed publish-subscribe. The next example shows how to send a message to services listening on a defined path in the actor system. Here, you send a message to the /user/echo path, which has the echo service you created on the cluster listening:

```
var response = await clusterClient.Ask("Hello echo service");
```

Once a connection is established between a cluster receptionist and a ClusterClient, the client becomes an extension of the cluster. During usage, heartbeats are sent between the receptionist and the client to ensure that both are still available. If the receptionist fails to respond to heartbeats, the system switches to using a different receptionist hosted in the cluster. By extension, because this information is being sent and received by the client, you can register an actor to receive messages from the cluster client informing it when more contact points have been added. The cluster-Client uses the SubscribeContactPoints message to do this:

```
clusterClient.Tell(SubscribeContactPoints.Instance);
```

Similarly, in the cluster, you can register an actor to receive notifications when new clients connect to the actor system. In this case, sending a SubscribeClusterClients message to the receptionist notifies an actor when new clients connect to the cluster:

```
clusterReceptionist.Tell(SubscribeClusterClients.Instance);
```

The ClusterClient and cluster receptionist provide a safe means of communicating with an Akka.NET cluster without the need to proxy through an external network protocol such as HTTP. By using the ClusterClient and the cluster receptionist, you can also get an experience that is almost equivalent to your client being a node in the cluster.

12.8   Case study: Clustering, scaling, cluster management

Big data processing has become a core component of many modern applications, providing valuable insight and analytics to both the business and the consumer. A big data–processing pipeline needs to ingest data from tens or hundreds of disparate data sources, joining rows quickly and efficiently across datasets before finally unlocking the insight contained within. In many instances, this is achievable using a single server capable of processing all the data sources. But as datasets grow in size and count, you may encounter many difficulties. You may be limited by the amount of memory on the machine. If there's not enough RAM to hold all the datasets, you have to use techniques that cache files to the hard disk, possibly increasing latency. You may be performing computationally intensive operations that take longer and longer to complete. In an industry where users and businesses increasingly expect immediate results, it's imperative that businesses match these expectations to remain competitive.

In this chapter, you saw how to scale out an actor system across multiple nodes, thanks to Akka.NET's clustering components. You can think of a big data pipeline as a sequence of actors. Each actor takes in the results from the previous actor and other datasets before performing mapping, joining, or filtering operations, after which the results are passed to the next actor in the chain. Figure 12.8 shows two datasets mapped to a similar format, joined together based on a common key, and filtered to remove unwanted lines. This maps to four distinct actors, two for performing the mapping stage on the initial two datasets, one for performing the join, and the final one for filtering the data.

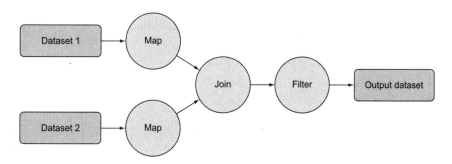

Figure 12.8   Big data jobs are composed of several distinct stages. By using Akka.NET clustering, you can partition each of these stages across a cluster of machines without needing to deal with network topology.

But as datasets grow in size, a single server might struggle with processing. Because actors are simple to scale, though, you can transparently move the actors around a cluster of machines. The decision on where to host actors is made internally by the Akka.NET runtime, meaning that you can focus on the data-processing pipeline itself rather than the difficult task of coordinating work across multiple machines.

Summary

In this chapter, you learned

- Extending many of the concepts you saw when using Akka.Remote to allow you to transparently scale actor systems across multiple nodes
- Patterns used in Akka.Cluster that allow you to design applications that can scale across machines
- Features of Akka.NET that make it easier for you to write distributed applications

Akka.NET and reactive programming in production

Throughout the book, we've looked at several small case studies, each chapter detailing how an Akka.NET feature is applicable in a real-world scenario. In chapter 2, you also saw how to design an e-commerce website using the principles of the Reactive Manifesto. In this chapter, you'll see how to combine these approaches by designing a reactive system from the ground up using Akka.NET functionality.

This chapter focuses on designing and developing an IoT application using Akka.NET. Sensors and consumer electronics have advanced in recent decades, and it's now possible to create ultra-low-cost and ultra-low-power sensor devices capable of recording data and sending it through an internet connection for collection elsewhere. In this chapter, we'll look at this type of system in the context of designing a smart-home application, in which there are several sensors per room collecting data to provide feedback about the overall state of the house. For example, a smart home might have movement sensors to detect motion, temperature sensors to control heating and air conditioning, and carbon monoxide detectors to detect the presence of gas. These sensors collect data at a fixed frequency and send it to a backend system so it can be accessed from anywhere in the world, allowing a homeowner to see the status of their home whether they're at home, at work, or on holiday. The application must support use by multiple people. With potentially many users and an even larger number of sensors, vast amounts of data are sent through the system. The system must provide quick feedback to users after data has been collected; and it must scale with the expected load, while continuing to be responsive in the presence of ever-changing data. In view of the concepts considered in chapter 1, a reactive architecture provides an ideal solution.

Figure 13.1 illustrates how a smart home might look. It has multiple rooms, and each room has multiple sensors for collecting data. The data is sent to a backend system, where it's processed. In this chapter, we'll only focus on building the backend system from the point of data collection onward; we won't focus on how to build the physical devices for the smart home.

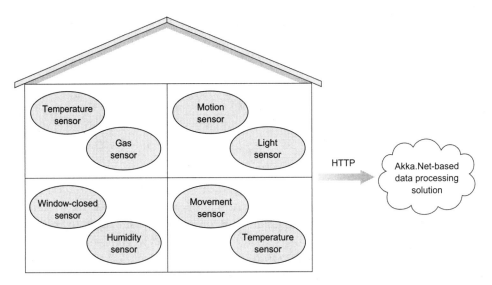

Figure 13.1 A smart home with multiple sensors forms the context for this chapter's case study.

Once data has been collected in the system, it must be aggregated in real time and understandable to users of the application, providing feedback about the home's state. The time-series aggregated data can be stored in a database for later presentation in graphs, and graphs should be dynamically updated when new data arrives.

13.1 *Designing with actors*

So far, you've seen at a high level that the application must receive data readings from IoT devices at a given frequency and aggregate those readings into a format that can be presented to users as graphs and warnings. You want to follow the principles of the Manifesto, so that you can build a larger, responsive system by scaling out as the load grows; you also want to handle errors by isolating them, forestalling knock-on effects on other system components.

When designing systems with Akka.NET, it's often beneficial to think of the smallest possible component you can use that can exist independently of other components: in this case, one actor per sensor in each smart home. This approach allows you to easily add more and more sensors to the system, without developing a backlog of messages to be processed. It will also be possible to isolate errors, should a sensor send faulty data through the system.

But the sensors exist as part of a broader context that contains a number of other linked components. Notably, sensors are deployed in rooms, and although you want to see data from individual sensors, you also want to see a broad overview of the state of a single room. Broadening the context further still, individual rooms are constituent parts of a house, and you want to see an overview of the status of the house as a whole. Although you could create a single actor responsible for the entire house that receives readings from every deployed sensor, that would create a potential bottleneck. An alternative is to create a hierarchy representing the overall application structure. This would allow performing aggregations on a sensor level and then pushing aggregated data up to the room level, where further aggregations could be done before pushing those aggregations up to the house level. We'll look at further benefits of the hierarchical approach in the next section, where we'll consider the failure-handling capabilities that come with this design.

In addition to performing aggregations on data, you also want to create alerts. As you collect data, you'll be on the lookout for anomalies indicating a sensor event, which could indicate an event of interest. For example, when using a motion sensor, several constant readings of movement would suggest movement in the home, something that should be investigated. But, at the same time, you don't want to send a notification every time movement is detected, or the user may receive hundreds of notifications every day. There should be some logic in place that continues to perform aggregations but doesn't send data. Although you could set a flag in the actor, this could increase the complexity of the code, especially as the number of potential states grows. For example, you should also consider what would happen if you wanted to reset an actor after a certain period of time, or allow for other functionality, such as a cool-down timer. In such cases, you can create state machines using the functionality you saw in chapter 4. This allows you to change an actor's behavior at runtime to an entirely new function for incoming messages, rather than trying to combine everything in a single handler function.

13.2 Handling failure

Failure is a part of every software project. In addition to possible software failure, you need to factor in the hardware components of an IoT application, such as the possibility of a faulty sensor, which can lead to a sensor sending invalid data. If invalid readings are sent to the processing backend, the likely cause is sensor failure. If a sensor fails, you need to ensure that it doesn't affect other system components. In chapter 6, you saw the benefits when parent actors supervise their spawned child actors; in the same manner, you can build a hierarchy of actors for this smart-home application.

Fortunately, you have a very hierarchical data model in place as it stands. Every sensor is deployed in a room, and each room exists as part of a house. This means that, at the very top level, an actor represents a house. Deployed under the house actor are a number of actors for each room, and each room has a number of sensor actors deployed. If a sensor starts to fail, it will propagate the error up to the room, which will isolate that sensor's errors from the other sensors. If the sensor fails on a frequent

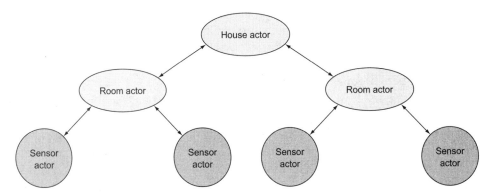

Figure 13.2 The smart-home hierarchy of actors

basis, its parent actor can escalate the error up to the level of the house and display the error more prominently in the application. This results in the hierarchy shown in figure 13.2. By modeling your application as a hierarchy of components where the child actors are responsible for the most critical work, your system isolates failure in the smallest individual component.

13.3 *Designing for scale*

Given the rise in popularity of IoT devices, your system could see continuous growth in coming years, leading to more data passing through it—something you need to consider. To maintain a reactive application, you must persist data in a database, in a format optimized for reading. To do that, you'll create a database-writer actor whose sole responsibility is to receive a record, which is then inserted into a database. You'll create an actor dedicated to this task primarily as an optimization. You could create a database connection per sensor, but that could lead to performance problems caused by connections not being reused. It would also disallow creating batches of writes against the database, because you'd have to send every row for every sensor, rather than writing a number of rows at once for a selection of sensors.

You'll create a system that looks like figure 13.3. Here, you see several sensors, all sending data to a single actor responsible for writing data into the database. But it's likely that the number of sensors will grow, forcing more data through the database-writer actor. As more data is forced through this actor, the message queue will grow, eventually delaying database writes and reducing application responsiveness, contradicting the aims of reactive architecture. To ensure that your system can stay responsive, you need to eschew bottlenecks, which limit system throughput. Fortunately, in your case, you can deploy multiple database writers, and thanks to Akka.NET's routers, you can treat a collection of writer actors as a single actor. You can add more writers as the load increases, ensuring that your application scales successfully with the expected load.

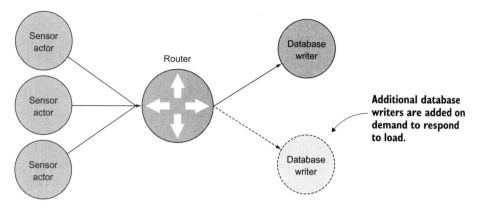

Figure 13.3 Multiple actors send input to a router, which passes the input to a database-writer actor. If its message queue grows too large, another database-writer actor can be added.

13.4 Handling configuration

You'll design your system to be maintainable and testable, including running the application and its dependencies in multiple environments to verify that all functionality works as expected. You'll also want to ensure separation of the various environments. For example, you'll run the application locally on a development machine, as well as in a production environment. It's important to use different databases for these two purposes so that you don't include test data in your production database or risk customer data by using it in a test environment.

In the last section, you designed a database-writer actor responsible for pushing aggregated data into the database in an efficient manner. By parameterizing the connection string that this actor uses, you can run the same application both in production and locally on a development machine without issue. But you'll also have a configuration for routers, which are common across both environments. In chapter 5, you saw how to create configuration files that can be accessed by actors across the system.

In your application, you'll create three configuration files: one common file holding the overall actor-system configuration, and two files providing environment-specific settings, notably, connection strings for the database. By splitting environment-specific settings into two files with different responsibilities, you can override the connection strings and merge the two types of files.

13.5 Ingesting data

With an internal infrastructure in place, your system is ready to receive data from the IoT devices deployed in people's homes. You'll create a publicly accessible API through which the devices can send messages. This API will be responsible for data-transmission security, as well as for converting data from an efficient protocol (HTTP) into the actor-system format.

In chapter 10, you saw that you can write a custom protocol that interacts directly with the actor system with Akka.IO; but here, you'll use an HTTP connection endpoint. This offers a number of benefits, including preexisting security solutions, which will help to protect user data when it's sent to backend systems. As these devices are deployed in homes with stable internet connection, you'll also have sufficient bandwidth to send data through HTTP, rather than needing to heavily optimize a protocol.

Although your actor system will hold all the system state, you should ensure that your ingestion nodes are stateless, so that you can quickly provision more of them on demand. You can achieve this by separating the core actor system (which holds your state) from the edge nodes (responsible for data ingestion), and then connecting the two together using Akka.NET remoting, as you saw in chapter 8. Because the data only flows from devices to the system in its current state, the ingestion nodes simply act as a pipeline stage, converting the messages from one format to another: HTTP to Akka.NET. This creates an architecture that resembles figure 13.4, in which messages are sent from sensor devices to the ingestion nodes, where they're forwarded to the actor system.

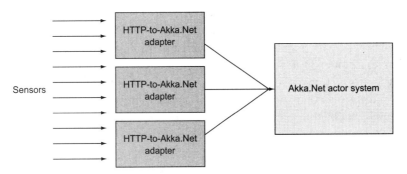

Figure 13.4 Messages are sent from sensor devices to ingestion nodes, where they're converted and forwarded to the actor system.

13.6 Testing

With your actors designed and ready, it's important to verify that they function as expected. You can do this by creating a test project that exercises the expected behavior of the actors by sending a number of messages when the application runs in production. In chapter 9, you saw how to test actors using a number of different methods, either testing them in isolation or testing how they integrate with other actors. These tests should be designed to test as much of the functionality of the actors as possible, to eliminate any surprises when the system runs in production and new messages are delivered.

With a suite of tests, you can verify system integrity when actor changes occur, allowing you to catch errors before the application goes live. You can further integrate the tests you write with a continuous-integration server. By constantly testing the quality of the build as changes are checked in to source control, fewer bugs will slip into the production environment than if you were testing manually.

13.7 Real-time integration

One key feature you want in your application is the ability to push new data to clients as soon as it becomes available, allowing users to respond to it appropriately. For example, if a user has a motion detector installed in their smart home and they have the web page open, they'll want immediate notification if movement is detected, so they can take appropriate action.

You can use one of the techniques we looked at in chapter 10 to achieve this by adding a WebSocket connection outside of the actor system. Whenever a user navigates to a web page with a WebSocket protocol, the actor system is notified that the user is connected. The actor system can register the WebSocket as a subscriber to any events published by the system: for example, a room sensor. Figure 13.5 illustrates what happens when a user navigates to a web page with a WebSocket connection and how the actor system is responsible for managing event subscription.

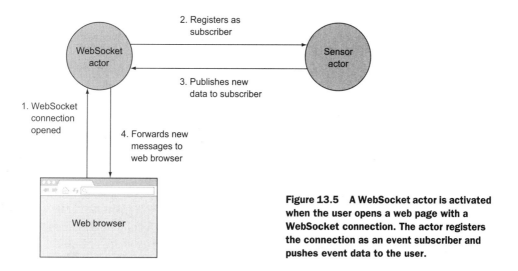

Figure 13.5 A WebSocket actor is activated when the user opens a web page with a WebSocket connection. The actor registers the connection as an event subscriber and pushes event data to the user.

13.8 Data persistence

You know how to write data in a database in an optimized time-series schema, but you'll also want to store other pieces of static data as sensor metadata, including the time period you should use when performing aggregations for a given sensor. Some sensors may need a finer level of granularity than others. With a motion sensor, you want to receive an alert as soon as a number of events have occurred, whereas with a temperature sensor, you might be happy to use a broader timescale. This data will be configured by users, so you need to persist it in the event of sensor restart or redistribution onto a different node.

Although you could choose to persist the data in a fashion similar to the database-writer actor, a better option in this scenario is to use Akka.Persistence, which we looked at in chapter 11. With Akka.Persistence, you include a simplified data store as part of an actor's definition. With the persistence components, you can persist events that flow through an actor. In this case, you'll choose not to persist sensor readings; instead, you'll store the events that change an actor's behavior, including events that influence message output, as defined by your application.

13.9 *Cluster scale-out*

As more customers use your service, you'll need more computing resources to handle the increased amount of data flowing through the system. Because your system actors are designed to be independent, you can locate them on any machine you want: there are no direct dependencies between any two actors. This means you can use the cluster-sharding capabilities of the Akka.NET clustering tools to distribute the sensors on different machines, as you saw in chapter 12. Given the hierarchy you developed (where you have a top-level actor for each home; each home has several rooms; and each room has several sensors), by partitioning the actor system at the home level, you can maintain the locality of all sensors and rooms, which are children of the home. This ensures that components that need to communicate with each other are located on the same machine; communication between them will be faster than if they were located on different machines. This opens up future opportunities for information sharing between sensors.

You can add more machines to the cluster, either manually or using the autoscaling capabilities provided by many cloud providers. In chapter 12, you saw that you can connect more nodes to the cluster in response to increased demand at any point in the application's life, and they'll become part of the cluster without manual intervention. In addition to this, Akka.NET clustering can detect node failures and reallocate resources from a cluster with healthy nodes. In this way, you can build elastically scalable systems that are resilient in the face of failures more significant than those affecting only small system components.

Conclusion

You can see how components fit together when you design systems using Akka.NET. Although there's no single one-size-fits-all solution to every problem, this chapter has given you an idea of the considerations you need to make when architecting broader solutions. When this understanding of system design with Akka.NET is combined with a solid understanding of the principles of the Reactive Manifesto, it presents an opportunity to create systems that are robust and scalable. Having seen this broader case study, along with the smaller case studies included in each chapter, you should now have an understanding of how the individual components of Akka.NET fit into a larger reactive system architecture, as well as how to develop those individual components using Akka.NET.

index

A

Ack message 100
Acknowledgement event 98
active record pattern 193
actor address 37
actor model 8, 10
actor passivation 233
actor reference 38
actor selection 38
actor systems 33–35
   composing 127–148
      Akka.NET remoting 129–130
      Akka.Remote security 143–147
      communicating with remote actors
         132–137
      elastically scaling across machines 137–140
      failure handling across machines
         140–143
      preparing to use remoting 130–132
   loading configurations into 69
   testing 167–168
ActorOf method 36, 60–61, 227
actorRefProvider 239
actors 26–33, 43–58
   addresses 37–39
   changing states of 15
   communicating through 180–182
   communicating with 36–40
   configuring deployments of 60–64
   converting FSM into 52–54
   defining 29–33
   deploying 33–36
   designing with 244–245
   e-commerce applications with 13–19
      data transfer between services 16–17
      making purchases 15–16

      reactive shopping cart 13–14
      scaling work with routers 17–18
   FSM actors 54–57
   hierarchy of 34–35
   in shards, communicating with 232
   integration testing 158–164
      asserting message responses 159–161
      creating test specifications 158–159
      test probes 163–164
      time-based testing 161–163
   lifecycles of 88–91
   overview of 26–28
   references 37–39
   remote deployment of 135–136
   restarting 82
   restricting remote actor targets 144–147
   sending messages to 39
   spawning 35–36, 63
   storing state with Akka .Persistence 192–213
   storing state within 20
   testing
      Akka.TestKit 153–154
      testing distributed applications with Multi-
         Node TestKit 164–171
   unit testing 154–158
      spawning test actors 155–156
      testing FSMs 157–158
      validating internal data 156–157
   uses for 28–29
   watching for deaths of 91–93
      DeathWatch 91–93
      reaper pattern 91–93
   writing persistent actors 195–197
   See also remote actors
ActorSelection 39, 99
ActorSystem 154, 227
AddItem event 196

addresses
  of actors 37–39
  remote actor system addresses 132–133
AddressTerminated property 142
Akka.Cluster module, building clustered applications with 214–242
  cluster clients 238–240
  cluster sharding 228–233
  cluster singleton 225–228
  cluster-aware routers 219–223
  distributed publish-subscribe 233–238
  working with cluster gossip 223–225
Akka.Cluster.Sharding module 228
Akka.DI.AutoFac NuGet project 66
akka.io toolkit
  integrations with 184–190
  sending data through 188–190
Akka.Logger.NLog 72
Akka.NET
  advantages of 7
  disadvantages of 8
  overview of 8–10
Akka.Persistence module 195–201
  configuring journals 199–201
  performance tuning of 201–212
    async write journals 203–204
    at-least-once delivery 204–208
    snapshot stores 201–203
    upgrade strategies for applications using event sourcing 208–212
  storing actor state with 192–213
  writing persistent actors 195–197
Akka.Remote module
  installing 130
  security 143–147
    limiting messages sent over networks 144
    restricting remote actor targets 144–147
Akka.TestKit module 153–154
all-for-one strategy 82
AllRoles property 224
API-user errors 96
application-level failures 78–96
  actor lifecycles 88–91
  fail-fast programming 86–88
  interface-level failures 94–95
  responding to 79–81
  supervision trees 81–86
    cumulative errors 84
    Decider function 83–84
    specifying actors to restart 82
  watching for deaths of actors 91–93
    DeathWatch 91–93
    reaper pattern 91–93
applications 25–42
  handling message loss 97–100

setting up 26
  upgrade strategies for 208–212
  See also clustered applications; distributed applications, testing with MultiNode TestKit
ArgumentException 85, 94
ArgumentNullException 94
ArithmeticException 84–85
Ask method 175
ASP.NET framework 175–178
asserting message responses 159–161
asterisk wildcard 38
async write journals 203–204
asynchronous logging 72
asynchronous operations 31
at-least-once delivery 97, 204–208
at-least-once messaging 205
AtLeastOnceDeliveryActor 205, 207–208
at-most-once delivery guarantee 97
AuthenticatedMessageEnvelope class 145
AutoFacDependencyResolver 66
autoscalers 110

B

bandwidth constraints 191
barriers 168–169
Become 45–47
behavioral tests 152
behaviors 43–58
  runtime, setting 44–47
    Become 45–47
    Unbecome 45–47
  switchable 45
best-effort router 114
Blackhole method 170
blackholing 170
blocking operations 29
bottleneck point 216
Bound message 187
broadcast pool 107, 110
broadcast support, in routers 125
BroadcastEnvelope 125
browsers 182–184
browsing state 15
ByteString 188–189

C

CartOverview message 159
cascading failures 140
child actors 16
circuit breaker pattern 47
CLR (Common Language Runtime) 30
cluster clients 238–240

cluster singleton 225–228
ClusterActorRefProvider 217, 239
cluster-aware routers 219–223
  creating groups 219–221
  creating pools 222–223
ClusterClient 238, 240
clustered applications 214–242
  cluster clients 238–240
  cluster sharding 228–233
  cluster singleton 225–228
  cluster-aware routers 219–223
  distributed publish-subscribe 233–238
  working with cluster gossip 223–225
ClusterRouterGroup class 221
ClusterRouterPool 223
clusters
  defined 216
  gossip 223–225
    handling messages 224–225
    retrieving cluster states 224
  of machines, scaling out across 20
  scaling out 250
  sharding 228–233
    communicating with actors in shards 232
    creating new shards 229–232
    handling passivation in shards 233
ClusterSingletonManager 226
ClusterSingletonProxy 227
code duplication, preventing 31
codebase 87
CommandFailed message 188
command-line tooling 26
commands 196
common configuration, test specification 166
Common Language Runtime (CLR) 30
CommonConfigurationProperty 166
concurrency models 50–52
Configuration method 176
configuration parameters 74
ConfigurationFactory.Parse method 69
configurations 59–75
  actor deployments 60–64
  DI containers 66–67
  handling 247
  journals 199–201
  loading into actor systems 69
  remoting for projects 130–132
  routers to use multiple machines 138–139
  why necessary 60
  with HOCON 67–70
Confirm command 206
ConfirmDelivery event 207
Connected message 187
consistent hashing 116–120
ConsistentHashableEnvelope 118

consistent-hashing router 117
ConsistentHashingGroup 221
ConsistentHashingPool class 117
Console.ReadLine 29
constructor guards 30
constructors 60
containers 66–67
Context property 32
Context.Parent 141
Context.Path.Parent 141
Context.Stop 88
Context.Watch 142
Create method 86
Create static method 36
CreateTestProbe method 164
CRUD (create, read, update, delete) 8
cumulative errors 84
custom constructors 60
custom dispatchers 61
custom loggers 73
custom mailboxes 60
Customers actor 145

D

data
  ingesting 247–248
  internal, validating 156–157
  persistence of 249–250
  sending through akka.io 188–190
  transferring between services 16–17
data jobs 241
data migrations 209
DatabaseCommunicationActor 86
DatabaseNotAvailableMessage 45
deadLetters actor 34, 73, 89
deaths of actors 91–93
DeathWatch 91–93, 142
Debug method 72
Decider function 83–84
Decider.From function 85
default state 49
DefaultResizer 110
defining actors 29–33
Deliver method 207
delivery. *See* at-least-once delivery
dependency graphs 65
dependency injection. *See* DI
deploying
  actors 33–36
    actor systems 33–35
    configuring deployments 60–64
    remotely 135–136
    spawning actors 35–36
  loggers 72–73

DeploymentComplete barrier 168
design patterns 14
DI (dependency injection) 59–75
    containers 66–67
    overview of 64–65
dispatchers 61
distributed applications, testing with MultiNode
        TestKit 164–171
    barriers 168–169
    MultiNode specs 165–167
    testing for network failure 169–171
    testing individual actor systems 167–168
distributed computing 215
distributed publish-subscribe 233–238
    point-to-point messaging 236–237
    topic messaging 234–236
DistributedPubSubMediator 234
distributing work 106–111
    groups 109–111
    pools 109–111
    routers 106–108
domain model 209
double forward slash character 68

E

e-commerce applications
    publishing 19–20
    with actors 13–19
        changing states of actors 15
        data transfer between services 16–17
        making purchase 15–16
        reactive shopping cart 13–14
        scaling work with routers 17–18
elastically scaling across machines 137–140
enabled property 220
end-to-end tests 152–153
EnterBarrier method 168
Environment property 183
environment settings 74
environments, reacting to changes in 20–21
Equals 55
error kernel patterns 88
error-handling code 87
errors
    cumulative 84
    in applications, responding to 79–81
escalate directive 83
event sourcing
    overview of 193–194
    upgrade strategies for applications using
        208–212
events 48, 196
ExceededException error 208
exceptions 79

ExistenceConfirmed property 142
ExpectMsg method 159–160
ExpectNoMsg method 161
extensibility points 34
external dependencies 64

F

Fact attribute 159
fail-fast programming 86–88
Failure class 94
failure detector 216
Failure message 120, 123
failures 76–102
    application-level 78–96
        actor lifecycles 88–91
        Akka.NET supervision trees 81–86
        fail-fast programming 86–88
        responding to application errors 79–81
        watching for deaths of actors 91–93
    handling 245–246
    handling across machines 140–143
        remoting DeathWatch 142
        supervisor strategies across networks 141
    interface-level 94–95
    of networks 169–171
    overview of 77–78
    transport-level 96–101
fault tolerance 19, 216
finite state machine. See FSMs
Forward method 146
freemium model 40
FSMActor class 54, 57, 157, 195
FSMs (finite state machines) 47–57
    in concurrency models 50–52
    converting into actors 52–54
    finite state machine actors 54–57
    overview of 48–49
    testing 157–158

G

GetCartOverview message 159
GetData message 45
GetLogger method 71
Global.asax file 176
gossip in clusters 223–225
    handling cluster gossip messages 224–225
    retrieving cluster states 224
Gossip protocol 216
GoTo method 55
graphs 65
GreeterActor 35
groups 109–111, 219–221

H

hash character 69
hashing 116–120
hash-mapping delegate 117
hierarchy
  designing 102
  of actors 34–35
HOCON (Human Optimized Configuration
      Object Notation)
  configuring with 67–70
  overview of 67–69
hubs 179

I

IActorRef 37, 93, 99, 131, 133, 163
IAppBuilder 176
IConsistentHashable interface 117
idempotence property 100
Identify message 39
IEventAdapter interface 210–211
IEventSequence interface 211
IMessageExtractor interface 230
In block, TestKit 162
index variable 63
ingesting data 247–248
Initialized message handler 51
installing Akka.Remote 130
integration testing actors 158–164
  asserting message responses 159–161
  creating test specifications 158–159
  test probes 163–164
  time-based testing 161–163
integrations 173–191
  real-time 249
  with akka.io 184–190
    creating listening sockets 185–188
    sending data through akka.io 188–190
  with ASP.NET 175–178
  with SignalR 179–184
    communicating through actors 180–182
    connecting to user web browsers 182–184
interface-level failures 94–95
internal data 156–157
IoT (Internet of Things) 5, 174
IPossiblyHarmful interface 144
IsRecovering 199
IsRecoveryComplete 199
ItemAdded event 196
ItemIdentifier event 210

J

JoinChatroom message 235
journals 196, 199–201, 209
  See also async write journals

K

key-value pairs 116, 119

L

lazy connections 132
Leader property 224
lifecycles of actors 88–91
listening sockets 185–188
LocalActorRef 37
locked state 52
loggers 72–73
logging 59–75
  advantages of 70–71
  customizing logger deployment 72–73
  writing to logs 71–72
Logging class 71

M

machines
  configuring routers to use multiple 138–139
  elastically scaling across 137–140
  handling failures across 140–143
    remoting DeathWatch 142
    supervisor strategies across networks 141
  scaling out across clusters of 20
  See also FSMs (finite state machines)
Manifest method 210
MapSignalR 182
max-nr-of-instances-per-node 222
MaxUnconfirmedMessages property 208
Members property 224
MessageConfirmed event 206–207
message-driven applications 4
MessageReceived message 180
messages
  asserting responses 159–161
  handling cluster gossip messages 224–225
  loss of 97–100
  preparing for next 44
  sending 39–40
  sending to remote actors 133–135
  sent over networks, limiting 144
MessageSent event 206
messaging
  point-to-point 236–237
  topic 234–236

methods, overriding 32
MultiNode TestKit
    specifications 165–167
    testing distributed applications with 164–171
        barriers 168–169
        for network failure 169–171
        individual actor systems 167–168
MultiNodeConfig class 166
MultiNodeFact attribute 166
MultiNodeSpec class 166
multiple independent actors 18

N

networks
    limiting messages sent over 144
    supervisor strategies across 141
    testing for failure 169–171
NLP (natural language processing) 101
nodes 216
NuGet package management system 26
NullReferenceException 79

O

one-for-one strategy 82
ORM (object relational mapper) 193
overriding methods 32
OWIN (Open Web Interface for .NET) 176, 182

P

packet latency 140
Parallel Library (TPL) 31
ParseString 69
Passivate message 233
passivation in shards 233
pattern-matching API 31
payment-gateway actor 17, 20
peer-to-peer cluster 216
Persist method 203, 210
PersistAsync method 203–204
PersistenceId 206
persistent
    actors, writing 195–197
    data 249–250
persistent connections 179
PersistentActor class 195
PersistentConnection class 182–183
point-to-point messaging 236–237
PoisonPill class 88, 91, 198
pools 109–111, 222–223
PostStop method 90
predicates 52

PreRestart method 89
PreStart method 90
PrivateMessageUser message 237
probes. See test probes
processing 27–28
production 243–250
    cluster scale-out 250
    data persistence 249–250
    designing for scale 246
    designing with actors 244–245
    handling configurations 247
    handling failures 245–246
    ingesting data 247–248
    real-time integration 249
    testing 248–249
programming. See fail-fast programming
Props 61–63
    creating 62–63
    problems with 63
    spawning actors with 63
Protocol Buffers serializer 210
protocol identifier 37
proxy actor 141
Publish message 236
publishing e-commerce applications 19–20
publish-subscribe functionality 21
purchase-completion state 15
purchases 15–16

Q

question mark wildcard 38

R

random routing 112–113
random-number generator (RNG) 112
Reactive Extensions (Rx) 6
Reactive Manifesto 4–6
reactive programming
    advantages of 3–10
    reactive systems vs. 6–7
reactive systems
    design of 12–13
    reactive programming vs. 6–7
real-time integration 249
reaper pattern 91–93
ReaperActor 93
ReceiveActor class 31, 46, 181, 195, 229
ReceiveCommand method 196
Received message 187
ReceiveRecover method 198
ReceiveTimeout event 98–99, 233
redelivery-burst-limit property 208

references to actors 37–39
RegisterService method 239
RegisterSubscriber 239
remote actors
    communicating with 132–137
    restricting targets 144–147
    sending messages to 133–135
    system addresses 132–133
remote deployment of actors 135–136
remote supervision actor 141
RemoteActorRefProvider 131, 217, 239
RemoteDeploy 136
RemoteRouterConfig 139
remoting
    configuring for projects 130–132
    DeathWatch 142
    overview of 129–130
    preparing to use 130–132
reproducible deployment 62
resilient applications 4
responsive applications 4
restart directive 83
restarting actors 82
resume directive 83
RNG (random-number generator) 112
roles 166
round-robin pool 112
round-robin routing 113–114, 138
round-robin-group 109
RoundRobinPool class 113, 223
routers
    cluster-aware 219–223
        creating groups 219–221
        creating pools 222–223
    configuring to use multiple machines 138–139
    overview of 106–108
    scaling work with 17–18
    smallest-mailbox 114–115
    tail-chopping 122–124
routing
    consistent hashing 116–120
    random 112–113
    round-robin 113–114
    scatter-gather first-completed 120–121
    strategies for 111–124
running state 89
RunOn method 168
runtime behaviors 44–47
    Become 45–47
    switchable behaviors 45
    Unbecome 45–47
Rx (Reactive Extensions) 6

S

SaveSnapshot message 202
scalability 19, 216
scaling 103–126
    designing for 246
    distributing work 106–111
        groups 109–111
        pools 109–111
        routers 106–108
    elastically across machines 137–140
    out 104–106
        across cluster of machines 20
        clusters 250
    routing strategies 111–124
        consistent hashing 116–120
        random routing 112–113
        round-robin routing 113–114
        scatter-gather first-completed 120–121
        smallest-mailbox routers 114–115
        tail-chopping routers 122–124
    up 104–106
    work with routers 17–18
scatter-gather first-completed 120–121
ScatterGatherFirstCompletedGroup class 120
scheduling actors 34
search actor 18
seed nodes 216
Sender property 33, 63
sending
    data through akka.io 188–190
    messages 39–40
    messages to remote actors 133–135
SendMessage command 180, 183
SendToAll message 237
serializing messages 14
services, transferring data between 16–17
SetReceiveTimeout method 99
sharding
    clusters 228–233
    communicating with actors in shards 232
    creating new shards 229–232
    handling passivation in shards 233
shopping carts 13–14, 16, 20
short-lived actors 35
SignalR library 179–184
    communicating through actors 180–182
    connecting to user web browsers 182–184
single actors 18
single targets 18
singleton. See cluster singleton
smallest-mailbox routers 114–115, 139
SmallestMailboxPool class 115
snapshot store 201
SnapshotOffer message 202

snapshots 201–203
sockets 185–188
spawning
   actors 35–36
   actors with Props 63
   test actors 155–156
specific configuration modifications 166
specifications, MultiNode TestKit 165
SqlServerJournal class 200, 211
Start method 231
starting state 88
StartProxy method 232
StartsWith method 55
Startup.cs file 176
stashing 51–52, 198
State property 224
state transition diagram 48
state transition table 49
StateData property 157
stateless operations 18
StateName property 157
states 48
   of actors 28, 43–58
      changing 15
      storing with Akka .Persistence 192–213
   of clusters, retrieving 224
   storing within actors 20
StateTimeout message 56
StatsD protocol 184, 189
Stay method 55
StockIdentifier property 211
stop directive 83
storing
   actor states with Akka .Persistence 192–213
   snapshots 201–203
   states within actors 20
SubscribeClusterClients message 240
Success class 94
supervision strategies 82
supervision trees 81–86
   cumulative errors 84
   Decider function 83–84
   specifying actors to restart 82
SupervisorStrategy method 85
switchable behaviors 45
Sys property 159
system actor 34

T

tail-chopping routers 122–124
TailChoppingPool class 125
tcp value 132
Tcp.IOError message 189

Tcp.PeerReset message 189
Tcp.Write message 189
TcpManager 186, 188
Tell method 39, 94
temp actor 35
Terminated message 93
terminating state 89
test attribute 158
test conductor 165, 169
test probes 163–164
test-actor references 155
TestActorRef 156
TestConductor property 170
TestFSMRef 157
testing 248–249
   actors 151–172
   distributed applications with MultiNode TestKit
      164–171
      barriers 168–169
      for network failure 169–171
      individual actor systems 167–168
      MultiNode specs 165–167
   integration testing actors 158–164
      asserting message responses 159–161
      creating test specifications 158–159
      test probes 163–164
      time-based testing 161–163
   unit testing actors 154–158
      spawning test actors 155–156
      testing FSMs 157–158
      validating internal data 156–157
TestKit class 158
TestProbe 167
TestTransport property 169
TicketBarrierActor 157
time-based testing 161–163
TimeoutException 84
TimeSpan 56
ToJournal method 210
topic messaging 234–236
TPL (Parallel Library) 31
transferring data between services 16–17
transient failure 80
transitions by actors 89–91
transport-level failures 96–101
trusted-selection-paths element 146
turnstile FSM 49
TypedActor class 32
types, testing 152

U

Unbecome 45–47
UnderlyingActor property 156

unit testing actors 154–158
  spawning test actors 155–156
  testing FSMs 157–158
  validating internal data 156–157
unlocked state 52
Unstash 52
UnstashAll 52
UntypedActor class 29, 31, 45
UpdateState method 206–207
upgrading strategies for applications 208–212
Use method 176
user actor 34
user experience (UX) 12
UserConnected message 180
UserDisconnected message 180
UserRegistration message 95
UserService.Login.Latency bucket 185
UX (user experience) 12

V

validating internal data 156–157
virtual-nodes factor 118
Visual Studio package-management GUI 26

W

warn-after-number-of-unconfirmed-attempts
    208
web browsers 182–184
WebSocket protocol 249
WebsocketActor 182
When method 56
wildcard-address approach 107
wildcards 38
WithDeploy 136
WithHashMapping method 117
WithRouter method 108
write journals. *See* async write journals
writing
  persistent actors 195–197
  to logs 71–72

X

xUnit runner 155

C# in Depth, Fourth Edition
by Jon Skeet

ISBN: 9781617294532
528 pages
$49.99
March 2019

Functional Programming in C#
How to write better C# code

by Enrico Buonanno

ISBN: 9781617293955
408 pages
$44.99
August 2017

For ordering information go to www.manning.com

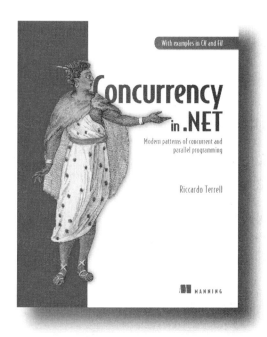
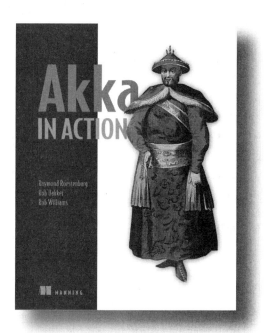

MORE TITLES FROM MANNING

Reactive Design Patterns
by Roland Kuhn with Brian Hanafee
and Jamie Allen

ISBN: 9781617291807
392 pages
$49.99
February 2017

*Functional and Reactive
Domain Modeling*
by Debasish Ghosh

ISBN: 9781617292248
320 pages
$59.99
October 2016

For ordering information go to www.manning.com

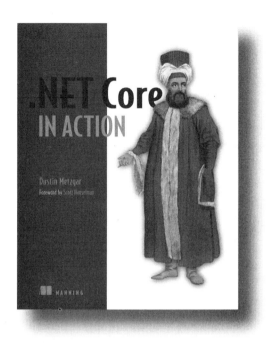

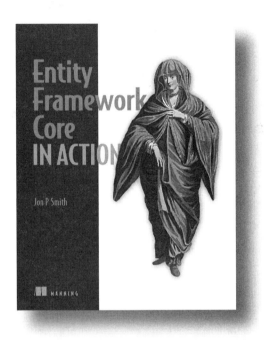

Entity Framework Core in Action
by Jon P Smith

ISBN: 9781617294563
520 pages
$49.99
July 2018

ASP.NET Core in Action
by Andrew Lock

ISBN: 9781617294617
712 pages
$49.99
June 2018

For ordering information go to www.manning.com

Get Programming with F#
A guide for .NET developers
by Isaac Abraham

ISBN: 9781617293993
592 pages
$44.99
February 2018

F# Deep Dives
Edited by Tomas Petricek
   and Phillip Trelford

ISBN: 9781617291326
372 pages
$49.99
December 2014

For ordering information go to www.manning.com

Learn Azure in a Month of Lunches
by Iain Foulds

ISBN: 9781617295171
384 pages
$44.99
August 2018

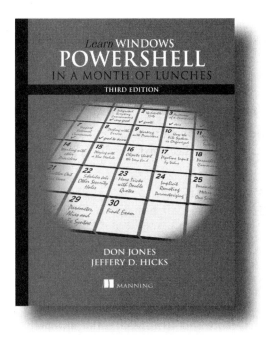

Learn Windows PowerShell in a Month of Lunches, Third Edition
by Don Jones and Jeffery Hicks

ISBN: 9781617294167
384 pages
$44.99
December 2016

For ordering information go to www.manning.com

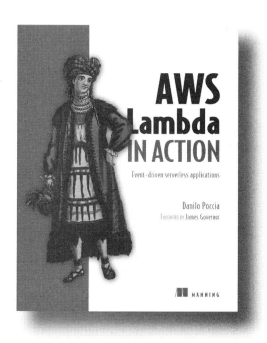

AWS Lambda in Action
Event-driven serverless applications
by Danilo Poccia

ISBN: 9781617293719
384 pages
$49.99
November 2016

Google Cloud Platform in Action
by JJ Geewax

ISBN: 9781617293528
632 pages
$59.99
August 2018

For ordering information go to www.manning.com

MORE TITLES FROM MANNING

Linux in Action
by David Clinton

  ISBN: 9781617294938
  384 pages
  $39.99
  August 2018

Learn Linux in a Month of Lunches
by Steven Ovadia

  ISBN: 9781617293283
  304 pages
  $39.99
  November 2016

For ordering information go to www.manning.com